REA

FRIENDS
OF ACPL

304.109

INDIGENOUS PEOPLES AND THE
FUTURE OF AMAZONIA

D1496403

ALLEN COUNTY PUBLIC LIBRARY
FORT WAYNE, INDIANA 46802

You may return this book to any location of
the Allen County Public Library.

DEMCO

Indigenous Peoples and the Future of Amazonia

Arizona Studies in Human Ecology

EDITOR

Robert McC. Netting (University of Arizona)

ASSOCIATE EDITORS

Peggy F. Barlett (Emory University)

James F. Eder (Arizona State University)

Benjamin S. Orlove (University of California, Davis)

Indigenous Peoples and the Future of Amazonia

An Ecological Anthropology of an Endangered World

Edited by
Leslie E. Sponsel

The University of Arizona Press
Tucson & London

Allen County Public Library
900 Webster Street
PO Box 2270
Fort Wayne, IN 46801-2270

The University of Arizona Press
Copyright © 1995
Arizona Board of Regents
All rights reserved

⊗ This book is printed on acid-free, archival-quality paper.
Manufactured in the United States of America

00 99 98 97 96 95   6 5 4 3 2 1

Library of Congress Cataloging-in-Publication Data

Indigenous peoples and the future of Amazonia : an ecological
    anthropology of an endangered world / edited by Leslie E. Sponsel.
        p.   cm. — (Arizona studies in human ecology)
    Includes bibliographical references (p.   ) and index.
    ISBN 0-8165-1458-5 (acid-free paper)
    1. Human ecology—Amazon River Region.   2. Ethnology—Amazon River
Region—Methodology.   3. Indians of South America—Amazon River
Region—Social conditions.   4. Biotic communities—Amazon River
Region.   5. Biological diversity—Amazon River Region.   6. Amazon
River Regions—Environmental conditions.   I. Sponsel, Leslie E.
(Leslie Elmer), 1943–   . II. Series.
GF532.A4I53   1995
304.1'09811—dc20   94-39431
                                                                          CIP

British Library Cataloguing-in-Publication Data
A catalogue record for this book is available from the British Library.

Contents

Foreword

My people, the Ye'kuana, believe that the social world is constantly changing and falls naturally into disorder and decomposition. Changes occur inevitably and steadily worsen everything, producing pain, anguish, and despair, but we never lose hope of renewal, for when chaos finally closes one of the cycles of change, it heralds the beginning of a time of renewed hope in a reborn world.

So history is a result of the many cycles of life that arise, change, decompose, and destroy themselves only to be reborn. This belief was transmitted to us by our ancestors and reflects lessons learned through living so close to nature; it could be telling us that the peoples of Amazonia have always known that the world is changing and that each cycle demands answers consonant with the environmental conditions of the moment.

My generation lives in a cycle that probably began about a thousand years ago. The way of life of this cycle is one in which we have maintained local diversity by spreading ourselves out in small groups. Each group has its own traditions and customs that identify the group as different from others. These traditions have helped many of us to survive and resist 500 years of confrontation with peoples who are philosophically very different from us.

Although we have struggled, studied, and adapted in the face of a multitude of conflicts created by this confrontation, it seems that the destruction of the present cycle is imminent. I would like to point out some of the consequences of this situation. First, our political leadership has been weakened, leaving us with the presence of token leaders. Second, our traditional patterns of using natural resources have been altered by new ecological and economic conditions. Previously, different groups would complement each other through specialization (for example, in the Venezuelan Amazon the Ye'kuana concentrated more on agriculture, the Hiwi on gathering and fishing, the Yanomami on gathering and hunting, and so forth). These patterns have been upset by invasions of colonizers as well as by other kinds of expropriation. Thus the conditions of harmony and understanding with the environment are getting rarer, which in turn contributes to the ever faster destruction of the forest resources.

Third, as the frontier advances with the presence of more and more people, our territories are closed in or we are pushed onto marginal lands. Our land, a territorial base that we need to fully develop our way of life, cannot be reduced to a little plot that some government decides to allow us to keep. We need adequate space not only because it is our source of sustenance but also because the land gives us dignity and respect so that each one of us can feel really human. And fourth, we suffer from waves of new and old diseases while we watch our forests and resources being irrationally exploited. The need for specialized medical care forces us to leave our homes for the cities where the care is available.

In the face of such instability, caused by the many external forces threatening our traditional lifestyles, it is imperative that scientific research no longer ignore our presence or consider us as mere objects of their studies. This opinion is shared by all Amazonian Indians with whom I have had the opportunity to discuss such matters. The fabulous resources of Amazonia have remained almost intact, thanks to the many generations who knew how to conserve them. We have never been selfish, nor do we intend to reserve the resources for ourselves, but we do demand respect for our right to benefit from their exploitation alongside the members of the dominant societies.

Furthermore, especially since we offer our knowledge and experience to scientific research, we have the right to demand solutions to the new problems created by the same societies that want our knowledge. Our wisdom will disappear with the forest. We consider it important that in reading the analyses of the data offered by the scientists in this book, readers should ask themselves: What is missing in the analysis? What is the value of indigenous ecological knowledge? And if this knowledge is no longer relevant, who then can offer us solutions for the future?

Simeon Jiménez

I wish to contribute one further point, already touched upon by Simeon Jiménez, which is intimately connected to my work in Amazonian ethnology: If it is true that contemporary scientists have been unable to induce favorable socioeconomic changes in Amazonia, what role is there left that we can play? This question produces feelings of bitterness for many of us; we have proven impotent when faced with a world based on political expediency that either ignores or distorts our published results and promotes changes that demonstrate little concern for the well-being of the peoples and environments that need to be protected. Many of us at first avoided facing the agonizing implications of this question, but increasingly we have to ask ourselves, What should the nature of science be, if not to serve the needs of all human beings?

Nelly Arvelo-Jiménez

As two people who have been intimately involved with the struggle for indigenous rights in the Venezuelan Amazon over the past 25 years, we affirm that the defense of indigenous rights and the conservation of the environment and its resources are inseparably tied. We have struggled for respect; not only should indigenous voices be heard but the ideas of indigenous people should be taken seriously, because these are the people who are directly affected by the social and ecological upheaval produced by the presence in Amazonia of conquistadores and colonizers, both old and new.

Simeon Jiménez and Nelly Arvelo-Jiménez

Translated by Andrew L. Cousins

Indigenous Peoples and the Future of Amazonia

Introduction

Leslie E. Sponsel

As we approach the beginning of the next century and millennium, the major challenge for anthropological research on human ecology in Amazonia is to understand the relationship between cultural and environmental variation through time and space, especially with reference to the survival and well-being of contemporary indigenous societies. But if we are to increase the relevance of anthropological research for these communities—beyond continuing to document traditional adaptations of indigenous populations to their ecosystems—then two themes deserve much more attention: (1) indigenous adaptations to the challenges presented by the cultural and environmental impacts of Western society, and (2) the immediate application of anthropological research to the needs, interests, priorities, and rights of indigenous societies, such as in providing information directly to them, recognizing their intellectual property rights, and promoting their self-determination (Baker 1991; Messer 1993; Sponsel 1991, 1992).

Previous inventories of anthropological research on human ecology in Amazonia have focused either on the main categories of subsistence—hunting, fishing, gathering, and farming (Clay 1988; Hames and Vickers 1983)—or on adaptations to different biomes—floodplain and lowland forest, upland forest, savannas, and black waters and other types of waters (Meggers 1971; Moran 1993; also see Roosevelt 1980:chs.1–3; Sponsel 1986; Steward and Faron 1959). This book is distinctive in its attempt to focus on the implications and applications of research in ecological anthropology for problems of indigenous survival and well-being. Our effort follows from a recognition of the markedly increasing gravity and urgency of cultural and environmental changes in Amazonia, which demand much greater practical relevance from the anthropological community. It is no exaggeration to say that the Amazon, including the indigenous peoples who reside there, are endangered (Amnesty International 1992; Bodley 1990; Gross 1990, Miller 1993; NACLA 1989; Sponsel 1991, 1992, 1993, 1994; Stone 1993; Urban 1985).

For this book I invited contributors to explore some aspects of one or more of three topics on ecological anthropology in Amazonia: (1) recent trends and future needs in basic and applied research; (2) subjects that have been neglected because much of the previous research concentrated on the hypothesis that animal protein is the limiting factor on indigenous populations; and (3) problems of indigenous survival, well-being, and ongoing adaptation in the face of challenges such as cultural change, disease, economic development, and deforestation. Most of the contributors deal with more than one of these three topics.

The authors are specialists in one or more of the following: archaeology, biological anthropology, ethnology, ethnography, nutritional anthropology, medical anthropology, biological ecology, ecological anthropology, and ethnoecology. Although an earnest effort was made to include authors who reside in each of the nine countries of the Amazon, only representatives from Brazil (Coimbra), Peru (Chicchón), and Venezuela (Holmes) proved to be available.

The thirteen essays in this book provide a fairly representative sample of contemporary research on anthropological aspects of human ecology in the Amazon. However, it has not been feasible to cover ecological aspects of other important topics in anthropology such as fishing (Goulding 1980; Gragson 1992; Smith 1981; Sponsel and Loya 1993), optimal foraging theory (Bettinger 1991:chs. 4–5; Smith and Winterhalder 1992), ethnobiology (Berlin 1992; Plotkin 1993; Plotkin and Famolare 1992; Posey and Overall 1990; Prance and Kallunki 1983; Schultes and Raffauf 1990), demography (Denevan 1992; Hern 1994), ethnohistory (Ferguson and Whitehead 1992), trade networks (Sponsel 1986:81), physiological responses to heat and other environmental stresses (Frisancho 1993), housing (Kroeger 1980), religion (Reichel-Dolmatoff 1971, 1976), gathering (Clay 1988), commercial exploitation and conservation of wildlife (Redford and Padoch 1992; Robinson and Redford 1991), extractive reserves (Browder 1992; Fearnside 1989), *caboclos* (also variously called criollos, mestizos, or *ribereños*) (Hecht and Cockburn 1989; Hiraoka 1985, 1989; Padoch 1988; Romanoff 1992), mining (Berwick 1992; Cleary 1990), militarization (Nietschmann 1987; Schmink and Wood 1992:chs. 3–4;

Treece 1989), ecofeminism (Diamond and Orenstein 1990; Rodda 1991), radical ecology or radical environmentalism (Manes 1990; Merchant 1992), and Marxist anthropology (Bettinger 1991:ch. 6; Dickens 1992; Harris 1987; Roseberry 1988). These lacunae, as well as the lack of a thorough literature review, reflect mostly the concerns of the editor and publisher to keep the book's price (based on its page length) manageable for students. For literature surveys and other background information, see Moran (1993) and Sponsel (1986).

Geographical as well as topical coverage is necessarily limited; case studies were not available from the Amazonian countries of Guyana, Surinam, and French Guiana. The regional gaps are unfortunate, especially because the Brazilian portion of the Amazon tends to dominate research as well as the media, and the Amazonian portions of other countries receive comparatively little attention.

In concluding, I should note that there is healthy academic disagreement among the authors, and each can be held responsible only for his or her own contribution.

Acknowledgments

I wish to express my deep appreciation for the collective efforts of all the authors, the two anonymous external reviewers, the staff of the University of Arizona Press, especially Christine Szuter and Robert Netting, and the manuscript editor, Jane Kepp. My wife, Poranee Natadecha-Sponsel, also deserves credit for her understanding and encouragement while I was consumed by the preparation of this volume. Indigenous and academic colleagues, including students, have contributed in various ways to this book, but they are too numerous to mention individually. Any royalties from this book will be invested in the production of Spanish and Portuguese editions, and thereafter the remainder will be donated to appropriate indigenous advocacy organizations. This book is dedicated to the descendants of the original peoples of Amazonia.

References Cited

Amnesty International
1992   *Brazil, "We are the Land": Indigenous Peoples' Struggle for Human Rights.* New York: Amnesty International USA.

Baker, Leslie, ed.
1991   Intellectual Property Rights: The Politics of Ownership. *Cultural Survival Quarterly* 15(3).

Berlin, Brent
1992   *Ethnobiological Classification: Principles of Categorization of Plants and Animals in Traditional Societies*. Princeton: Princeton University Press.

Berwick, Dennison
1992   *Savages: The Life and Killing of the Yanomami*. London: Hodder and Stroughton.

Bettinger, Robert L.
1991   *Hunter-Gatherers: Archaeological and Evolutionary Theory*. New York: Plenum Press.

Bodley, John H.
1990   *Victims of Progress*. Mountain View, Calif.: Mayfield Publishing.

Browder, John O.
1992   The Limits of Extractivism. *BioScience* 42(3):173–82.

Clay, Jason W.
1988   *Indigenous Peoples and Tropical Forests: Models of Land Use and Management from Latin America*. Cambridge, Mass.: Cultural Survival, Inc.

Cleary, David
1990   *Anatomy of the Amazon Gold Rush*. Iowa City: Iowa University Press.

Denevan, William M., ed.
1992   *The Native Population of the Americas in 1492*. Madison: University of Wisconsin Press.

Diamond, Irene, and Gloria Feman Orenstein
1990   *Reweaving the World: The Emergence of Ecofeminism*. San Francisco: Sierra Club Books.

Dickens, Peter
1992   *Society and Nature: Towards a Green Social Theory*. Philadelphia: Temple University Press.

Fearnside, Philip M.
1989   Extractive Reserves in Brazilian Amazonia. *BioScience* 39(6):387–93.

Ferguson, R. Brian, and Neil L. Whitehead, eds.
1992   *War in the Tribal Zone: Expanding States and Indigenous Warfare*. Santa Fe, N.M.: School of American Research Press.

Frisancho, Roberto A.
1993   *Human Adaptation and Accommodation*. Ann Arbor: University of Michigan Press.

Goulding, Michael
1980   *The Fishes of the Forest: Explorations in Amazonian Natural History*. Berkeley: University of California Press.

Gragson, Ted L.
1992   Fishing the Waters of Amazonia: Native Subsistence Economies in a Tropical Rain Forest. *American Anthropologist* 94(2):428–40.

Gross, Anthony
1990   Amazonia in the Nineties: Sustainable Development or Another
         Decade of Destruction? *Third World Quarterly* 12(3):1–24.

Hames, Raymond B., and William T. Vickers, eds.
1983   *Adaptive Responses of Native Amazonians.* New York: Academic Press.

Harris, Marvin
1987   Cultural Materialism: Alarums and Excursions. In *Waymarks*, edited by
         Kenneth Moore, pp. 107–26. Notre Dame, Ind.: University of Notre
         Dame Press.

Hecht, Susanna, and Alexander Cockburn
1989   *The Fate of the Forest: Developers, Destroyers and Defenders of the Amazon.*
         New York: Verso.

Hern, Warren M.
1994   Health and Demography of Native Amazonians: Historical Perspective
         and Current Status. In *Amazonian Indians from Prehistory to the Present:
         Anthropological Perspectives*, edited by Anna C. Roosevelt, pp. 123–49.
         Tucson: University of Arizona Press.

Hiraoka, Mario
1985   Mestizo Subsistence in Riparian Amazonia. *National Geographic
         Research* 1(2):236–46.
1989   Agricultural Systems on the Floodplains of the Peruvian Amazon. In
         Fragile Lands of Latin America: Strategies for Sustainable Development,
         edited by John O. Browder, pp. 75–101. Boulder, Colo.: Westview
         Press.

Kroeger, A.
1980   Housing and Health in the Process of Cultural Adaptation: A Case
         Study Among Jungle and Highland Natives from Ecuador. *Journal of
         Tropical Medicine and Hygiene* 83:53–69.

Manes, Christopher
1990   *Green Rage: Radical Environmentalism and the Unmaking of Civilization.*
         Boston: Little, Brown.

Meggers, Betty J.
1971   *Amazonia: Man and Culture in a Counterfeit Paradise.* Chicago: Aldine-
         Atherton.

Merchant, Carolyn
1992   *Radical Ecology: The Search for a Livable World.* New York: Routledge.

Messer, Ellen
1993   Anthropology and Human Rights. *Annual Review of Anthropology*
         22:221–49.

Miller, Marc S., with the staff of Cultural Survival, Inc.
1993   *State of the Peoples: A Global Human Rights Report on Societies in Danger.*
         Boston: Beacon Press.

Moran, Emilio F.
1993   *Through Amazonian Eyes: The Human Ecology of Amazonian Populations.*
         Iowa City: University of Iowa Press.
NACLA (North American Conference on Latin America)
1989   War in the Amazon. NACLA Report 23(1):12–40.
Nietschmann, Bernard
1987   Militarization and Indigenous People: The Third World War. *Cultural
         Survival Quarterly* 11(3):1–16.
Padoch, Christine
1988   People of the Floodplain and Forest. In *People of the Tropical Rain Forest,*
         edited by Julie Sloan Denslow and Christine Padoch, pp. 127–40.
         Berkeley: University of California Press.
Plotkin, Mark
1993   *Tales of a Shaman's Apprentice.* New York: Penguin.
Plotkin, Mark, and Lisa Famolare, eds.
1992   *Sustainable Harvest and Marketing of Rain Forest Produce.* Washington,
         D.C.: Island Press.
Posey, Darrell A., and William Leslie Overall, eds.
1990   *Ethnobiology: Implications and Applications.* Proceedings of the First
         International Congress of Ethnobiology, vols. 1–2. Belém, Brazil:
         Museu Goeldi.
Prance, Ghillean T., and J. A. Kallunki, eds.
1983   *Ethnobotany in the Neotropics.* New York: New York Botanical Garden.
Redford, Kent H., and Christine Padoch, eds.
1992   *Conservation of Neotropical Forests: Working from Traditional Resource
         Use.* New York: Columbia University Press.
Reichel-Dolmatoff, Gerardo
1971   *Amazonian Cosmos: The Sexual and Religious Symbolism of the Tukano
         Indians.* Chicago: University of Chicago Press.
1976   Cosmology as Ecological Analysis: A View from the Rainforest. *Man*
         11:307–18.
Robinson, John G., and Kent H. Redford, eds.
1991   *Neotropical Wildlife Use and Conservation.* Chicago: University of
         Chicago Press.
Rodda, Annabel
1991   *Women and the Environment.* Atlantic Highlands: Zed Books.
Romanoff, Steven
1992   Food and Debt Among Rubber Tappers in the Bolivian Amazon. *Human
         Organization* 51(2):122–35.
Roosevelt, Anna C.
1980   *Parmana: Prehistoric Maize and Manioc Subsistence Along the Amazon
         and Orinoco.* New York: Academic Press.

Roseberry, William

1988   Political Economy. *Annual Review of Anthropology* 17:161–85.

Schmink, Marianne, and Charles H. Wood

1992   *Contested Frontiers in Amazonia.* New York: Columbia University Press.

Schultes, Richard Evans, and Robert F. Raffauf

1990   *The Healing Forest: Medicinal and Toxic Plants of the Northwest Amazonia.* Portland: Timber Press.

Smith, Eric Alden, and Bruce Winterhalder, eds.

1992   *Evolutionary Ecology and Human Behavior.* New York: Aldine de Gruyter.

Smith, Nigel

1981   *Man, Fishes, and the Amazon.* New York: Columbia University Press.

Sponsel, Leslie E.

1986   Amazon Ecology and Adaptation. *Annual Review of Anthropology* 15:67–97.

1991   Sobrevivirá la antropología al siglo XX? Reflexiones sobre la mutua relevancia entre indígenas y antropólogos. *Arinsana* 7(13):65–79.

1992   Information Asymmetry and the Democratization of Anthropology. *Human Organization* 51(3):299–301.

1993   The Yanomami Holocaust Continues. In *Who Pays the Price?* edited by Barbara Johnston, pp. 37–46. Washington, D.C.: Island Press.

1994   The Current Holocaust in the Brazilian Amazon: Ecocide, Ethnocide, and Genocide Against the Yanomami Nation. In *International Human Rights and Indigenous Peoples*, edited by C. Patrick Morris and Robert K. Hitchcock.

Sponsel, Leslie E., and Paula C. Loya

1993   Rivers of Hunger? Indigenous Resource Management in the Oligotrophic Ecosystems of the Rio Negro, Venezuela. In *Tropical Forests, People and Food: Biocultural Interactions and Applications to Development*, edited by C. M. Hladik et al., pp. 435–46. London: Parthenon.

Steward, Julian H., and Louis C. Faron

1959   *Native Peoples of South America.* New York: McGraw-Hill.

Stone, Roger D.

1993   *Dreams of Amazonia.* New York: Penguin.

Treece, Dave

1989   The Militarization and Industrialization of Amazonia: The Calha Norte and Grande Carajas Programmes. *The Ecologist* 19(6):225–28.

Urban, Greg

1985   Developments in the Situation of Brazilian Tribal Populations from 1976 to 1982. *Latin American Research Review* 20(1):7–25.

PART I

ENVIRONMENTAL VARIATION AND ADAPTATION

Cultural and environmental systems are dynamic in many respects, including their variation through time and space. Variations in the environment often influence variations in culture, and vice versa, as the two systems interact. The following chapters by Betty Meggers and Robert Carneiro focus on the temporal dimension of variation, the former emphasizing environmental changes in prehistory, and the latter, changes in the course of cultural evolution. The chapter by Emilio Moran focuses on spatial variation in the environment, whereas William Balée explores how indigenes changed their environment.

In chapter 1, Meggers argues that Amazonia is a region marked by climatic variability, and this variability has been further aggravated by several short- and long-term fluctuations during the past 5,000 years. Interrelated changes in climate and biotic communities temporarily altered the carrying capacity of regions inhabited by human societies, with profound impacts on the distribution and size of their populations as well as on their cultural adaptations. Meggers finds correlations between episodes of drought and discontinuities in the archaeological record at 1,500, 1,000, and 700 years ago that imply repeated disruptions of local groups. Several prominent features of Amazonian social organization and ideology are intelligible as mechanisms for coping with environmental uncertainty. Meggers concludes by linking the future with the past through cautioning that human adaptation and economic development in the long term inevitably will be affected by the environmental instability of Amazonia.

In chapter 2, Carneiro concentrates on demographic and social changes in relation to spatial variations in the environment (floodplain and interior forests) that contributed to the evolution of chiefdoms. As populations naturally increased along the more productive floodplains, so did resource competition, which eventually grew into warfare that was managed through the evolution of the sociopolitical institution of chiefdoms. This population pressure on the resource base was influenced as much, if not more, by social circumscription (the presence of neighboring villages and tribes) as by physical circumscription (the constraints of the relatively narrow floodplain). These factors help explain why chiefdoms emerged in certain parts of Amazonia and not in others.

Carneiro's explanation considers chiefdoms in Amazonia to have developed in situ rather than having diffused from the Andean or Circum-Caribbean area. He views warfare as the critical factor in the origin of the chiefdom as well as of the state. In exploring the ecological basis of the chiefdom in Amazonia, Carneiro also provides a useful historical review of the literature and includes some criticisms of archaeologist Anna Roosevelt's interpretations of prehistory in Amazonia. In part Carneiro bases his criticism on a consideration of some of the neglected ethnohistory of Amazonia.

In chapter 3, Moran explains that historically there has been a tendency on the part of scholars and policy makers to aggregate the Amazon region into two basic types of environments—the floodplain (*várzea*) and the interior forest (*terra firme*). He asserts that this aggregation ignores variability and constrains comparison and generalization between study sites. Moran emphasizes that Amazonia is characterized by diversity rather than uniformity. He elucidates the biological and cultural ecology of Amazonia by subdividing the várzea into three types of ecosystems and the terra firme into five types. This classification reflects the multiplicity of ecosystems, which vary in their geological, biotic, and human histories. By applying a finer scale of resolution, Moran's strategy of disaggregation promotes a better understanding of the specific constraints and opportunities for human adaptation in each of these different types of ecosystems in Amazonia.

Disaggregation also has important practical implications for economic development and biological conservation. For example, Moran points to the special considerations that policy makers should give to the more fragile and less resilient ecosystems such as the oligotrophic (nutrient poor) ones associated with white sands and black waters, as along the Rio Negro in the northwest region of Amazonia.

Like Moran, Balée in chapter 4 is also concerned with developing a more refined approach to the environment, but his method is that of historical ecology. Balée applies ethnobotany to analyze the ecology of the biocultural landscape in diachronic perspective. He argues that under the pressures of colonialism, some societies shifted from farming to foraging in the fallow lands of past farming societies in their advanced successional stages. Thus, through historical ecology, the past illuminates the present, and vice versa. The research of Balée and others on historical ecology is challenging the idea that the Amazon and other areas of supposed wilderness are pristine—unaffected by human use and management.

1

Judging the Future by the Past

The Impact of Environmental Instability on Prehistoric Amazonian Populations

Betty J. Meggers

Amazonia remains the last terrestrial portion of our planet to excite our imaginations. Its immense area, magnificent vegetation, exotic fauna, and distinctive indigenous people give it a mystery that nearly five centuries of exploration have failed to dispel. Politicians, developers, and anthropologists, as well as the general public, perceive various kinds of hidden and potential assets awaiting exploitation. Biologists, climatologists, and ecologists are beginning to reveal a different kind of mystery: How has the most diverse biota on earth developed in the context of the greatest edaphic and climatic adversity, the evolutionary equivalent of making a silk purse from a sow's ear?

Arguments among anthropologists over whether and to what extent Amazonia is suitable for sustained, intensive subsistence production have depended primarily on observations of surviving indigenous groups. Although many of these groups exhibit social and ideological behavior that can be understood as adaptations to environmental constraints, their low population densities and egalitarian social organization have often been attributed instead to decimation and deculturation since European contact. The abundance of archaeological sites and the eyewitness accounts of early explorers have been cited as further evidence that dense and sedentary populations existed during pre-Columbian times (e.g., Myers 1992; Smith 1980). If surviving groups are decultured and decimated remnants, they are irrelevant for estimating the potential of the region for supporting intensive human occupation now and in the future. It is important, therefore, to establish whether population density and settlement duration were significantly higher during pre-Columbian times.

Until recently, neither the ecological nor the archaeological data were sufficient to assess human carrying capacity and to estimate except in general terms whether it was achieved by the indigenous populations (Meggers 1974). It is now evident that Amazonia is a region of marked climatic instability, which has been aggravated by several short- and long-term fluctuations during the past five millennia. Variations in rainfall exert a domino effect on the food chain, first disrupting the reproductive cycles of plants, then of herbivores dependent upon them, then of carnivores, and finally of humans.

This account will review the effects of climatic instability on the biota most relevant for human survival and the archaeological evidence that episodes of aridity played a significant role in human history. The discussion is divided into four parts: (1) climatic instability, (2) prehistoric settlement behavior, (3) correlations between climatic and cultural change, and (4) sustainable long-term carrying capacity.

Climatic Instability

Most evaluations of the potential of Amazonia for sustained, intensive exploitation incorporate the assumption that the present climate and biota are stable configurations, although geological, climatological, and biological evidence is making it increasingly clear that this impression is wrong. Seasonal and periodic short-term variations in the timing and intensity of precipitation are characteristic, and since the Pleistocene there have been intervals lasting decades or centuries when the climate was wetter, drier, or cooler than now. These fluctuations caused significant and repeated disruptions of the local vegetation, altering the conditions of survival both for herbivores and for their predators. Being omnivores, humans were doubly vulnerable. This situation is fundamental not only for understanding prehistoric cultural adaptation but also for constructing viable programs for sustainable exploitation of the region in the future.

Two levels of environmental fluctuation can be distinguished: (1) seasonal and periodic oscillations of short duration and temporary impact on the biota, and (2) longer episodes sufficiently intense to have catastrophic effects. The first kind establishes the ceiling on carrying capacity, whereas the second kind lowers the ceiling by causing temporary changes in the abundances and distributions of subsistence resources.

Variations in Seasonality

The two principal components of the climate are temperature and rainfall. In Amazonia, both fluctuate considerably from one year to the next.

Although average monthly temperatures seldom vary more than two degrees over most of the region, the southwest is vulnerable to sudden drops to near freezing during the Patagonian winter, causing massive mortality among birds, fish, and mammals (Nimer 1979).

Rainfall is highly erratic compared to most other parts of the world. The standard deviations for mean winter rainfall during the 16-year period from 1962 through 1977 ranged from 6 to 12 in Amazonia, Malaysia, and coastal southeast Africa. Elsewhere, they seldom exceeded 3 and were often as low as 0.5 (Shukla 1987:fig. 16a). The number of days with rain, the intensity of precipitation, the onset and termination of the dry season, the amount of rain during the dry season, and the monthly and annual rainfall all fluctuate unpredictably within and among subregions. Minor variations in the severity of the dry season or the onset of precipitation suppress flowering and fruiting (Fearnside 1986:50). Although mammals tend to maintain population densities at levels sustainable by the minimal rather than the average productivity of the most vulnerable resource, they experience famine during especially bad years (Leigh, Rand, and Windsor 1982). In this context, the impression that game is underexploited by human hunters may reflect failure to recognize strategies that enhance survival during years of exceptional stress.

Fluctuations in rainfall also affect the regimes of the rivers, not only in the immediate region but throughout their lower courses. Records kept at Manaus from 1902 to 1973 reveal large annual deviations in maximum and minimum water levels (fig. 1.1) and similar inconsistencies in the timing and rate of rise and fall, all of which have deleterious effects on the aquatic fauna. When the crest is low, fish that disperse into flooded forests during high water face increased competition for food, and much of the landscape is deprived of its annual coating of fertile silt. When the minimum level is unusually low, aquatic animals are crowded into small, oxygen-depleted ponds where mortality is high. If the water rises too rapidly, it drowns the clutches of eggs laid on sandbars by turtles. If it drops too quickly, it traps fish in shrinking pools with fatal consequences.

Human exploitation of the floodplain requires coping with these vicissitudes. A prolonged inundation shortens the next growing season for wild and cultivated plants; a premature rise destroys or reduces the harvest. The abundance of easily captured fish during low water is a short-term benefit because the tropical climate precludes preservation for consumption during times of high water, when dispersal makes the fish more difficult to catch. The fact that the regime of the Amazon is determined by erratic rainfall in the distant headwaters makes predicting and preparing for local variations impossible.

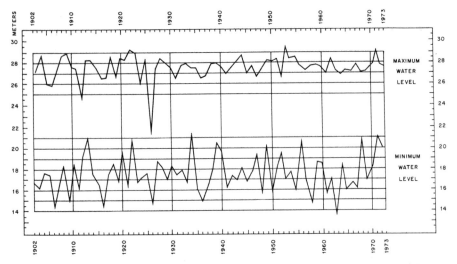

Figure 1.1. Variations in maximum and minimum water level at the mouth of the Rio Negro between 1902 and 1973. The fluctuating amplitude and temporal unpredictability of these oscillations place severe limitations on the reliability of floodplain agriculture and the productivity of aquatic plant and animal resources. (After Soares 1977:fig. 16.)

Long-Term Fluctuations

The assumption that the tropical forest remained unaffected by climatic changes during and since the Pleistocene has been refuted by geological, paleoclimatological, climatological, and biogeographical evidence (e.g., Ab'Sáber 1982; Markgraf and Bradbury 1982; Van der Hammen 1974). Drier and possibly cooler conditions between 18,000 and 10,000 B.P. reduced the extent of the rain forest, creating corridors of more open vegetation suitable for the dispersal of arid-adapted plants and animals (Haffer 1969; Ochsenius 1985). The period between 10,000 and about 8000 B.P. was moist and possibly warmer than today. Between 6000 and 4000 B.P., slightly cooler and drier conditions again prevailed. A shorter arid episode occurred between about 2700 and 2000 B.P., and briefer droughts have been detected at about 1500, 1000, 700, and 400 B.P. These oscillations have been invoked to account for the disjunct distributions, the numerous centers of endemism, and the high diversities of plants and animals in Amazonia (Prance 1982; Whitmore and Prance 1987).

　　Current dating establishes the presence of humans throughout South America by 12,000 B.P. Consequently, their movements and subsistence activities must have been affected by these oscillations, both directly and indirectly. Until recently, the only evidence for repeated disruptions was the heterogeneous distribution of indigenous languages (Meggers 1979). Sufficient archaeological evidence is now available to reconstruct settlement behavior during the past three millennia and to assess the impact of the arid episodes within this time span on human communities.

Prehistoric Settlement Behavior

Archaeological Evidence

Assessing the intensity of pre-Columbian occupation requires identifying social entities among prehistoric populations comparable to the endogamous communities among contemporary indigenous groups. The task is complicated by several kinds of factors. Contemporary societies are defined principally by language, kinship, marriage rules, and other intangible features seldom reflected in material culture. Furthermore, the preponderance of artifacts, from dwellings to ornaments, are manufactured from organic materials that decompose rapidly in humid heat and acid soils. Stone and pottery are exempt from these forms of degradation, but absence of local rock sources in most of central and western Amazonia makes pottery the only abundant surviving form of evidence. Since complete vessels are encountered only in exceptional circumstances, the effort to reconstruct human adaptation and cultural history depends on maximizing retrieval of the information encoded in sherds. The novelty of the procedures warrants their description as a basis for evaluating the resulting interpretations.

Field and Analytic Procedures / Prior to 1976, knowledge of Amazonian prehistory was restricted almost completely to a few widely separated parts of the region (Evans and Meggers 1968:fig. 80). In that year, the Smithsonian Institution and the National Research Council of Brazil (CNPq) agreed to cosponsor long-term archaeological survey in Brazilian Amazonia. Concurrent investigations were conducted in northern lowland Bolivia, where painted pottery and artificial mounds reminiscent of those at the mouth of the Amazon had been reported. The principal goal was to develop a space-time framework that would permit comparing regional chronologies, recognizing differences in cultural complexity, and tracing the times, directions, and intensities of interactions among regions.

The major tributaries of the Amazon were given priority for survey for two reasons: (1) they represent potential routes of movement to and from the main river, and (2) ceramic complexes along the middle Amazon display sufficient heterogeneity to suggest multiple sources of influence. The fieldwork followed uniform procedures within the limits of funds and local conditions. All sites encountered were assigned an identifying number, their surface characteristics and dimensions were recorded, one or more unselected surface collections were made, and one or more stratigraphic pits were excavated whenever possible. Classification of the pottery employed uniform categories to facilitate comparison within and among regions. A large number of carbon 14 dates was obtained to supplement relative chronologies and assist in their alignment.

Each sample of pottery (a surface collection or a level of a stratigraphic excavation) was separated initially into undecorated and decorated categories. The undecorated sherds were sorted according to differences in temper (sand, siliceous bark, sponge spicules, crushed sherd, crushed shell, etc.), and the relative frequencies of each temper category were calculated for each sample. Trends of increasing or decreasing frequency of the principal undecorated types in successive levels of stratigraphic excavations provided a framework for interdigitating samples and constructing a relative chronology, a procedure known as seriation (fig. 1.2). The decorated sherds were sorted by technique, their relative frequencies calculated, and the results plotted on the seriation chart to the right of the undecorated types from the same provenience. Because decorated sherds rarely exceeded 15 percent of unselected samples, usually represented several techniques with erratic occurrences, and included slipped and painted surfaces vulnerable to loss from erosion, they seldom showed sufficiently consistent trends to be useful for constructing detailed chronologies. The final state of analysis defined vessel shapes and evaluated their functional and chronological aspects.

Social Implications of Seriations / Samples that can be interdigitated into a single sequence have long been assumed to represent some form of social or historical configuration, but its specific nature has been undefined. To avoid possibly unwarranted ethnographic connotations, the term "phase" was adopted in 1954 to label the entity represented by a seriated sequence (Meggers and Evans 1957:13–24). The identification of dozens of phases defined by uniform criteria and the evaluation of their characteristics using evolutionary theory and ethnographic models now suggest they are the prehistoric counterparts of communities among contemporary groups (Meggers 1990).

Among animal populations, interbreeding minimizes variation by maintaining a common gene pool. If a segment of the population becomes partly or completely isolated, it will begin to diverge as a consequence of

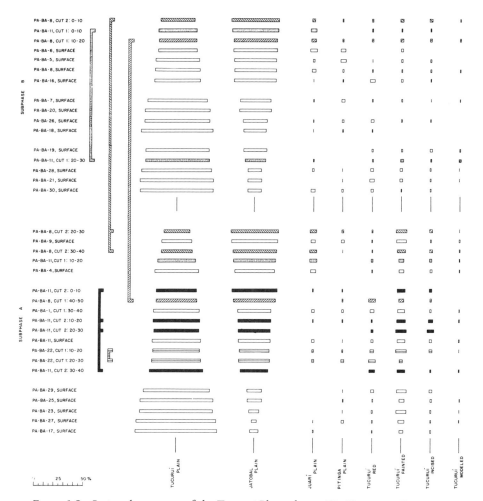

Figure 1.2. Seriated sequence of the Tucuruí Phase, lower Rio Tocantins. Stratigraphic evidence for an increase in Jatobal Plain and a decrease in Tucuruí Plain provides the framework for interdigitating the excavated samples and surface collections from other sites. The existence of two subphases, characterized principally by differences in the relative frequencies of Tucuruí Painted and Tucuruí Incised, implies that the community consists of two matrilocal, exogamous households. Their contemporaneity is established by the similar trends and relative frequencies of Tucuruí Plain and Jatobal Plain, and by the distributions of sites assigned to both subphases throughout the group territory. The existence of identical relative frequencies in the undecorated types in samples in the middle episode of Subphase A and the late episode of Subphase B imply contemporaneous villages. (Revised from Simões and Costa 1987.)

the founder principle and genetic drift. The former reflects initial differences in the representation of the antecedent genetic composition; the latter labels gradual directional change characteristic of traits not subject to natural selection. The same kind of incipient diversification following reduced interaction has been reported among semi-isolated human populations, not only genetically (Spielman, Migliazza, and Neel 1974), but also linguistically (D'Ans 1982:252; Salzano et al. 1977; Seeger 1981: 229–230), and culturally. Minor variations in origin myths, song repertoires, organization of dance festivals, and preparation of foods and beverages characterize Akawaio communities in eastern Guyana (Colson 1983/ 4:111–112). Variations in kinship terminology, dress, ornament, and ceremonies evolved among Panare communities in southeastern Venezuela during less than a century of separation (Henley 1982:11–14). Pronounced differences in village plan, diet, religion, and other traits emerged within a few decades of reduced interaction among Mundurucu groups on the upper Tapajós (Murphy and Murphy 1954). Although less attention has been paid to technology, analogous diversifications have been reported in basketry construction (Newton 1981:281), hammock weaving (Newton 1974), bow length and cross section (Hartmann 1976), and personal ornament (Henley 1982:13; Seeger 1981:230).

The ethnographic data document both the existence of minor distinctions among territorially segregated communities that share a common language and culture (e.g., the Akawaio) and the process of divergence followed reduced interaction among segments of an ancestral community (e.g., Panare, Mundurucu). The similarity between the ethnographic examples and the gradual, unobtrusive, and directional changes in the relative frequencies of undecorated pottery types that characterize seriated sequences implies that all are attributable to the operation of cultural drift under similar circumstances. If so, a phase defined by a seriated sequence corresponds to a semiautonomous community of the kind prevalent among surviving indigenous groups (Meggers 1990; Meggers and Evans 1980).

Correlating Ethnographic and Archaeological Patterns

If a phase is the prehistoric equivalent of a community, the characteristics and distributions of the constituent habitation sites in time and space can be used to reconstruct settlement behavior. Four aspects are particularly susceptible to identification: (1) territorial boundaries, (2) village movements, (3) village size and permanence, and (4) number of contemporary villages.

Territories / Surviving indigenous groups exhibit four principal kinds of territorial configurations: (1) isolated, (2) contiguous, (3) overlapping, and (4) interspersed.

Isolated territories, consisting of a core area that is exclusive to the community and separated from those of other communities by unoccupied regions, have been reported among the Yukpa-Yuka (Ruddle 1971), the Yukuna (Jacopin 1972), and the eastern Yanomamo (Smole 1976). Recognizing this pattern archaeologically requires differentiating it from spurious discontinuities attributable to absence of investigation, and no reliable examples have been identified thus far.

Contiguous territories have one or more common frontiers. Akawaio territories abut along rivers, the boundaries often coinciding with intersecting tributaries; by contrast, the interior limits are often separated by unclaimed land (fig. 1.3; Colson 1983/4). A similar pattern has been reported for the Encabello (Vickers 1983). Among the Piapoco, rivers may define frontiers (Vidal 1989:fig. 1). Contiguous distributions are the most easily detected archaeologically because they are implied by abrupt changes in the phase affiliations of sites along a river (fig. 1.4; Simões and Costa 1987). This pattern has been identified throughout the lowlands. When boundaries coincide with differences in river conditions, they often persist in spite of replacements of the phases.

Overlapping or fluctuating boundaries have been reported among the Matisgenka (Rosengren 1981/2), Wayapi (Grenand 1980), and Piaroa (Kaplan 1975), but may not be identifiable archaeologically since the shared regions usually seem to be exploited for hunting rather than residence. No prehistoric examples have been verified.

Interspersal of villages occupied by speakers of different languages is characteristic in southeastern Colombia, where it may be a recent phenomenon (Jackson 1983:map 2). Although archaeological sites belonging to different phases are often interspersed, stratigraphic evidence and carbon 14 dates indicate the phases are successive rather than contemporary.

In summary, where sufficiently intensive survey has been conducted, the spatial distributions of phases imply the existence of contiguous territories, the most common variety of settlement behavior among contemporary indigenous communities.

Village Movement and Reoccupation / Two principal kinds of village movement have been reported ethnographically: (1) centripetal and (2) directional. Centripetal movement within a territory is characteristic among established populations. Successive moves may be short or long,

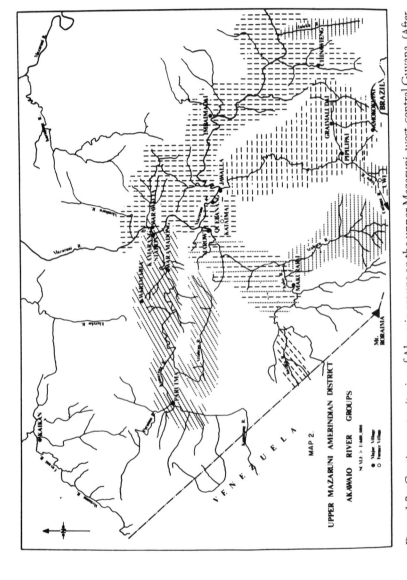

Figure 1.3. Contiguous territories of Akawaio groups on the upper Mazaruni, west-central Guyana. (After Colson 1983/4:108.)

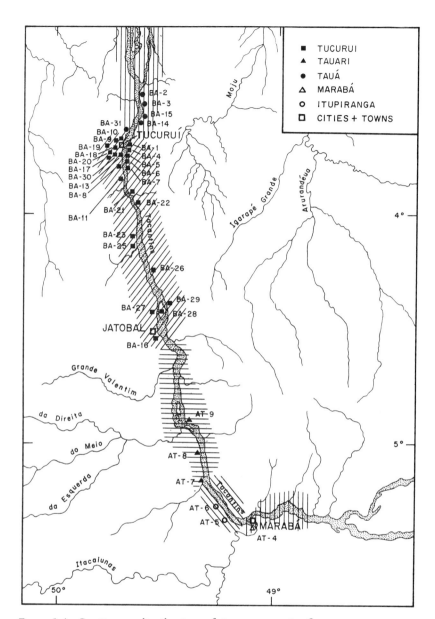

Figure 1.4. Continuous distributions of sites representing five contemporary phases on the lower Rio Tocantins, implying contiguous territories comparable to those among the Akawaio. The boundaries are stable and coincide with changes in the productivity of aquatic resources.

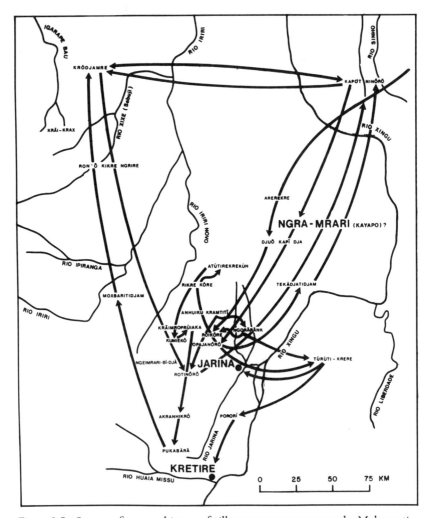

Figure 1.5. Seventy-five-year history of village movement among the Mekranoti, southeastern Amazonia, displaying a centripetal pattern characterized by long and short moves and reoccupation of several sites. (Based on Verswijver 1978.)

village permanency varies, and some locations are reoccupied repeatedly. The Mekranoti moved 36 times during some 75 years, returning 10 times to previously occupied sites (fig. 1.5; Gross 1983). Centripetal movement and reoccupation have also been reported among the Siona-Secoya (Vickers 1983), the Tatuyo (Dufour 1983), the Yanomamo (Hames 1983), and other groups. Directional movements, by contrast, appear to be opportunistic responses to the withdrawal or extinction of the previous occupants of adjacent territories. This situation has been documented in southern Venezuela among the Panare (Henley 1982) and several Yanomamo groups (Chagnon 1968; Hames 1983). Long-distance moves to escape local disturbance, especially European intrusion, have also been reported (e.g., Gallois 1981).

Because a seriated sequence constitutes a relative chronology, it can be used to reconstruct the history of village movement by a phase. The reliability of the result depends on several factors, among them the completeness of the inventory of sites and the number of stratigraphic excavations at each site (which provides information on reoccupation). Where sufficient evidence exists, it generally suggests centripetal movement. The settlement history reconstructed for the Tucuruí Phase on the lower Tocantins (fig. 1.6) resembles that reported for the Mekranoti, both being characterized by combinations of long and short moves and by multiple reoccupation of certain sites. Although the replacement of one phase by another in many local sequences implies an initial directional movement by the invading group, no prehistoric example has been identified.

The archaeological evidence indicates that the centripetal pattern of village movement within a well-defined territory and the periodic reoccupation of favorable locations, characteristic among surviving indigenous groups, are pre-Columbian adaptations that were established by the beginning of the Christian Era.

Village Size / The most common kind of village reported ethnographically is a single, circular or oblong communal house occupied by one or more extended families. The smallest dimensions occur among the Piro (4 × 7 m) and Juruna (4.5 × 12.0 m). Intermediate sizes are represented by the Bora (16–20 m diameter), Cubeo (16 × 23 m), and Achuar (12 × 20 m). Except among the Shipibo, where length is said to exceed 100 m (Myers 1973:246), the largest dwellings occur in eastern Colombia, where structures about 50 m in diameter are reported to be common (Reichel Dussán 1988:146). The community may occupy a single house, two or more houses at the same location, or several houses several kilometers apart. Village populations range from a dozen to several hundred, with the majority between 30 and 100.

Inferring village size from archaeological evidence is complicated by the frequency of reoccupation and consequent enlargement of the surface dimensions of sites through time and by the absence of information on the relationship between refuse disposal and house area. As a general rule, we have assumed that sites with surface extents within the range reported for dwellings among surviving indigenous groups and superficial

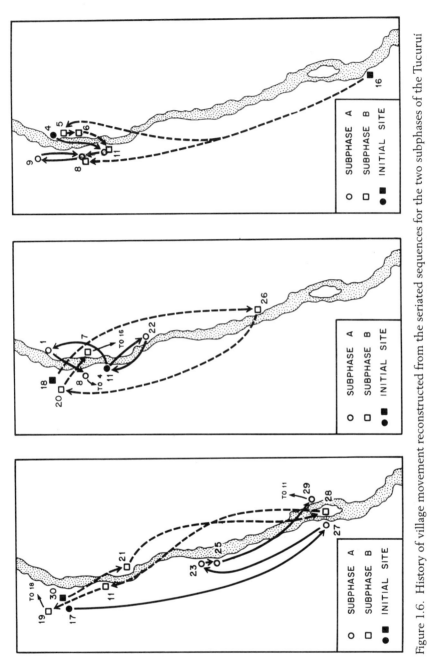

Figure 1.6. History of village movement reconstructed from the seriated sequences for the two subphases of the Tucuruí Phase. The centripetal pattern (depicted in three stages), the presence of long and short moves, and the reoccupation of some sites resemble the Mekranoti settlement history. Stratigraphic samples from the large number of sites represented only by surface collections would reveal numerous additional moves and reoccupations, but the general pattern should not be affected.

accumulations of refuse correspond to single episodes of occupation. Employing these criteria suggests substantial differences in village size among prehistoric groups. The minimum areas of sites of the Apuriné, Quinarí, Xapurí, Muru, Cajubim, and Jacamim phases in Acre are 8 × 15 m or less, comparable to the dimensions of Piro and Juruna houses. The smallest sites of the Tucuruí Phase on the lower Tocantins are also in this category. By contrast, the smallest sites of the Cacarapí, Curuá, and Pacajá phases on the lower Xingu and Tapajós measure 30 × 50 m, implying dwellings at the high end of the ethnographic size range.

A second clue to village size is provided by the positions of levels of stratigraphic excavations in the seriated sequence. All large sites from which stratigraphic information has been obtained show discontinuities within and among excavations. The former imply intermittent occupation of the location tested; the latter imply that no settlement extended over the entire archaeological site (Meggers 1991, 1992b; Miller et al. 1992). Hence, the surface extent of archaeological sites cannot be used to infer village size, as has often been assumed (e.g., Myers 1973; Roosevelt 1991:113–114).

Contemporary Villages / The most commonly reported settlement pattern among surviving indigenous Amazonian groups is a single village consisting of one communal dwelling. The opposite extreme is represented by the Yukpa-Yuko and Achuar, who may be dispersed among up to 16 isolated dwellings at different locations within the territory (Descola 1989:155; Ruddle 1971). The number may fluctuate as a consequence of temporary fissions and fusions.

In keeping with the theoretical assumptions underlying a seriated sequence, samples from different locations with essentially identical relative frequencies in the principal undecorated pottery types should represent contemporaneous settlements. One such set occurs in the seriated sequence for each subphase of the Tucuruí Phase. In the middle section of the seriation for subphase A, the relative frequencies of Tucuruí Plain and Jatobal Plain are equivalent except for the earliest and the two latest samples (see fig. 1.2). The surface collections from PA-BA-8 and PA-BA-5 in the late section of the seriation for subphase B are also equivalent. If each subphase represents an exogamous matrilocal group, then there should be at least two villages throughout the duration of the phase. The intermittent occurrence of one or two additional villages is consistent with the periodic fissioning reported among existing Amazonian groups.

Villages consisting of two or more dwellings at the same location have been identified at sites of the Jamarí and Matapí phases on the Rio Jamarí, a tributary of the right bank of the upper Madeira (Miller et al. 1992:figs. 69–71). There is insufficient evidence to define their dimensions, but their spatial distributions are compatible with those of multidwelling villages reported ethnographically.

Correlations Between Climatic and Cultural Change

Palynological evidence for several episodes of aridity during the past four millennia raises the question of their possible impacts on prehistoric human communities. Comparing the well-dated cultural sequences from lowland Bolivia (Llanos de Moxos), the middle Amazon (Silves/Uatumã and lower Xingu), and the mouth of the Amazon (Marajó) reveals that replacements in each region are contemporaneous with one another and with the arid episodes (fig. 1.7). Pottery making begins in most parts of the region about 2000 B.P., following an arid episode lasting several centuries. Subsequent discontinuities correlate with arid episodes at about 1500 and 700 B.P. (The concentration of cultural changes at about 1000 B.P. rather than 1200 B.P. probably reflects the greater precision of the archaeological chronology.)

The overlap in 1-sigma ranges of the carbon 14 dates for the preceding and succeeding phases indicates that the episodes were brief, and the cultural discontinuities imply that they were catastrophic. Short duration and severe impact are hallmarks of El Niño, and recent modeling of global climate reveals that drought in Amazonia is typically associated with such events (fig. 1.8). Both on the coast of Peru and in Amazonia, the impact even of Niños rated as very strong (exemplified by the 1982–83 event) is temporary. Massive destruction from flooding caused by substantially more severe "mega-Niño" events has been documented in the archaeological record of north coastal Peru at about 1500, 1000, and 700 B.P. (Moseley and Deeds 1982:table 2; Moseley, Feldman, and Ortloff 1981; Shimada 1985:363–66). The contemporaneous cultural replacements throughout Amazonia imply similarly devastating impacts on local subsistence resources, forcing the population to emigrate or adopt a dispersed and mobile way of life until normal conditions were restored (cf. Rindos 1984: 278). This interpretation is supported by the subsistence stress experienced by a Yanomami community during the drought provoked by the relatively mild 1972–73 event (Lizot 1974:7).

Repeated dislocations of human populations are also implied by the disjunct distributions of the principal language families and the large numbers of isolated languages in the neotropical lowlands (e.g., Greenberg 1987). Moreover, the chronologies of divergence of the families,

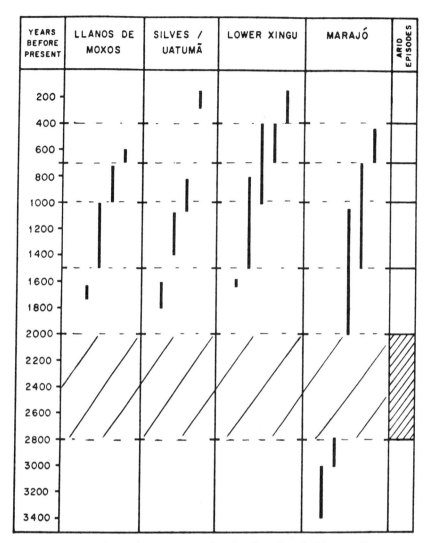

Figure 1.7. Correlations between episodes of aridity identified from pollen cores and discontinuities in the archaeological sequences from the Llanos de Moxos (northeastern Bolivia), the middle Amazon (Silves/Uatumã and lower Xingu), and mouth of the Amazon (Marajó Island). (Arid episodes after Ab'Sáber 1982 and Van der Hammen 1974.)

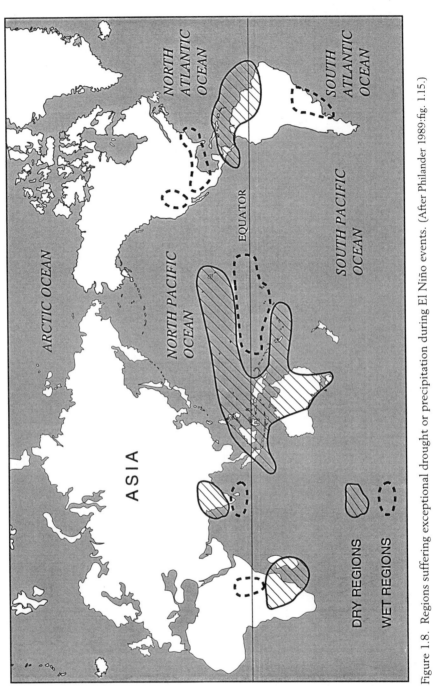

Figure 1.8. Regions suffering exceptional drought or precipitation during El Niño events. (After Philander 1989:fig. 1.15.)

languages, and dialects are compatible with the dates for the principal arid episodes. Arawakan separations have been estimated at about 1500, 1300, 1000, and 850 B.P. (Migliazza 1982:508), Cariban separations at about 1500 and 1000 B.P. (Migliazza 1982:504), and Tupian separations at about 1800, 1500, 1100, 1000, 800, 600, and 500 B.P. (Migliazza 1982:502). The numerous uncertainties in carbon 14 and lexicostatistical dating make it unlikely that this agreement is fortuitous.

Estimating Sustainable Carrying Capacity

Sustainable carrying capacity can be estimated from two principal kinds of evidence: (1) environmental factors that inhibit intensification of subsistence resources, and (2) cultural practices that mitigate their effects.

Environmental Perspectives

A few biologists and agronomists have estimated the sustainable productivity of subsistence resources. One analysis was conducted in an area about 7,000 km^2 on the upper Rio Negro of southern Venezuela (Clark and Uhl 1987). Combining figures on daily caloric requirements, amount of land necessary to supply manioc for one adult, and area available for growing manioc (taking into consideration fallow periods), Clark and Uhl estimated carrying capacity at 3.1 per km^2, or about seven times greater than the existing population, which depends on imported food. The discrepancy was explained when the productivity of fishing—the principal local source of protein—was examined. Calculating monthly catch per unit of effort gave a mean of 0.62 kg per hour, only one-third of the amount obtainable using similar technology on the Amazon. The estimated annual sustainable yield of 125 tons could supply 100 percent of the dietary protein for only 1,000 people or a population density of 0.14 per km^2. Clark and Uhl concluded that "given the scarcity of game . . . the low protein content of conuco [garden] crops, and the irregular availability of wild plant foods, it is difficult to imagine any combination of protein sources that would have permitted a regional population substantially greater than the 3000 present today. Indeed . . . it is even possible that today's population has exceeded the region's carrying capacity" (1987:21; see Gross 1975 and Ross 1978 for more extensive discussions).

A similar result was obtained from a computer simulation conducted to assess the sustainability of a human population of 24 per km^2, the density used to establish the sizes of allotments of land to colonists along part of the Transamazon Highway on the opposite margin of the lowlands. The high rates of failure among the settlers were predicted by the computer runs, which indicated that carrying capacity was substantially lower (Fearnside 1986). Studies comparing the costs and benefits of cattle raised on pasture created by deforestation, agriculture conducted using fertilizers and specialized technology, and plantation forestry all indicate that shifting cultivation is the only ecologically sustainable and economically successful form of exploitation. Jordan (1987:102, 105) has observed that "because the factors for plant production are well known, technologically sustainable agriculture theoretically can be carried out anywhere, in the Amazon, in the desert, or on a spacecraft. However, for agriculture to be meaningful for development, the technology must be economically feasible. . . . Although bureaucratic and logistical problems played a role, the major reason for lack of success seems to have been failure to consider environmental limitations of the Amazon Basin." (For more extended discussion, see Lamb 1987; Meggers 1992a).

Remedial Measures

Indigenous Amazonian groups maximize the productivity of biotic resources in a variety of ways. Their knowledge of wild plants is exhaustive. The Chácobo used 82 percent of the species in a sample hectare containing 360 species representing 221 genera (Boom 1987). The Jivaro collected 120 species of wild fruits and used an additional 600 species for house construction, cordage, implements, dyes, drugs, ornaments, and other purposes (Berlin 1987). The Kayapó exploited 250 species for fruits, nuts, and tubers (Posey 1983). Most groups use knowledge of the food preferences of game to enhance hunting success.

Agricultural practices minimize the impacts of uncertain weather, infertile soils, and disease. Small clearings supplement natural gaps that encourage secondary vegetation and enhance biotic diversity. Intercropping promotes conservation of nutrients. Planting multiple varieties reduces the risk of crop failure. The Kayapó, who grew 16 varieties of sweet potatoes, 17 varieties of manioc, and 8 varieties of maize, are typical (Posey 1983). The abundance of desirable wild species is enhanced by selective weeding and by transplanting (Balée 1989; Irvine 1989). Through these and other measures "the Amazonian Indians have overcome and made use of ecological variation (*terra firme*, floodplain, times of relative aridity, times of heavy rain, intense shade, little shade, etc.)" (Kerr and Clement 1980:254).

Various aspects of Amazonian settlement behavior and ideology also maximize long-term carrying capacity. Many groups reduce the pressure on game in the vicinity of the village by spending long periods hunting and gathering in distant parts of the forest (e.g., Good 1989:144). The belief that humans are part of nature and that an equilibrium must be maintained between the human world and the spirit world also fosters harmonious interaction (Reichel-Dolmatoff 1976; Smole 1989:117). The environmental degradation that follows increased sedentism testifies to the effectiveness of indigenous methods for maintaining population densities within limits that can be sustained indefinitely under normal conditions (Henley 1982:51–53; Ross 1978:10).

Conclusion

The archaeological and climatological evidence casts doubt on the validity of assertions that Amazonia supported dense sedentary populations prior to European contact. The archaeological record indicates that the subsistence and settlement behavior characteristic of surviving indigenous groups existed throughout the region by the Christian Era, when the adoption of pottery permits its detection. It also indicates that environmental and cultural stability were interrupted about 1500, 1000, and 700 B.P. by brief, severe droughts that reduced subsistence resources below the requirements of these small, well adapted, semisedentary communities, forcing their dispersal. The disjunct distributions and estimated chronologies of differentiation of the principal languages are additional evidence that emigration was a repeated response to temporary depletion of the local food supply.

Several prominent features of Amazonian culture become intelligible in the context of environmental uncertainty. Comprehensive and sophisticated knowledge of the characteristics of soils, the potential uses of plants, the habits of animals, and the interactions among the biota is not only relevant for maximizing subsistence productivity under normal conditions but also facilitates the adoption of alternative strategies when primary resources fail. The extensive trade networks that often link otherwise hostile groups and the specialized production of various kinds of objects by village or tribe, in spite of universal availability of the raw materials, are understandable as mechanisms for maintaining relations of interdependence to cushion against unpredictable local shortages (cf. Plog 1989:287). Similarly, sorcery and warfare, especially among closely related communities, inhibit tendencies for population densities and concentrations to exceed levels sustainable under normal conditions. The discontinuities in the archaeological record throughout the lowlands testify, however, that these measures were insufficient to offset the devastating impact of periodic famine associated with unpredictable mega-Niño events (Meggers 1994).

Thus, rather than constituting decultured remnants of former dense and sedentary populations, many surviving groups perpetuate patterns of behavior perfected during millennia of interaction with other components of the ecosystem. Although prehistoric communities along the banks of the Amazon may have been larger than those on the terra firme, the high densities reported by early explorers have not been supported by archaeological evidence. Here, as on the terra firme, discontinuities in the local chronologies testify to the disruptive consequences of El Niño–induced droughts.

Whether the early impacts of epidemics, slave raids, and other consequences of European invasion were more devastating than the disruptions provoked by periodic climatic fluctuations during the preceding 1,500 years remains to be established. The former initially affected a relatively small part of the region, whereas the latter were felt throughout the lowlands. There is another significant difference between the two kinds of events. The pre-Columbian catastrophes were provoked by local declines in rainfall, which temporarily affected the behavior of the biota. A decline in the productivity of primary foods could be compensated in part by enhanced use of secondary resources, such as manioc, perhaps fostering their domestication (Williams 1992). The European invasion, by contrast, has increasingly imposed alien forms of exploitation that are altering the biota in advance of climatic change. Accelerating disruption of the complex interactions on which the survival of the ecosystem depends threatens its permanent degradation (Shukla, Nobre, and Sellers 1990).

Whether we are capable of replacing our destructive methods with appropriate strategies is questionable. That we will do so before the damage becomes irreversible seems even less likely. The requisite knowledge exists, but its application is impeded by national and international political and economic forces (Hecht and Cockburn 1989). By converting the limitations into assets, the indigenous population has demonstrated that sustainable, long-term exploitation of this remarkable and challenging environment is possible. Their history warns us, however, that even the most appropriate strategies may be vulnerable during the catastrophic droughts that periodically afflict the region.

Acknowledgments

The archaeological fieldwork on which this analysis is based was conducted by Mário F. Simões, Museu Paraense Emílio Goeldi; Ondemar F. Dias, Instituto de

Arqueologia Brasileira; Eurico Th. Miller, Secretaria de Educação, Cultura e Turismo de Rondônia and Eletronorte; Celso Perota, Universidade Federal de Espírito Santo; and Bernardo Dougherty and Horacio Calandra, Universidade de La Plata, Argentina. I acknowledge my indebtedness to them with pleasure and gratitude. Major funding has been provided by the Neotropical Lowland Research Program of the National Museum of Natural History, Smithsonian Institution.

References Cited

Ab'Sáber, Aziz N.
1982   The Paleoclimate and Paleoecology of Brazilian Amazonia. In *Biological Diversification in the Tropics*, edited by G. T. Prance, pp. 41–59. New York: Columbia University Press.

Balée, William
1989   Cultura na vegetação da Amazônia brasileira. Coleção Eduardo Galvão, Museu Paraense Emílio Goeldi, pp. 95–109. Belém, Brazil.

Berlin, Brent
1987   Contributions of Native American Collectors to the Ethnobotany of the Neotropics. *Advances in Economic Botany* 1:24–33.

Boom, Brian M.
1987   Ethnobotany of the Chácobo Indians, Beni, Bolivia. *Advances in Economic Botany* 4.

Chagnon, Napolean
1968   *Yanomamo: the Fierce People*. New York: Holt, Rinehart and Winston.

Clark, Kathleen, and Christopher Uhl
1987   Farming, Fishing, and Fire in the History of the Upper Rio Negro Region of Venezuela. *Human Ecology* 15:1–26.

Colson, Audrey Butt
1983/4 The Spatial Component in the Political Structure of the Carib Speakers of the Guiana Highlands: Kapon and Pemon. *Antropológica* 59–62: 73–124.

D'Ans, André-Marcel
1982   L'Amazonie péruvienne indigène. Paris: Payot.

Descola, Philippe
1989   *La selva culta: Simbolismo y praxis en la ecología de los Achuar*. Quito: Ediciones Abya-Yala.

Dufour, Darna L.
1983   Nutrition in the Northwest Amazon: Household Dietary Intake and Time-Energy Expenditure. In *Adaptive Responses of Native Amazonians*, edited by Raymond B. Hames and William T. Vickers, pp. 329–55. New York: Academic Press.

Evans, Clifford, and Betty J. Meggers
1968   *Archeological Investigations on the Rio Napo, Eastern Ecuador*. Smithsonian Contributions to Anthropology 6. Washington, D.C.

Fearnside, Philip M.
1986   *Human Carrying Capacity of the Brazilian Rainforest.* New York: Columbia University Press.

Gallois, Dominique
1981   *Os Waiapi e seu território.* Boletim do Museu Paraense Emílio Goeldi 80. Belém, Brazil.

Good, Kenneth
1989   Yanomami Hunting Patterns: Trekking and Garden Relocation as an Adaptation to Game Availability in Amazonia. Ph.D. dissertation, University of Florida.

Greenberg, Joseph H.
1987   *Language in the Americas.* Stanford, Calif.: Stanford University Press.

Grenand, Pierre
1980   *Introduction à l'étude de l'univers Wayãpi: Ethnoécologie des Indiens du Haut-Oyapock (Guyana française).* Langues et Civilisations à Tradicion Orale 40. Paris: Société d'Etudes Linguistiques et Anthropologiques de France.

Gross, Daniel
1975   Protein Capture and Cultural Development in the Amazon Basin. *American Anthropologist* 77:526–49.
1983   Village Movement in Relation to Resources in Amazonia. In *Adaptive Responses of Native Amazonians,* edited by Raymond B. Hames and William T. Vickers, pp. 429–49. New York: Academic Press.

Haffer, Jurgen
1969   Speciation in Amazonian Forest Birds. *Science* 165:131–37.

Hames, Raymond B.
1983   The Settlement Pattern of a Yanomamo Population Bloc: A Behavioral Ecological Interpretation. In *Adaptive Responses of Native Amazonians,* edited by Raymond B. Hames and William T. Vickers, pp. 393–427. New York: Academic Press.

Hartmann, Thekla
1976   Cultura material e etnohistória. *Revista do Museu Paulista* 23:175–97.

Hecht, Susanna, and Alexander Cockburn
1989   *The Fate of the Forest: Developers, Destroyers and Defenders of the Amazon.* London: Verso.

Henley, Paul
1982   *The Panare: Tradition and Change on the Amazonian Frontier.* New Haven, Conn.: Yale University Press.

Irvine, Dominique
1989   Succession Management and Resource Distribution in an Amazonian Rain Forest. *Advances in Economic Botany* 7:223–37.

Jackson, Jean
1983   *The Fish People: Linguistic Exogamy and Tukanoan Identity in Northwest Amazonia.* Cambridge: Cambridge University Press.

Jacopin, Pierre-Yves
1972   Habitat et territoire Yukuna. *Journal de la Société des Américanistes* 61:107–39.

Jordan, Carl E., ed.
1987   *Amazonian Rain Forests: Ecosystem Disturbance and Recovery.* New York: Springer-Verlag.

Kaplan, Joanna O.
1975   *The Piaroa: A People of the Orinoco Basin.* Oxford: Clarendon Press.

Kerr, Warwick E., and Charles R. Clement
1980   Práticas agrícolas de consequências genéticas que possibilitaram aos índios da Amazônia uma melhor adaptação às condições ecológicas da região. *Acta Amazônica* 10:251–61.

Lamb, F. Bruce
1987   The Role of Anthropology in Tropical Forest Ecosystem Resource Management and Development. *Journal of Developing Areas* 21:429–58.

Leigh, Egbert G., Jr., A. Stanley Rand, and Donald M. Windsor, eds.
1982   *The Ecology of a Tropical Forest: Seasonal Rhythms and Long-Term Changes.* Washington: Smithsonian Institution Press.

Lizot, Jacques
1974   El río de los Periquitos: Breve relato de un viaje entre los Yanomami del Alto Siapa. *Antropológica* 37:3–23.

Markgraf, Vera, and J. Platt Bradbury
1982   Holocene Climatic History of South America. *Striae* 16:40–45.

Meggers, Betty J.
1974   Environment and Culture in Amazonia. In *Man in the Amazon*, edited by Charles Wagley, pp. 91–110. Gainesville: University Presses of Florida.
1979   Climatic Oscillation as a Factor in the Prehistory of Amazonia. *American Antiquity* 44:252–66.
1990   Reconstrução do comportamento locacional pré-histórico na Amazônia. Boletim do Museu Paraense Emílio Goeldi, Antropologia, 6(2):183–203.
1991   Cultural Evolution in Amazonia. In *Profiles in Cultural Evolution*, edited by A. Terry Rambo and Kathleen Gillogly, pp. 191–216. Anthropological Papers no. 85, Museum of Anthropology, University of Michigan, Ann Arbor.
1992a   Amazonia: Real or Counterfeit Paradise? *Review of Archaeology* 13:25–40.

1992b   Prehistoric Population Density in the Amazon Basin. In *Disease and Demography in the Americas*, edited by John W. Verano and Douglas H. Ubelaker, pp. 197–205. Washington, D.C.: Smithsonian Institution Press.

1994   Archeological Evidence for the Impact of Mega-Niño Events on Amazonia During the Past Two Millennia. *Climatic Change* 24:321–38.

Meggers, Betty J., and Clifford Evans

1957   *Archeological Investigations at the Mouth of the Amazon*. Bureau of American Ethnology Bulletin 167. Washington D.C.: Smithsonian Institution.

1980   Un método cerámico para el reconocimiento de comunidades prehistóricas. Boletín del Museo del Hombre Dominicano, año 9, num. 14:57–73.

Migliazza, Ernest C.

1982   Linguistic Prehistory and the Refuge Model in Amazonia. In *Biological Diversification in the Tropics*, edited by G. T. Prance, pp. 497–519. New York: Columbia University Press.

Miller, Eurico Th., et al.

1992   *Archeology in the Hydroelectric Projects of Eletronorte, Preliminary Results*. Brasília: Centrais Elétricas do Norte do Brasil S.A.

Moseley, Michael E., and E. E. Deeds

1982   The Land in Front of Chan Chan: Agrarian Expansion, Reform, and Collapse in the Moche Valley. In *Chan Chan: Andean Desert City*, edited by M. E. Moseley and K. C. Day, pp. 25–53. Albuquerque: University of New Mexico Press.

Moseley, Michael E., R. A. Feldman, and C. R. Ortloff

1981   Living with Crises: Human Perception of Process and Time. In *Biotic Crises in Ecological and Evolutionary Time*, edited by M. Nitecki, pp. 321–67. New York: Academic Press.

Murphy, Robert, and Yolanda Murphy

1954   *As condições atuais dos Mundurucu*. Instituto de Antropologia e Etnologia do Pará, publ. 8. Belém, Brazil.

Myers, Thomas P.

1973   Toward the Reconstruction of Prehistoric Community Patterns in the Amazon Basin. In *Variation in Anthropology*, edited by D. W. Lathrap and Jody Douglas, pp. 233–52. Urbana: Illinois Archaeological Survey.

1992   Agricultural Limitations of the Amazon in Theory and Practice. *World Archaeology* 24:82–97.

Newton, Dolores

1974   The Timbira Hammock as a Cultural Indicator of Social Boundaries. In *The Human Mirror*, edited by Miles Richardson, pp. 231–51. Baton Rouge: Louisiana State University Press.

1981   The Individual in Ethnographic Collections. In *The Research Potential of Anthropological Museum Collections*, edited by A. Cantwell, J. Griffin, and N. Rothschild, pp. 267–287. Annals of the New York Academy of Sciences 376.

Nimer, Edmon
1979   *Climatologia no Brasil*. Rio de Janeiro: Superintendência de Recursos Naturais e Meio Ambiente.

Ochsenius, Claudio
1985   Pleniglacial Desertization, Large-Animal Mass Extinction and Pleistocene-Holocene Boundary in South America. *Revista de Geografia Norte Grande* 12:35–47.

Philander, S. George
1989   *El Niño, La Niña, and the Southern Oscillation*. San Diego: Academic Press.

Plog, Fred
1989   The Sinagua and Their Relations. In *Dynamics of Southwest Prehistory*, edited by Linda S. Cordell and George J. Gummerman, pp. 263–91. Washington, D.C.: Smithsonian Institution Press.

Posey, Darrell A.
1983   Indigenous Ecological Knowledge and Development of the Amazon. In *The Dilemma of Amazonian Development*, edited by Emilio F. Moran, pp. 225–57. Boulder, Colo.: Westview Press.

Prance, Ghillean T., ed.
1982   *Biological Diversification in the Tropics*. New York: Columbia University Press.

Reichel-Dolmatoff, Gerardo
1976   Cosmology as Ecological Analysis: A View from the Rainforest. *Man* 11:307–18.

Reichel Dussán, Elizabeth
1988   Asentamientos prehispánicos en la Amazonía colombiana. In *Colombia Amazónica*, pp. 129–273. Bogotá: Universidad Nacional de Colombia y Fondo "José Celestino Mutis."

Rindos, David
1984   *The Origins of Agriculture: An Evolutionary Perspective*. Orlando, Fla.: Academic Press.

Roosevelt, Anna C.
1991   *Moundbuilders of the Amazon: Geophysical Archaeology on Marajo Island, Brazil*. San Diego: Academic Press.

Rosengren, Dan
1981/2 Proximity and Interaction: The Case of the Matsigenka of the Upper Urubamba, Southeastern Peru. Gøteborgs Etnografiska Museum, *Arstryck* 48–63.

Ross, Eric
1978   Food Taboos, Diet and Hunting Strategy: The Adaptation to Animals in Amazon Cultural Ecology. *Current Anthropology* 19:1–36.

Ruddle, Kenneth
1971   Notes on the Nomenclature and the Distribution of the Yukpa-Yuko Tribe. *Antropológica* 30:18–27.

Salzano, F. M., J. V. Neel, H. Gershowitz, and E. C. Migliazza
1977   Intra and Intertribal Genetic Variation within a Linguistic Group: The Ge-speaking Indians of Brazil. *American Journal of Physical Anthropology* 47:337–47.

Seeger, Anthony
1981   *Nature and Society in Central Brazil: The Suya Indians of Mato Grosso.* Cambridge, Mass.: Harvard University Press.

Shimada, Izumi
1985   Cultural Continuities and Discontinuities on the Northern North Coast, Middle-Late Horizons. In *The Northern Dynasties: Kingship and Statecraft in Chimor,* edited by M. E. Moseley and A. Cordy-Collins, pp. 297–392. Washington, D.C.: Dumbarton Oaks.

Shukla, Jagadish
1987   General Circulation Modeling and the Tropics. In *The Geophysiology of Amazonia,* edited by R. E. Dickinson, pp. 409–58. Chicago: University of Chicago Press.

Shukla, J., C. Nobre, and P. Sellers
1990   Amazon Deforestation and Climatic Change. *Science* 247:1322–25.

Simões, Mário F., and Fernanda de Araujo Costa
1987   Pesquisas arqueológicas no baixo rio Tocantins (Pará). *Revista Arqueologia* 4:11–27. Belém, Brazil.

Smith, Nigel J.
1980   Anthrosols and Human Carrying Capacity in Amazonia. *Annals of the Association of American Geographers* 70:533–66.

Smole, William J.
1976   *The Yanomama Indians: A Cultural Geography.* Austin: University of Texas Press.
1989   Yanomama Horticulture in the Parima Highlands of Venezuela and Brazil. *Advances in Economic Botany* 7:115–28.

Soares, Lúcio de Castro
1977   Hidrografia. In *Geografia do Brasil: Vol. I, Região norte.* Rio de Janeiro: Fundação Instituto Brasileiro de Geografia e Estatística.

Spielman, Richard S., Ernest C. Migliazza, and James V. Neel
1974   Regional Linguistic and Genetic Differences among Yanomama Indians. *Science* 184:637–44.

Van der Hammen, Thomas
1974   The Pleistocene Changes of Vegetation and Climate in Tropical South America. *Journal of Biogeography* 1:3–26.

Verswijver, Gustaaf
1978   Separations et migrations des Mekragnoti: Groupe Kayapó du Brésil Central. Boletin de la Société Suisse des Américanistes 42:47–59.

Vickers, William T.
1983   The Territorial Dimensions of Siona-Secoya and Encabello Adaptation. In *Adaptive Responses of Native Amazonians*, edited by Raymond B. Hames and William T. Vickers, pp. 451–78. New York: Academic Press.

Vidal O., Silvia M.
1989   Consideraciones etnográficas sobre la cerámica de los Piapoco. Asociación Venezolana de Arqueología, Boletín 5:36–59.

Whitmore, T. C., and G. T. Prance, eds.
1987   *Biogeography and Quaternary History in Tropical America*. Oxford: Clarendon Press.

Williams, Denis
1992   El arcaico en el noroeste de Guyana y los comienzos de la horticultura. In *Prehistoria Sudamericana: Nuevas Perspectivas*, edited by Betty J. Meggers, pp. 233–51. Washington, D.C.: Taraxacum.

2

The History of Ecological Interpretations of Amazonia: Does Roosevelt Have It Right?

Robert L. Carneiro

With her excavations at Parmana on the middle Orinoco and on Marajó Island at the mouth of the Amazon, Anna Roosevelt has staked a claim to being the leading archaeologist of Amazonia. Anyone professionally concerned with the culture history of this region cannot help but be interested in her latest pronouncements on the subject. Accordingly, I was prompted to read Roosevelt's article "Determinismo ecológico na interpretação do desenvolvimento social indígena da Amazônia" (1991a) as soon as it came into my hands.

In this work Roosevelt sets out to trace the advances made over the last half-century in interpreting Amazonian prehistory. Having carefully read her article, I must say that I find her treatment of the subject to be at odds with the facts—so much so that I feel compelled to offer a different version of this history, one that I think comes closer to the truth.

Roosevelt herself invites criticism of her views, speaking of "the good effect that healthy competition and intellectual debate among a number of strong scholars can have to foster progress" (1991b:115). I fully agree, and cheerfully accept her invitation.

My aim in this paper, however, is not simply to criticize and correct what I deem to be Roosevelt's errors. It is also to amplify, if possible, our understanding of Amazonian cultural development.

I should also make it clear that my quarrel is not with Roosevelt's current views on the determinants of this development. Leaving aside her "maize hypothesis," which I have criticized elsewhere (Carneiro n.d.) and which I will discuss later in this chapter, I find her ideas about how Amazonian chiefdoms arose to be in accordance with my own. (Indeed, I claim to have contributed to them!) But I would go farther and say a word of praise for Anna Roosevelt. In several of her works, especially those dated 1987 and 1991b, she has woven a fuller tapestry of Amazonian chiefdoms than anyone else has attempted so far. Still, among the golden threads of her fabric one can detect a few strands of horsehair. And these deserve to be removed and discarded.

Let us get down to cases. To begin with, Roosevelt's main argument in this paper (1991a) is a familiar one. She holds that Betty Meggers's views regarding the limiting effects of a tropical rain forest environment on the development of Amazonian culture were wrong. Meggers had argued that the rain forest could not give rise to chiefdoms, and if a chiefdom were introduced into Amazonia from the outside, it could not long survive there. This notion, Roosevelt contends, was mistaken, and the error mis-led an entire generation of Amazonianists. The result was, she says, that attempts to understand the true nature of Amazonian cultural develop-ment were stultified.

Fortunately, says Roosevelt, this error was eventually rectified. And indeed it was. But because of the foreshortened version of the rectifica-tion she presents, the novice reader is left to conclude that it was she herself who first discovered and corrected Meggers's errors. A closer look at the history of this rectification reveals a rather different story.

The first specific critique to be made of Roosevelt's article is that she paints with too broad a brush. It is true that Amazonianists today agree that in some of her views Meggers was wrong, that she underestimated the carrying capacity of the Amazon basin. But Roosevelt attributes this error to Meggers's adherence to the doctrine of "ecological determinism," pure and simple, and this is patently false. "Ecological determinism" was not to blame for this misstep. Only *one particular view of it* was. Thus Roosevelt's refutation of Meggers's version of "ecological determinism" leaves the general explanatory principle intact. It certainly does nothing to invalidate the view that ecological factors exerted a profound influence on the rise of Amazonian chiefdoms. Yet countless times in her paper Roosevelt inveighs against "ecological determinism" as if it were all of a piece.[1]

But there is an irony here, and it is this. Throughout her paper, as well as elsewhere in her writings, Roosevelt not only fails to banish ecological factors from her interpretations but actually adopts and applies them, repeatedly and effectively. Indeed, in the one single crumb she throws to Betty Meggers, Roosevelt acknowledges that the empirical research prompted by Meggers's theory "has brought out, quite properly, the rele-vance of ecological factors in Amazonian anthropology" (1991a:104).[2]

Moreover, Roosevelt goes well beyond this. Later in her paper, while noting that the first ceramic-yielding sites in Amazonia are found in *vár-zea* and estuarine environments, she says (1991a:118): "This association between ecologically favorable regions and cultural development is not very surprising given the abundance and concentration of subsistence re-sources which these areas present. Such resources could foster more permanent settlements and population growth which, in turn, initiated subsequent changes in the subsistence economy and in socio-political organization." Could anything be more ecological?

What Roosevelt does, in effect, is to stand Meggers's argument on its head. She asserts that not only did ecological factors not *limit* cultural development in the Amazon but that in certain favored areas they actu-ally *propelled* it. Indeed, one cannot read the body of Roosevelt's work without being impressed by the positive role she assigns to ecological factors. Thus, while purporting to deny ecological determinism as an explanatory principle, she warmly embraces particular applications of it.

I might note, in passing, that ecological interpretations of Amazonian culture history, with various ecological factors assigned either a positive or a negative role, have dominated Amazonian research for the last half-century, with no other point of view being even a serious competitor.[3]

In her unrelenting attacks on Meggers's views, Roosevelt shows a failure to grasp the recent state of Amazonianist thinking. She writes as if Meg-gers's theory was not only alive but also posed a continuing threat to current understanding (e.g., 1991a:104). The fact is, however, that this theory has been dead for 20 years. Indeed, Meggers herself implicitly laid it to rest in 1971 (1971:121–49).[4]

Another misconception—or misrepresentation—to be found in the ar-ticle under review involves the role played by ethnologists in assessing the validity of Meggers's theory. Repeatedly Roosevelt chastises ethnologists, charging not only that they failed to point out Meggers's errors but also that they actively helped to propagate them (e.g., 1991a:104, 105, 108, 114–15, 124, 128). "Empirical ethnographic works with an ecological determinist base," Roosevelt says, "were not effective in revealing the er-rors of the theory" (1991a:107). But this is simply not true. In my Ph.D. dissertation, "Subsistence and Social Structure: An Ecological Study of the Kuikuru Indians" (Carneiro 1957), a work with which Roosevelt (1980:279) is acquainted, I specifically challenged several of Meggers's notions about the limits imposed on Amazonian culture by a rain forest environment. And my arguments on this score were published a few years later (Carneiro 1960, 1961).

One comes away from Roosevelt's article with the impression that in the formation of our present understanding of the growth of Amazonian culture, ethnologists had no part. It was archaeologists, particularly herself, we are led to believe, who played the dominant, if not the exclusive, role. In order to argue this, however, Roosevelt has had to skip over many of the actual steps involved in achieving our current understanding of Amazonia. As an ethnologist who considers himself to have participated in forging this understanding, I feel that an effort is needed to set the record straight.

The Evolution of Amazonian Societies

In a series of papers beginning in 1960 (Carneiro 1960, 1961, 1964, 1970a, 1970b, 1970c, 1971, 1979, 1981, 1983, 1987a, 1987b, 1987c), I took up a number of issues relating to the evolution of Amazonian societies. In several of these papers I opposed Meggers's notion of Amazonia's limited cultural potential, bringing to bear both factual data and theoretical arguments. Not only did I point out the existence of indigenous chiefdoms in Amazonia at contact times, but I also proposed a theory to account for them. Because in her current paper Roosevelt, with only one exception,[5] passes over these publications in silence, I would like to review their main points here.

It was once widely held—and explicitly proclaimed by Betty Meggers (1954:807)—that because of the inhibiting effects of slash-and-burn cultivation in the tropical forests of Amazonia, Indian villages were forced to remain small. Indeed, Meggers went so far as to propose a limit of 1,000 persons on the size Amazonian villages could attain. In a paper first read in 1956 (but not published until 1960), I challenged this supposition. Citing ethnographic data I had collected among the Kuikuru of central Brazil in 1953–54, and employing a series of calculations incorporating these data, I was able to show that "with slash-and-burn as the only limiting factor, a village of some 2,000 persons could live on a permanent basis where the Kuikuru do now" (Carneiro 1961:232).[6]

In a second paper, published the following year (Carneiro 1961), I disputed several other commonly held notions about Indian culture in the Amazon—that slash-and-burn cultivators invariably must relocate their villages, that food productivity among them was low, that a surplus of food could not be produced or preserved, that there was little or no leisure time left after subsistence, and that tropical forest soils were uniformly poor.[7] Thus, 30 years before Roosevelt's current paper, I had already challenged Meggers's (1954:809) views that "the environmental potential of the tropical forest is sufficient to allow the evolution of culture to proceed only to the level represented by the Tropical Forest [autonomous village] culture pattern" and that "further indigenous evolution is impossible" (1954:809).

In later fieldwork among the Amahuaca of eastern Peru (1960–61), I took soil samples from garden plots, abandoned fields, and surrounding forest, and had them analyzed. Commenting on the results of this analysis, Dr. Hugh Popenoe of the department of soils at the University of Florida noted that "these are fairly good agricultural soils and with possible supplementary additions of nitrogen . . . could produce crops continuously" (quoted in Carneiro 1964:16n). These soil analyses, incidentally, might have been used to advantage by Roosevelt in arguing, as she does (but without citing any empirical evidence), that the newer soils of the Ucayali basin are more fertile than those of certain other parts of Amazonia (1991a:110).

I should point out, though, that at the time I wrote my two earlier papers (1960, 1961) I was evidently still unaware of the previous existence of chiefdoms along the Amazon. Nor was I fully cognizant of the important differences between riverine and interfluvial habitats. By the end of the decade, however, I was quite aware of this distinction and of its significance for peoples living in the two types of habitat. In a paper read in 1968 and published two years later, I wrote:

> From a cultural-ecological point of view the Amazon basin may be thought of as comprising two distinct types of habitat, one consisting of areas lying along the major rivers, and the other of areas located away from them. These two types of habitat differ strikingly in the amount of fish and other riverine food resources which they make available for human exploitation. In the small rivers and streams of the interfluvial areas, fish are relatively few in number and small in size. In such areas fishing can hardly serve as the major source of protein.   (Carneiro 1970b:245)

And I went on to discuss the differences in subsistence and settlement patterns a riverine environment made possible:

> A marked contrast to this situation is afforded by tribes living along the larger rivers. Since these rivers offer food in tremendous quantities, fishing comes more and more to displace hunting. Moreover, since the supply of riverine food is not only abundant but literally inexhaustible, tribes living on the major rivers seldom if ever face the need to move their villages because of a shortage of protein.   (Carneiro 1970b:245)

Then I looked at the contrast between interfluvial and riverine peoples as reflected in settlement patterns:

> Interfluvial peoples, forced to maintain a relatively high reliance on hunting, adopted agriculture only to a limited extent, and remained small in size and semi-nomadic in settlement pattern. Riverine peoples [on the other hand], finding it possible to subsist heavily on fish and other river animals, became more sedentary, embraced agriculture more fully, and developed larger villages. (Carneiro 1970b:245)

I then proceeded to characterize the general level of culture attained by these river dwellers, adding:

> Differences between interfluvial and riverine peoples went beyond those of size and settlement permanence. Social, political, and ceremonial distinctions of considerable magnitude arose as well. Indeed, where riverine resources were most bountiful of all, on the Amazon River itself, tribes such as the Omagua, Manao, and Tapajó approached and even attained a Circum-Caribbean [chiefdom] level of culture. (Carneiro 1970b:245)

Finally, in the same year, in an article entitled "A Theory of the Origin of the State," I noted:

> Early voyagers down the Amazon left written testimony of a culture along that river higher than the culture I have described for Amazonia generally. In the 1500s, the native population living on the banks of the Amazon was relatively dense, villages were fairly large and close together, and some degree of social stratification existed. Moreover, here and there a paramount chief held sway over many communities. (Carneiro 1970a:736)

Clearly, then, by 1970 I had recognized that chiefdoms had existed on the Amazon and had expressed it unequivocally in print. And I also noted that chiefdoms were not restricted to the Amazon but occurred as well on the Mojos plain of Bolivia (Carneiro 1970b:738n).

Let me make it clear, though, that I do not claim to be the first or the only one among contemporary Amazonianists to have recognized these facts. Donald Lathrap, for one, had done so as well, as I clearly acknowledged in my review of his book, *The Upper Amazon* (1970):

> Two opposing views of Amazonian prehistory exist. On the one hand there is the view of Meggers and Evans that Amazonia is an area of poor subsistence, where indigenous cultures could not rise above the level of small and simple autonomous villages. Those cultures which appear to transcend this level, such as Marajoara on Marajó Island, are interpreted by Meggers and Evans as intrusive. They came out of the Andes at a chiefdom level, but soon declined to a Tropical Forest level when subjected to the limitations of a rain forest environment. With this view Lathrap strongly disagrees. He contends that Amazonia, or at least its major rivers, amply rewarded its agricultural

and fishing peoples, and that along the Amazon proper, cultures evolved indigenously to the level of chiefdoms.   (Carneiro 1971:238)

Thus, eight years before Roosevelt had published a line on the subject, there were on record at least two clear statements that chiefdoms had arisen in Amazonia. And indeed, this was already the prevailing view among Amazonianists generally when Roosevelt first entered the field. It is fair to say, then, that Roosevelt absorbed this view rather than invented it.

During the 1970s I continued to focus my attention on chiefdoms, and in an article entitled "Factors Favoring the Development of Political Leadership in Amazonia" (1979) I attempted to summarize and synthesize my knowledge of these complex polities, noting:

> This step in political evolution occurred in two areas of Amazonia: along the Amazon River itself, and in the Mojos plain of what is now Bolivia. Amazon River tribes which attained multi-village chiefdoms included the Omagua, Manao, and Tapajó, while in the Mojos plain chiefdoms developed among the Mojo, Bauré, Manasí, and Cayuvava. These chiefdoms did not long survive white contact, and so the details of their organization never became [well] known. But their existence is indisputable.   (Carneiro 1979:88–89)

In this same article I went on to quote from Carvajal's account of Orellana's voyage down the Amazon in 1542, during which the Spaniards encountered a number of chiefdoms. At one point, Carvajal wrote: "We arrived in the provinces belonging to Machiparo [apparently an Omagua chief], who is a very great overlord and one having many people under him. . . . It took us [two days and two nights] . . . to get out of the territory occupied by the subjects of this great overlord" (Medina 1934:190, 198). And after leaving the Omagua behind, the Spaniards encountered still other chiefdoms, including Oníguayal and Paguana (Medina 1934: 199, 200, 202).

Turning to the Bolivian llanos, I noted that "while the chiefdoms of the Mojos plain may not have attained quite the same scale as those along the Amazon, the power of their political leaders was nonetheless substantially greater than that of a typical Tropical Forest chief" (1979:89). And I proceeded to quote from a monograph by Alfred Métraux, written as early as 1942, that showed a clear recognition of the high level of political organization attained in the Mojos area (Métraux 1942:129). (The portrayal of Mojos societies as full-fledged chiefdoms was further extended by William Denevan in *The Aboriginal Cultural Geography of the Llanos de Mojos of Bolivia* [Denevan 1966:43–50, 104–105, 108–110], a work I had already cited in "A Theory of the Origin of the State" [1970a:738n].)

After reviewing the solid evidence for the existence of chiefdoms in two separate areas of Amazonia, I continued as follows: "The question remains: what special conditions were present along the Amazon River and in the Mojos plain that enabled multi-village chiefdoms to arise there when they did not do so in other parts of Amazonia?" (1979:89). And I proceeded to discuss such things as the availability of várzea, the huge quantities of aquatic food resources found in the waters of the Amazon, and other ecological factors, including population pressure and warfare, that seemed to me involved in the process of chiefdom formation (Carneiro 1979:89–91).

In yet another article, "Further Reflections on Resource Concentration and Its Role in the Rise of the State" (1987a), I took a closer look at how the clustering of wild food resources along the Amazon had contributed to the emergence of chiefdoms there. In doing so, incidentally, I openly acknowledged a valid criticism of my earlier discussion of chiefdom formation on the Amazon that Roosevelt (1980:37–39) had made in her book *Parmana*. And I modified my original argument in order to take account of her strictures (Carneiro 1987a:248–50).

It should be evident, then, that over the course of three decades, I as well as others have devoted considerable attention to the fact that chiefdoms could and did arise in Amazonia and to why they had done so. With that much settled, let us turn now to what Roosevelt has to say in her recent paper (1991a) about when and where these chiefdoms arose.

Roosevelt's Views on the Evolution of Chiefdoms

Since excavating the site of Parmana on the middle Orinoco, Roosevelt has moved her archaeological investigations to the Island of Marajó and has dug in the very area where Meggers and Evans first unearthed and described the chiefdom-level culture of Marajoara. But unlike her predecessors, Roosevelt (1991b:3) concluded from her work there that "Marajoara society was not an ephemeral, ill-adapted manifestation but a successful, long-term adaptation that continuously occupied its habitat . . . for hundreds of years." Indeed, she even went so far as to call Marajoara "one of the great tropical chiefdoms of the world" (Roosevelt 1991b:119).

Roosevelt's excavations on Marajó and her later surface survey of Santarém (the capital of the old Tapajó chiefdom) gave her a fuller notion of the extent and antiquity of Amazonian chiefdoms. The gist of her current ideas about these matters are contained in the article under discussion.

First, let us see what date Roosevelt assigns to the earliest Amazonian chiefdoms. I should note that Meggers and Evans (1957:422) had attributed the relatively late date of about A.D. 1250 to the beginning of Marajoara, the archaeological phase of Marajó they associated with a sub-Andean or Circum-Caribbean — that is, a chiefdom level — of culture. But Roosevelt has pushed back the date for initial Marajoara by nearly 1,000 years, dating it now at A.D. 400 (1991b:1). Nevertheless, she does not seem to regard Marajoara as the earliest chiefdom in Amazonia.

Since a chiefdom is, first and foremost, a form of political organization, it leaves no direct evidence of itself. Its presence must be inferred from the recovery of material objects that indirectly reflect its existence. The commonest and most easily retrievable of such evidence is elaborate pottery, the theory being that such pottery could be produced only by full-time specialists, who in turn could not arise until a chiefdom, with the means of supporting them, was firmly in place.

On page 113 of her article Roosevelt (1991a) writes as follows: "Between 4000 and 3000 B.P. [2000–1000 B.C.], societies with elaborately decorated ceramics and with wide-mouthed bowls in abundance give evidence of an efficient horticulture, based on the cultivation of tropical root crops." If we take "elaborately decorated ceramics" as indicating a chiefdom, this would *appear* to place the first Amazonian chiefdoms back as early as 1500 B.C. But Roosevelt probably does not mean to imply this, since later she speaks of "the beginning of the Christian era, when the first signs of the organization of chiefdoms make their appearance" (1991a: 126).

I certainly am not competent to judge the date of the emergence of chiefdoms on Marajó or elsewhere in the Amazon. As an ethnologist, I have no basis for challenging Roosevelt's estimate of this date. Archaeological facts and not ethnological theory must determine it. Nonetheless, I am keenly interested in the date she assigns to this event because it bears heavily on theory — the theory Roosevelt presented at length in *Parmana* (1980) on what triggered the rise of Amazonian chiefdoms in the first place.

Simply stated, Roosevelt held that only with the advent of maize were the Indian villages of the middle Orinoco (and the Amazon) able to obtain enough protein to allow them to become sedentary, a condition generally held to be a prerequisite of chiefdom formation. At the site of Parmana, Roosevelt found that the introduction of maize coincided with archaeological evidence for a jump in population, and this jump in turn coincided, she thinks, with the emergence of chiefdoms. Accordingly, her inference was that the introduction of maize had given the initial impetus to the rise of Orinocoan chiefdoms.

Parmana, however, was only one case. Later, working on Marajó Island on the lower Amazon, Roosevelt had an opportunity to see whether the introduction of maize at this site again coincided with, and appeared to precipitate, the origin of chiefdoms. If it did, her theory would be strengthened; if it didn't, it would be overturned.

Before examining what Roosevelt found on Marajó, a little more background to her maize theory is in order. It is clear that for this theory to hold, riverine food resources—fish, turtles, manatees, and so forth— would have had to be insufficient to provide Indians living on the Orinoco and the Amazon with the amount of protein they required. Thus, in arguing for her maize hypothesis in *Parmana*, Roosevelt needed to minimize the availability of riverine protein to the Indians living on those rivers. And so she did (1980:95–112).

Having found from my own field experience among the Kuikuru, as well as from a reading of the relevant literature, how extraordinarily abundant fish were in the larger rivers of Amazonia, it seemed to me that Roosevelt's theory would not stand up. In a paper entitled "The Ecological Basis of Amazonian Chiefdoms," written in 1986 but not yet published, I marshaled considerable evidence against it. Since the reasons for my opposition to the maize theory are stated in full in that paper, I will not repeat them here in any detail. The essence of my argument is that the Orinoco and the Amazon can be shown to have supported fish, turtles, and manatees in such vast numbers that they could—and did—provide all the protein the natives living along those rivers could possibly need. And these virtually inexhaustible riverine resources made it possible for villages to remain sedentary and for native populations to grow dense—conditions that Roosevelt and I agree were necessary for chiefdoms to emerge.

"The Ecological Basis of Amazonian Chiefdoms" is, however, still in press. So in order that my argument against the maize theory not appear to rest on mere assertion, I give here the sources of the evidence I cited against it: Gumilla (1963:219–32); Medina (1934:192, 193, 204, 207, 409, 414–15, 419, 430); Ursúa (1861:31); and Acuña (1891:50–55). In March 1987 I presented Anna Roosevelt with a copy of this paper, which shortly thereafter she acknowledged having read.

Now back to the present debate. It is curious that in Roosevelt's current paper, with its sweeping account of Amazonian cultural development, there is no specific mention of her maize theory. Even more surprising, neither is it mentioned in her recent book, *Moundbuilders of the Amazon* (1991b). Indeed, maize, so conspicuously the theoretical centerpiece of *Parmana* that an old engraving of a maize plant occurs as a decorative motif on the first page of every chapter, does not even appear in the index of *Moundbuilders of the Amazon*.

What status, then, does Roosevelt now accord to the maize theory? In her current assessment, was maize, after all, a sine qua non for the rise of Amazonian chiefdoms? Let us see what answer we can glean from a close inspection of her latest article.

On page 117 she notes that the absence of carbonized seeds from the earlier levels of Marajó, as well as the evidence provided by the isotopic study of skeletal remains, indicates that "the first Amazonian societies with elaborate ceramics [presumably chiefdoms] depended principally on plant cultivation [of manioc] and . . . obtained their protein principally from the abundant riverine fauna." Then on page 125 she notes that "maize became the principal food source of tropical lowlands only shortly before the Christian era, *well after the rise of complex societies in this region*" (emphasis mine).

It would appear, then, that Roosevelt has quietly abandoned her maize hypothesis. She no longer seems to hold that the cultivation of this plant was a prerequisite for the emergence of chiefdoms. But if she has in fact renounced her maize theory, why does she do it so unobtrusively? Why leave it to others to ferret out this significant demarche from the interstices of her work? It seems to me that a theory so boldly trumpeted at its inception should not be laid to rest so silently. If this is, indeed, the demise of the maize hypothesis, it deserves a decent burial, and not simply deposition in an unmarked grave.

But Roosevelt, who opposes Meggers in so many ways, has chosen to emulate her in this regard. In chapter 4 of her book *Amazonia: Man and Culture in a Counterfeit Paradise* (1971), Meggers described the Omagua and Tapajó, of the upper and lower Amazon, respectively, as being full-blown chiefdoms. Yet nowhere in the book does she concede that portraying them as such constitutes, ipso facto, a renunciation of her thesis that chiefdoms could not arise in Amazonia.[8]

Now, although Roosevelt seems to have demoted maize from the place it once held as the trigger mechanism for the rise of Amazonian chiefdoms, she nonetheless continues to accord it an important role in the sustenance of somewhat later chiefdoms. Thus she writes: "The chemical composition of the bones of prehistoric human skeletons in Amazonia ($n = 36$) shows that there was little or no consumption of maize until shortly before the Christian era, after which its cultivation became the principal food source on the middle Orinoco, the upper Ucayali, and the lower Amazon" (1991a:125). And speaking of Amazonian chiefdoms at the time of first white contact, she says that "their subsistence systems were intensive and concentrated on the cultivation of seed crops, including maize" (1991a:121).

She may be right. Although she incorrectly downplays the productivity of manioc (see Carneiro 1983:95), maize may nevertheless have come to surpass it in importance among a number of Amazonian chiefdoms. At any rate, I am not prepared to dispute the point. I know from my own fieldwork that the Amahuaca of eastern Peru relied more heavily on maize than on manioc, and that the average family among them harvested some 25,000 to 30,000 ears of corn a year (Carneiro 1964:17).

But the importance of maize to later Amazonian chiefdoms is a separate issue. Our concern here is to determine the root cause of chiefdoms, so our focus must remain on what conditions existed just prior to their emergence. And if the cultivation of maize was not one of them, it is important to give this fact proper emphasis.

The Role of Ecological Factors in the Evolution of Amazonian Chiefdoms

In the rest of this paper I would like to set aside criticism and deal more positively with the interplay of some of the ecological factors that gave rise to Amazonian chiefdoms. In doing so I will look especially at two major types of agricultural land available to peoples living along the Amazon: *terra firme* and várzea.

While Roosevelt devotes a good deal of space to a fairly technical discussion of the soil types of Amazonia (1991a:108–11) and refers in several places to terra firme and várzea (e.g., 1991a:109, 111, 112), she never clearly distinguishes between them. Nor does she draw the full implications of their differences for native systems of agriculture. Let me, therefore, attempt to do so.

As Brazilians use the term, terra firme is land lying high enough above the adjacent rivers so that it never floods. Most of the Amazon Basin, including virtually all the land between the large rivers—the so-called "interfluves"—consists of terra firme.

Várzea refers to low-lying land along the Amazon and other major rivers that seasonally overflow their banks and inundate their surroundings.[9] Because the sediment deposited by the annual flooding of such rivers is rich in mineral nutrients, várzea has high agricultural value.[10] And because its fertility is replenished every year, it need not be fallowed after only two or three years of cultivation, as is usually true for terra firme. Instead, it may be planted year after year. Being agricultural land of prime quality, várzea was much sought after—and fought for—by the Indians who lived in its vicinity (Medina 1934:190).

Despite its high fertility, várzea has certain drawbacks. Since it is underwater half the year, it cannot be cultivated year-round. Whatever crops are planted on it must be harvested within six months or so. This presents a problem for manioc, the tubers of which normally take 16 to 18 months to reach optimal size. However, the Indian cultivators who once lived along the Amazon had found a partial solution to this problem. They had developed a variety of manioc—called *mandioca puré* in Brazil—that yields tubers of edible, if not optimal, size in just 6 months (Loureiro 1986:27).

The short várzea growing season, however, posed no problem at all for maize. Maize grows extremely fast in the tropics. I have seen maize planted by Amahuaca Indians living on the Ucayali River grow to a height of 13 feet and produce full, ripe ears in exactly two months. Thus, not only could maize ripen on várzea during its short growing season, but it also could easily produce two crops a year. Moreover, maize needs the high fertility of várzea soil, whereas manioc will yield at least five tons of roots per acre even when cultivated on poor, acid soils (Carneiro 1983:95).[11]

In addition to its short growing season, várzea has another drawback, one that would have made it unwise, if not impossible, for native agriculturalists to rely on it exclusively. It is that várzea cannot be counted on for cultivation every year. I was in Manaus in early August of 1975, by which time the floodwaters of the Amazon should have substantially receded. But the rainy season that year had seen the river crest at a very high level, and thus it was taking longer than usual for it to give back the land it had flooded. A lot of várzea that should have been high and dry and ready for planting by then was still under water.[12]

The implications of this uncertainty for native agriculturalists should be clear: they could not afford to put all their eggs in one basket. Várzea could never have been the only land reserved for growing crops. Some reliance must also have been placed on terra firme. The innumerable villages that once dotted the margins of the Amazon must—at least in certain years—have been forced to make use of terra firme. In years of excessive flooding, then, terra firme would have served as a kind of "crop insurance."

Although the early chroniclers appear to be silent on this point, the general rule for pre-Columbian cultivators was probably this: During ordinary years, raise all maize and as much manioc as possible on várzea, but be ready to turn to terra firme for both crops during years when floodwaters fail to recede quickly enough.

On the two occasions I have traveled on the Amazon—in 1975 and 1991—I noted that high bluffs, the tops of which provide terra firme, are to be found here and there along the river. I especially remember a hilltop near Manaus called Morro de Santantonio, which lies within the angle formed by the Rio Negro and the Solimões as they converge to form the Amazon proper. Plenty of várzea lies around the base of this hill, while the top, which stands well above high water, affords an ample amount of terra firme. Unquestionably this must have been a choice site for an Indian village—indeed, for the capital of a pre-Columbian chiefdom. Besides providing high land, secure from flooding even during very rainy years, the hilltop affords a view of both the Rio Negro and the Solimões looking upstream and of the Amazon looking downstream. In those early warlike days, the approach of enemy canoes from any direction could easily have been detected while they were still a considerable distance away.

My surmise that this was a prime site for native settlement was confirmed by a little surface survey. The present-day road that cuts around the downstream end of the hill has left an exposed embankment from which potsherds protrude throughout much of its profile. So far as I know, this site has never been systematically excavated, although I understand that Mario Simões dug a few test pits here some decades ago.

Cultural Development on the Lower Amazon

Using a longer focus, let me now attempt—with Roosevelt's help—to sketch the broad outlines of cultural development on the lower Amazon. Even before the coming of agriculture, the riverine food resources of this river, being extraordinarily bountiful, drew early Indian populations to its banks. Resource concentration was at work and produced the expected results. As Roosevelt (1991a:126) notes, "Paleo-Indians spread throughout the interior of the whole region at the beginning of the Holocene, and soon afterwards, in areas of rich soils and productive waters, people established themselves in large settlements subsisting on the intensive taking of fish, mollusks, and, in some areas, the products of certain trees" (see also p. 115). We have evidence of this form of subsistence in the huge shell mounds—*sambaquis*—that are found here and there along the Amazon (Roosevelt 1991a:115–16).

There is a striking parallel here (which Roosevelt alludes to [1991a: 110, 112, 113]) between the cultures of the Amazon at this time and those of the European Mesolithic and North American Archaic. In parts of the eastern North American woodlands, for example, the Archaic period saw a reorientation of subsistence from big game hunting to the exploitation of aquatic resources. And this change was likewise accompanied by the early establishment of large, sedentary villages. At the Koster site on the

Illinois River, for instance, "as early as 6500 B.C. . . . [Archaic peoples] were eating enormous quantities of freshwater fish and mussels," and by 3900 B.C., well before the coming of agriculture, there was already a series of large, permanent villages in the region (Struever and Holton 1979:155–56).

Summarizing the picture of Eastern Woodlands culture during this period, Emerson and McElrath (1983:231) write: "The small, constantly shifting, mobile bands of hunters and gatherers still dominate many scholars' research on the Archaic . . . [but] there is little evidence to support this latter model for the Terminal Late Archaic cultures of the American Bottom. Data indicate that these cultural groups had adopted a sedentary life-style as a result of their exploitation of the rich environment of the river valley."

Thus it is that in different parts of the world similar environments led to similar cultural adaptations, providing yet another example of the power of ecological factors to shape cultures in parallel ways.

Writing of the period of sambaqui shellfish gatherers, Roosevelt (1991a: 116) remarks: "This early adaptation to intensive foraging was not ephemeral. It flourished as a self-sustaining system for no less than 4,000 years." Now, the fact that these foragers were already largely sedentary was to have a profound effect. It permitted them to begin experimenting with the domestication of local food plants that heretofore had been gathered wild. The flora thus exploited included mostly seed plants, notably, Roosevelt tells us, chenopodium (1991a:121).[13] No doubt the rich várzea soil made these experiments in domestication rewarding enough to encourage the sambaqui dwellers to turn increasingly to agriculture as a means of supplementing their diet.

The next important event in the subsistence history of Amazonia, which occurred around 2000 B.C., was the introduction of manioc (Roosevelt 1991a:117). Once adopted and grown as a staple crop by riverine peoples, manioc proved to be "productive enough to become the primary source of calories," relegating the local domesticates to a subsidiary role (1991a:116). This new and broader subsistence base made possible a higher level of culture. Roosevelt (1991a:117) notes that "the first Amazonian societies with elaborate ceramics depended principally on the cultivation [of manioc] for their calories," their protein continuing to come "primarily from the abundant riverine fauna" (1991a:117). Later, around 200 B.C., maize was introduced to the Amazon, further widening the subsistence base. Over time, then, crop plants came to rival and eventually surpass riverine fauna as the major source of food (Roosevelt 1991a: 116, 117).

The abundant and reliable food supply that agriculture and fishing together assured to these native populations spurred their growth. Within perhaps a few centuries of the full-scale adoption of agriculture, the growing density of occupation along the Amazon gave rise to population pressure. As choice farmland, especially várzea, came into short supply, villages began competing with one another for it, and the ensuing warfare became progressively more intense. At first it led to the victors' simply dispossessing the losers of their land, but later the result was the subjugation and incorporation of the enemy groups themselves. The outcome of this process (which I have described in detail elsewhere [e.g., Carneiro 1970a, 1979, 1981, 1987a]), was supravillage aggregation and integration, giving rise to the first Amazonian chiefdoms.

But the process did not stop there. Fighting over river frontage continued, and successive conquests led to the formation of larger and larger chiefdoms. This increase in the size of political units was accompanied by their internal elaboration, including such things as the development of powerful chiefs, the emergence of social classes, the elaboration of arts and crafts, and a number of related features. Eventually, polities of impressive size and complexity developed along the Amazon and were still flourishing there in 1542 when Orellana navigated its length. The early chroniclers provided tantalizingly sketchy accounts of these great chiefdoms, and a few archaeologists—Anna Roosevelt preeminent among them—are now attempting to provide us with more and more details of their material remains. These data, when sufficiently well assembled, should help us piece together a fuller picture of their emergence, expansion, and florescence.

Indeed, Roosevelt has already begun doing this herself. Although she says little about the precise mechanisms and processes of chiefdom formation, she sees chiefdoms emerging in much the same ways I have previously described (e.g., Carneiro 1970a, 1979, 1981, 1987a). Thus, she considers their rise to be "linked in a causal manner to the presence of concentrated resources favorable to agriculture" (1991a:126) and as occurring "at a time of increased population density in the floodplains" (1991b:114; see also 1991a:126, 1991b:436). And she does not shy away from warfare as the instrument by which village autonomy was surmounted and once-independent communities welded together into multivillage chiefdoms (1991a:120, 126–27, 128, 1991b:407, 411, 422–23). In the end, she sees some of the chiefdoms that emerged in Amazonia as attaining extraordinary dimensions (1991a:118–19, 120–21, 1991b:436), a few of them even appearing to her "to have been urban in scale and complexity" (1991b:

113). Establishing this claim as fact, however, will require considerably more evidence.

Factors Preventing the Rise of Chiefdoms

But now, what about the many Amazonian groups that failed to evolve into chiefdoms? Where were they located and what held them back? For the most part, the villages that remained autonomous were situated in the interfluvial regions. Roosevelt's treatment of the interfluves is somewhat ambivalent. On the one hand, she recognizes that some interfluvial soils on terra firme are relatively fertile (1991a:108–11, 130). But by and large she regards such soils as inferior, writing, for example, of the "nutrient-poor terra firme forest habitats" (1991b:19) and remarking that "anthropologists are correct in concluding that most of the interfluvial areas which Indians now occupy are inadequate for supporting large populations and for intensive use of the land" (1991a:133; see also pp. 108, 112, 113).[14]

It was the poverty of these soils, precluding, in her opinion, high crop yields, that she holds primarily responsible for the failure of the large, sedentary populations needed for the rise of chiefdoms to have developed in the interfluves.

I am prepared to argue, however, that it was not the quality of interfluvial soils that held back chiefdom formation there. For one thing, where manioc is the staple crop, soil fertility is seldom an overriding consideration. Even when grown on poor soil, manioc is capable of yielding abundantly. As I have already noted, the Kuikuru, who plant all their manioc on highly acid terra firme, are nonetheless able to harvest 5 to 6 tons of roots per acre.[15]

There is a curious sidelight here. In a number of places in her article, Roosevelt (1991a:108, 129, 130) comes close to implying that the interfluvial areas of Amazonia were, in precontact times, virtually uninhabited. While she does not actually say this, she repeatedly indicates that tribe after tribe now living in the interfluves was pushed there by direct or indirect European pressure. At one point she remarks that "instead of viewing the Amazonian Indians of the ethnographic present as an example of an original adaptation to tropical forest, it might be more correct to start thinking of them as ecologically and economically marginal survivors of colonial expansion" (1991a:130). Again she writes, "A more plausible explanation for the [simple] life-styles of the present-day [Indian] populations" than the poverty of their interfluvial habitats "might be found in their historical status as refugees from colonial expansion" (1991a:130). And once more she speaks of "the movement of Indians from varzeas . . . to more remote parts of the interfluves, with the aim of avoiding the disruption of conquest" (1991a:129).

To be sure, a good many interfluvial tribes *are* refugees from better habitats along the larger rivers. But surely not all. Many of the tribes now inhabiting the interfluves were there well before 1500. And if Roosevelt does not want to be understood as arguing the contrary, she should take pains to make herself clear on this point.

Turning to another issue, one of the reasons Roosevelt gives for the heavy yields of agriculture along the Amazon (besides the high fertility of várzea) is "intensive cultivation" (1991a:107, 111, 126, 1991b:2, 25). I wonder about this. In the interfluves, intensive cultivation is not required to produce a good crop, either from manioc or from maize. The Amahuaca of the upper Inuya, for example, never fence their cornfields and seldom weed them. Maize grows so rapidly that it soon towers over any weed that might try to compete with it for sunlight. Thus, in the two months it takes maize to mature, virtually no work is bestowed on it from the time the kernels are planted till the ripened ears are picked. And as we have seen, even with this indifferent treatment Amahuaca maize is still able to produce very abundantly.

Manioc cultivation in the interfluves likewise does not require intensive labor. It is true that in the upper Xingu, where the Kuikuru live, manioc plots must be fenced to protect them from deer and peccaries. But the work required to fence a manioc plot does not constitute what I suppose Roosevelt to mean by "intensive cultivation." It amounts to far less labor than that involved in, say, terracing or irrigation. And if moderate amounts of labor were all that were needed to produce substantial yields of maize and manioc on terra firme, why would it have taken much more labor to do so on várzea?

It is true that the building of raised fields to safeguard farmland from flooding, as was done on the Mojos plain (and perhaps also along certain stretches of the Amazon), did require a large initial investment of labor. But it seems to me that little extra work would have been needed after that. Indeed, quite possibly less labor was involved in raised field cultivation overall than in slash-and-burn, because in the latter, large tracts of forest must be cleared and fenced every year.

The relatively high yields of manioc and maize on terra firme mean that virtually any interfluvial tribe could have enjoyed a secure subsistence, insofar as agriculture was concerned. Many years ago (Carneiro 1961:49–52) I showed that not only could the slash-and-burn cultivation of manioc on terra firme provide villages with a secure subsistence, but it could also allow a village to attain a large size and to remain sedentary. Manioc cultivation, therefore, cannot be considered the limiting factor in keeping interfluvial villages from developing into chiefdoms.

But if the swidden cultivation of manioc—or maize—did not preclude the emergence of chiefdoms in the interfluves, what did? What other element in the subsistence economy of interfluvial tribes restricted their development? In earlier pages, I have already suggested the answer, but let me examine the matter in more detail.

First of all, the term *interfluvial*, as applied to Indian villages in Amazonia, is something of a misnomer. No Amazonian village is completely removed from any river. The constant need for water dictates that every village must have ready access to at least a small stream. What is really meant by an "interfluvial" village is one that lies far enough away from a *large* river to be unable to exploit it.

A basic question about the subsistence of any Amazonian village is: What is its primary source of protein? We have seen that the large rivers whose inundations provide rich várzea soil also provide aquatic protein in huge amounts. So abundant is this aquatic biomass that under native methods of exploitation it could never be exhausted or even seriously depleted. With such a plentiful source of protein at its doorstep, any village living along a major river could remain completely sedentary.

In interfluvial areas, the situation was usually quite different. The Amahuaca of the upper Inuya afford a good example. Where the Amahuaca lived in 1961, the Inuya was so narrow that in many places I could easily jump over it. And it was so shallow that the fish it supported were few and small. Clearly, the upper Inuya could not begin to supply the Amahuaca with the amount of protein they required. It was hunting to which they turned for the bulk of their protein (Carneiro 1970c).

Although the Amahuaca lived in tiny settlements, and although the surrounding forest was reasonably well stocked with game, it did not take long for a community to deplete the animals in its immediate vicinity. Even though they harvested large amounts of maize, the Amahuaca were forced to move their settlements every few years in order to keep abreast of their major source of protein. And when they did so, families would occasionally have to leave behind in their corncribs ears of corn they had not managed to consume (to be eaten later by crickets and mice). This strikes me as pretty strong evidence that, so far as the duration of settlements is concerned, what hunting requires can override what agriculture permits.

With regard to the effect of hunting, I would say that the Amahuaca are typical of most interfluvial tribes. It is not low yields of manioc or maize or the exhaustion of the surrounding soil that usually leads interfluvial peoples to move. This movement is more often a direct result of their reliance on hunting and the ready depletion of game. Ecological factors operating in the interfluves surely militated against the emergence of chiefdoms there. But, to repeat, it was not agricultural deficiencies that were responsible. It was the fact that, not being able to derive from fishing the major share of their protein, the natives of the interfluves had to rely on hunting and be subjected to its demands and limitations.

Before concluding this paper, I would like to take a closer look at the upper Xingu, the habitat of the Kuikuru, because this region illustrates the workings of the ecological factors I have just described. Looking at a map of Amazonia, one might easily conclude that the upper Xingu basin is a typical interfluvial region. After all, it is headwater territory, where rivers are usually narrow and shallow. But the facts are otherwise. The tributaries that join together to form the Xingu, especially the Kuluene and the Kuliseu, are broad and deep and are bountifully stocked with fish. And the same holds true of the various lakes that lie between these rivers. Since fishing in these waters is so rewarding, fish have become almost the only source of animal protein utilized by the Xinguanos. If hunting was once important among them (as I suspect it was), it certainly is negligible today.[16] The subsistence of present-day upper Xingu villages, based on plentiful harvests of manioc and bountiful catches of fish, has allowed them to remain essentially sedentary for a century or more (Carneiro 1961:48–49).

We may think of the upper Xingu as something of a "halfway house" between the várzea habitats of the lower Amazon and the terra firme habitats of the interfluves. On the one hand, the Xinguanos plant their manioc not on várzea, which hardly exists in the upper Xingu, but on terra firme, well away from the rivers. But on the other hand, with regard to what its rivers and lakes provide in the way of fish, the upper Xingu is certainly more like the Amazon than like the typical interfluve.

As one might expect, the sociopolitical organization of the Xinguanos reflects their favorable ecological conditions. Even today, after a hundred years of contact, upper Xingu villages are reasonably large and their ceremonialism quite elaborate. And, significantly, there are signs that the culture of the Xinguanos was once a good deal more complex than it is now. Certain ethnographic vestiges, as well as some striking archaeological remains, attest to this. It is a safe guess, I think, that the upper Xingu once had very sizable villages, strong political leadership, some degree of social stratification, considerable warfare, and extensive defensive works. I am not quite ready to say that the upper Xingu was once an area of chiefdoms, that is, of multivillage polities ruled by paramount chiefs. But I certainly would not discount the possibility. And, I might add, what I have read in Roosevelt's work about the chiefdoms of the lower Amazon has inclined me more and more to this opinion.

Just as "ecological determinism" would lead us to predict, wherever the appropriate environmental conditions were present—even in such a seemingly unlikely area as the very headwaters of an Amazon tributary—a marked elaboration of culture took place. And in certain favored areas, this elaboration may even have approached the level once widely found along the Amazon River itself.

Conclusion

In the foregoing pages I have tried to show that by 1988, the year Anna Roosevelt delivered the paper here discussed, I had already argued vigorously and repeatedly for a view of Amazonian cultural development categorically different from the narrow one originally proposed by Betty Meggers. I had asserted—and buttressed my assertions with facts—that the Amazon was not a single, homogeneous, restrictive environment capable of supporting only small, simple, egalitarian, and autonomous villages. Instead, I pointed to the existence of imposing chiefdoms along much of the Amazon, as well as in the Mojos plain, as proof of the very opposite. And I carried the argument further by specifying in detail the ecological factors that prompted these chiefdoms to emerge, as well as the evolutionary steps that marked their growth.

Thus, the picture painted by Anna Roosevelt in her article of 1991—a picture that would lead newcomers to suppose that only with her work did we gain the first true understanding of Amazonian culture history—is badly out of focus. Roosevelt's real contributions to unraveling the details of Amazonian prehistory are too numerous and too well known for her not to acknowledge her predecessors in this endeavor and to have them share with her some of the credit for our current knowledge of the cultural processes that characterized the prehistory of this great region.

Notes

1. Only in one place, near the very end of her article (p. 132), does she even begin to qualify this blanket indictment by modifying "ecological determinism" with the word "simplistic."

2. In this and other passages quoted from Roosevelt's article the translation from Portuguese to English is mine.

3. I should point out, however, that in her latest book, *Moundbuilders of the Amazon*, Roosevelt appears to flirt with ideological and symbolic interpretations, noting that "social and symbolic archaeology" are "sometimes touted in opposition to processual archaeology" (1991b:117), but indicating that she regards this opposition as "unprofitable" and asserting that "the general theoretical approach adopted in this . . . inquiry is one that combines materialist and idealist approaches" (1991b:4–5).

4. Meggers's original claim that more complex (chiefdom-level) cultures could not arise indigenously in Amazonia is surely dead. But she has since modified her views on this score. First, she recognized that várzea soils were significantly more fertile than interfluvial soils and *could* support more complex cultures (1984:629). More recently, though, because the Amazonian archaeological survey program she has directed has failed to find any of the large village sites reported by the sixteenth-century chroniclers, she has come to question the veracity of those early reports (1992:203).

5. The one exception is her citation (Roosevelt 1991a:112, 126–27)—and general acceptance—of the theory of environmental circumscription, as modified to fit Amazonian conditions, that I presented originally in Carneiro 1970a:736–37 and amended in Carneiro 1987a:248–50.

6. I later cited ethnohistorical evidence uncovered by Curt Nimuendajú (1939:12) that in 1824 the Apinayé had actually had a village of 1,400 people (Carneiro 1961:51).

7. Prior to this, Edwin Ferdon (1959) had already pointed out certain shortcomings in Meggers's argument about the limits ostensibly placed on agricultural production by tropical forest soils.

8. However, speaking of the fertility but at the same time uncertain availability of várzea, on which Amazonian chiefdoms relied, Meggers (1971:149) wrote as follows: "Adaptation to this situation set a ceiling on cultural development and it seems probable that várzea groups, such as the Omagua and Tapajós, had achieved the maximum level of cultural elaboration consistent with these local environmental conditions" (1971:149). So, in a way, Meggers still clings to a vestige—an eroded remnant—of her theory of environmental limitation.

9. For a discussion of the subtleties and nuances of just what should and should not be called várzea, see Chernela (1989:239).

10. This is true of whitewater rivers like the Solimões and the Amazon, but evidently not of blackwater rivers like the Rio Negro: "The blackwater floodplain contrasts dramatically with the whitewater floodplain: its nutrient source materials [deriving ultimately from the ancient, eroded Guiana shield] are characteristically poor and its waters are not laden with silts. Flooding does not improve the adjacent soils in blackwater rivers and does not increase their potential agricultural productivity" (Chernela 1989:246).

11. This is not to say that manioc cannot benefit from being grown on fertile soil. It can. The Kuikuru told me that if manioc cuttings were planted in the rich black earth normally reserved for maize, they would produce tubers as big around as a man's thigh.

12. To her credit, Meggers (1971:149) was among the first anthropologists to point out this shortcoming of várzea. Noting its "unique natural productivity," she went on to say, "This natural productivity has two important defects, however: 1) it is highly seasonal; and 2) it is subject to unpredictable fluctuations. Cultural mechanisms were developed to compensate for seasonality, but the food shortages that resulted from premature or prolonged inundation could not be predicted or offset." I would agree with "predicted" but would question "offset."

13. It is another striking parallel between the Amazon and Mississippi basins that the attempts at domestication that began in each area independently both hit upon chenopodium as a promising local food plant to experiment with (Roosevelt 1991a:115, 121; Smith 1989:1568).

14. In *Moundbuilders of the Amazon* (1991b:437) she reiterates that "the theory that low-nutrient tropical forests are inimical to cultural development is still viable."

15. Roosevelt lists the Kuikuru among groups who cultivate soils "rich in nutrients" (1991a:130). However, this is not the case, as she would have discovered by consulting my article on Kuikuru manioc cultivation (Carneiro 1983:77).

16. My conjectural thumbnail reconstruction of the history of Kuikuru subsistence and settlement pattern is as follows: When the ancestors of the Kuikuru first entered the upper Xingu basin centuries ago, they relied on hunting about as much as fishing. But as they discovered the fish-wealthy lakes in the basin, they settled down near one of them, continuing to hunt but increasing their dependence on fishing. Finally, when game in the vicinity became depleted, they faced the choice of either moving their village to stay abreast of the game or staying put, placing more and more reliance on fishing and gradually abandoning hunting. They did the latter.

References Cited

Acuña, P. Cristóval de
1891   *Nuevo descubrimiento del gran río de las Amazonas. Colección de libros que tratan de América, raros y curiosos*, vol. 2. Madrid.

Carneiro, Robert L.
1957   Subsistence and Social Structure: An Ecological Study of the Kuikuru Indians. Ph.D. dissertation, Department of Anthropology, University of Michigan.
1960   Slash-and-Burn Agriculture: A Closer Look at Its Implications for Settlement Patterns. In *Men and Cultures*, edited by Anthony F. C. Wallace, pp. 229–34. Philadelphia: University of Pennsylvania Press.

1961   Slash-and-Burn Cultivation among the Kuikuru and Its Implications for Cultural Development in the Amazon Basin. In *The Evolution of Horticultural Systems in Native South America: Causes and Consequences, a Symposium*, edited by Johannes Wilbert, pp. 47–67. *Antropológica*, Supplement Publication no. 2. Caracas: Sociedad de Ciencias Naturales La Salle.

1964   Shifting Cultivation Among the Amahuaca of Eastern Peru. Beitrage zur Völkerkunde Südamerikas. Festgabe für Herbert Baldus zum 65, edited by Hans Becher. *Völkerkundliche Abhandlungen* 1:9–18. Des Niedersachsischen Landesmuseums, Abteilung für Völkerkunde, Kommissionsverlag Munstermann-Druck GMBH, Hannover.

1970a   A Theory of the Origin of the State. *Science* 169:733–38.

1970b   The Transition from Hunting to Horticulture in the Amazon Basin. Proceedings of the Eighth International Congress of Anthropological and Ethnological Sciences, Tokyo and Kyoto, 1968. Vol. 3, *Ethnology and Archaeology*, pp. 144–48.

1970c   Hunting and Hunting Magic Among the Amahuaca of the Peruvian Montaña. *Ethnology* 9:331–41.

1971   Review of *The Upper Amazon*, by Donald W. Lathrap. *American Journal of Archaeology* 75:238–39.

1979   Factors Favoring the Development of Political Leadership in Amazonia. *El Dorado* (Greeley, Colo.) 4:86–94. (Reprinted in *Leadership in Lowland South America*, edited by Waud H. Kracke, pp. 4–8. *South American Indian Studies* [Bennington, Vt.] no. 1, 1993.)

1981   The Chiefdom: Precursor of the State. In *The Transition to Statehood in the New World*, edited by Grant D. Jones and Robert R. Kautz, pp. 37–79. New York: Cambridge University Press.

1983   The Cultivation of Manioc Among the Kuikuru Indians of the Upper Xingú. In *Adaptive Responses of Native Amazonians*, edited by Raymond B. Hames and William T. Vickers, pp. 65–111. New York: Academic Press.

1987a   Further Reflections on Resource Concentration and Its Role in the Rise of the State. *BAR* [British Archaeological Reports] *International Series* no. 349, pp. 245–60.

1987b   Cross-Currents in the Theory of State Formation. *American Ethnologist* 14:756–70.

1987c   Village Splitting as a Function of Population Size. In *Themes in Ethnology and Culture History, Essays in Honor of David F. Aberle*, edited by Leland Donald, pp. 94–124. Folklore Institute. Meerut, India: Archana Publications.

n.d.   The Ecological Basis of Amazonian Chiefdoms. *South American Indian Studies*. Forthcoming.

Chernela, Janet M.

1989   Managing Rivers of Hunger: The Tukano of Brazil. *Advances in Economic Botany* 7:238–48.

Denevan, William
1966   *The Aboriginal Cultural Geography of the Llanos de Mojos of Bolivia.*
        Ibero-americana, no. 48.

Emerson, T. E., and D. L. McElrath
1983   A Settlement-Subsistence Model of the Terminal Late Archaic Adapta-
        tion in the American Bottom, Illinois. In *Archaic Hunters and Gatherers
        in the American Midwest*, edited by James L. Phillips and James A.
        Brown, pp. 219–41. New York: Academic Press.

Ferdon, Edwin
1959   Agricultural Potential and the Development of Culture. *Southwestern
        Journal of Anthropology* 15:1–19.

Gumilla, P. José
1963   *El Orinoco ilustrado y defendido.* Biblioteca de la Academía Nacional de
        la Historia, no. 68. Caracas.

Lathrap, Donald W.
1970   *The Upper Amazon.* New York: Praeger.

Loureiro, Antonio
1986   *A grande crise (1908–1916).* Manaus, Brazil: T. Loureiro & Cia.

Medina, José Toribio
1934   *The Discovery of the Amazon According to the Account of Friar Gaspar de
        Carvajal and Other Documents.* American Geographical Society Special
        Publication, no. 17.

Meggers, Betty J.
1954   Environmental Limitation on the Development of Culture. *American
        Anthropologist* 56:801–24.
1971   *Amazonia: Man and Culture in a Counterfeit Paradise.* Chicago: Aldine-
        Atherton.
1984   The Indigenous Peoples of Amazonia, Their Cultures, Land Use Pat-
        terns and Effects on the Landscape and Biota. In *The Amazon: Limnology
        and Landscape Ecology of a Mighty Tropical River and Its Basin*, edited by
        H. Sioli, pp. 627–48. Dordrecht, Netherlands: Dr. W. Junk Publishers.
1992   Prehistoric Population Density in the Amazon Basin. In *Disease and
        Demography in the Americas*, edited by John W. Verano and Douglas H.
        Ubelaker, pp. 197–205. Washington, D.C.: Smithsonian Institution
        Press.

Meggers, Betty J., and Clifford Evans
1957   *Archeological Investigations at the Mouth of the Amazon.* Bureau of
        American Ethnology Bulletin 167. Washington, D.C.: Smithsonian
        Institution.

Métraux, Alfred
1942   *The Native Tribes of Eastern Bolivia.* Bureau of American Ethnology Bul-
        letin 134. Washington, D.C.: Smithsonian Institution.

Nimuendajú, Curt
1939   *The Apinayé.* Catholic University of America, Anthropological Series,
        no. 8. Washington, D.C.
Roosevelt, Anna C.
1980   *Parmana: Prehistoric Maize and Manioc Subsistence Along the Amazon
        and Orinoco.* New York: Academic Press.
1987   Chiefdoms in the Amazon and Orinoco. In *Chiefdoms in the Americas,*
        edited by Robert D. Drennan and Carlos A. Uribe, pp. 153–84.
        Lanham, Md.: University Press of America.
1991a   Determinismo ecológico na interpretação do desenvolvimento social
        indígena da Amazônia. In *Origens, adaptações e diversidade biológica do
        homem nativo da Amazônia,* organized by Walter A. Neves, pp. 103–41.
        Museu Paraense Emílio Goeldi, Coleção Emilie Snethlage. Belém,
        Brazil.
1991b   *Moundbuilders of the Amazon: Geophysical Archaeology on Marajó Island,
        Brazil.* San Diego: Academic Press.
Smith, Bruce D.
1989   Origins of Agriculture in Eastern North America. *Science* 246:1566–71.
Struever, Stuart, and F. A. Holton
1979   *Koster: Americans in Search of Their Prehistoric Past.* New York: Anchor
        Press/Doubleday.
Ursúa, Pedro de
1861   *The Expedition of Pedro de Ursúa and Lope de Aguirre, Translated from
        Pedro Simón's Sixth Historical Notice of the Conquest of Tierra Firme.*
        Translated by William Bollaert. The Hakluyt Society, publication no. 18.
        London.

3

Disaggregating Amazonia

A Strategy for Understanding Biological and Cultural Diversity

Emilio F. Moran

We are fortunate to be living in a period when Amazonia is no longer a terra incognita, no longer a region characterized simply as green hell, or as paradise. Over the past several decades, an increasing number of scholars in biology, anthropology, and geography have undertaken research into Amazonian ecosystems and in doing so have begun to tear the veil that hid the reality of Amazonia: its enormous environmental and cultural diversity—a diversity that makes our statements about it always partial views of the whole.

Despite general acceptance of the great diversity that Amazonia represents, treatment of the region by both scholars and policy makers tends to aggregate the region into two broad types of landscapes: *terra firme*, or uplands, making up 98 percent of the region, and *várzea*, or floodplains, making up about 2 percent (e.g., Meggers 1971). Exceptions to this tendency include Denevan (1976), Schubart and Salati (1982), Vickers (1984), and Prance and Lovejoy (1985). The terra firme–várzea classification fails to distinguish between regions in their degree of fragility and resilience or their primary and secondary productivity—to name just two important sets of criteria for structural and functional diversity in Amazonian ecosystems.

Despite the virtual explosion of research in Amazonia over the past 20 years (Barbira-Scazzocchio 1979; Hames and Vickers 1983; Hemming 1985; Herrera and Moran 1984; Moran 1983; Prance and Lovejoy 1985; Salati et al. 1984; Schmink and Wood 1984; Sioli 1984; and Wagley 1974, to list just a few of the edited collections that attempt to capture the rapidly developing literature; see also reviews by Moran [1982] and Sponsel

[1986]), we are still limited by our inability to compare results from one site to another. Findings from one site either are viewed as generalizable to the entire region or are presented as having unique, site-specific characteristics.

Most anthropologists accept the terra firme–várzea dichotomy and place data from areas as ecologically different as the Xingu basin, the Rio Negro basin, and the central Brazilian savannas into the category of "terra firme adaptations" (or into the even more aggregating "lowland South America"). Thus, evidence from ecosystems with widely different soils, above-ground biomass, and water regimes is used to support radically opposing views explaining cultural evolution, village size, and population mobility (see Gross 1975 vs. Beckerman 1979; Harris 1977 vs. Chagnon 1968). The distinction between terra firme and várzea glosses over important differences, especially within the vast terra firme.

Because the terra firme–várzea descriptive scheme has been widely used by biological and social scientists, it has found its way into government policies toward the Amazon. The treatment of the terra firme as a vast homogeneous region leads to policies which presume that the outcome of development projects can be constant across the region. This became patently manifest in the planning documents for the Transamazon Highway. In one document, for example, projections were made as to farmers' expected grain output that did not make allowances for variation in soil quality, slope, and climate (Ministerio da Agricultura 1972). The same yield expectations were used for areas to be occupied between the Tocantins and Madeira rivers. Four years later, farmers' performance was measured against this fixed standard, without adjustments for variable conditions (Moran 1981).

The Amazon is a very diverse region, with a multiplicity of ecosystems that reflect the variable geologic history, vegetations that have been present, and past human uses. Alarming rates of species and cultural loss have taken place in recent years — and we do not even have a framework within which to understand the significance of the losses. Are *all* ecosystems of Amazonia equally biodiverse? Has deforestation in one area the same impact as in another? What is the evidence for prehistoric environmental modification? Are ecosystems with species dominance more "manageable" or more fragile than those in which dominance is absent? Is endemicity greater in some areas of Amazonia than others? If so, what are the implications? Have native Amazonians passively adapted to the constraints of Amazonia, or have they actively modified ecosystems to meet their needs and, in doing so, created anthropogenic ecosystems? These and many other questions like them suggest themselves immediately when we consider Amazonia as an area characterized by variability rather than by homogeneity.

The major challenge for research in ecological anthropology in Amazonia in the decade ahead is to understand the relationship between cultural and ecological variation through time and space. Whether human populations have simplified ecosystem diversity or whether they are responsible for creating some of the diversity we see today has relevance for future management efforts in the Amazon. Until we disaggregate Amazonia we will persist in destroying its biological and cultural diversity.

Studying Human Adaptive Strategies

The persistence of the terra firme–várzea scheme is no accident. It is a scheme broad enough to speak across the biological and social sciences, allowing the integration of findings from each. Any framework that would hope to improve on this dichotomy must be based on criteria that are meaningful across a range of biological and social science disciplines.

One approach that has been used elsewhere (Moran 1979), which addresses the varied concerns of the physical, biological, and social sciences, is based on human adaptability to constraints. The study of human adaptability emphasizes the plasticity of human responses. It uses a broad array of data that includes physiological, behavioral, and cultural adjustments to specific problems and opportunities confronted by inhabitants of a particular environment. This approach focuses on how human populations, in interacting with each other and their environments, attempt to accommodate themselves to specific resources and situations that they face. As a result, the environment ceases to be either an overgeneralized context for human action or a determining force and becomes instead a constraint or opportunity to which a human population may or may not respond (Moran 1979:5).

This approach is applicable to a region as diverse as Amazonia. Such an approach clearly identifies constraints and opportunities and the human responses to them. Constraints such as low biological productivity, low above-ground biomass, high frequency of plants with toxic secondary compounds, and drought-related stress require adjustments by resident organisms. Tables 3.1 and 3.2 illustrate the ecosystems and constraints and opportunities that are discussed briefly in this chapter and at greater length elsewhere (Moran 1990). Choosing a constraint or limiting factor as the basis for understanding biological and human responses allows researchers to focus on the dimensions of human action that have immediate significance for the actors, and it requires, at least initially, that all levels of response to the problem be considered. Both site-specific and aggregate data are important in answering distinct questions, but they may not be used as proxies for each other.

Such a scheme, however, is insufficient by itself. It serves as a useful point of departure for understanding the interrelations of people with their habitat. People interact at several levels and with things other than the habitat. They interact with each other as individuals and as members of social groups. And whether as individuals or as members of groups, they interact also with external forces. This latter focus in research has become increasingly important in ecological anthropology and has been labeled by several investigators as "political ecology" (Sheridan 1988; Wolf 1982). In this chapter I begin with a consideration of habitat diversity in Amazonia and then return to considerations of political economy, political ecology, and history.

The Major Ecosystems of the Amazon

In what follows I would like to propose a framework for Amazonia that focuses on both constraints and opportunities and that permits finer distinctions than are now possible using the gross dichotomy between terra firme and várzea.

Várzea Ecosystems

The várzea should be disaggregated into at least three distinct regions — the upper floodplain, the lower floodplain, and the estuary. The variability present in this aquatic environment, however, is much greater than this threefold division would imply and merits further disaggregation based on future studies of these areas (see Table 3.1 for a summary of the constraints and opportunities present in the floodplain ecosystems).

The *upper floodplain* is highly variable in environmental characteristics, depending on the geological areas from which its sediments are derived. A recent research report on the alluvial soils of the upper Amazon concludes that upper floodplain soils are significantly diverse in chemical and physical properties. Soils carried by streams with headwaters in the eastern Peruvian cordillera (e.g., Rio Mayo) generally have both high base status and pH values (6.5 to 8.5). Those developing in sediments eroded from the calcareous sedimentary deposits of the Andean foothills of both Ecuador and Peru (e.g., Rio Cashiboya) tend to be slightly acid (pH 5.0 to 6.5) but present no serious chemical or mineralogical constraints. By contrast, floodplain alluvial soils originating in the eastern portion of the Peruvian basin (e.g., Rio Yavarí floodplain) tend to be strongly acid (pH

Table 3.1 Amazonian Várzea Ecosystems: Constraints and
         Opportunities

Estuary	Lower Floodplain	Upper Floodplain
Daily cycle of flooding with the tides	Reduced floodplain Fed by effluents from Guiana and Brazilian shields	Higher incidence of whitewater rivers with nutrient-rich sediments from Andes
Rich alluvial deposition year-round		
Less species-diverse, greater dominance	Great seasonal fluctuations in river level	Meandering rivers creating diversity in aquatic habitats
Many plants of economic value	Species-diverse, little dominance	Fish-rich várzea lakes
Rich riverine and marine fisheries	Rich riverine resources	More seasonal pattern of flooding

Source: Moran 1990.

4.0 to 5.0) and have levels of aluminum saturation exceeding 85 percent (Hoag et al. 1987:78–79).

Thus, anthropologists will need to specify the qualities of the alluvium in the upper floodplain—rather than simply allude to the presence of alluvium—if they are to understand the constraints and opportunities under which a population lives. In those areas of the upper floodplain with high acidity, lower nutrient content, and high aluminum saturation, population densities tend to be lower because of lower crop productivity. Furley (1979) has noted that the floodplains in the Rondônia region tend to be very acid hydromorphic gleys that are of less agricultural value than the high base-status soils of the terra firme of Rondônia—an observation that should put everyone on guard against the common generalization that várzea soils are more fertile than terra firme soils. What is true in the aggregate may not be true at a finer scale of resolution and may lead one unwittingly to overlook differences between local areas occupied by populations one is studying.

Two other constraints present in the upper floodplain that should be included in the analysis of human adaptability are altitude and slope. It is generally understood that above-ground plant biomass and productivity tend to decline with altitude in the rain forest, and this trend has important consequences for animal biomass and productivity, the efficiency of hunting effort, and other matters hotly debated in the anthropological literature (Vickers 1984). Although slope is not generally given much attention in research on lowland South America, it requires management to avoid soil loss. In the upper floodplain slope can be expected to have particular significance.

On the positive side, the region is enriched by meandering rivers that create numerous habitats for terrestrial animals and fish. Humans in this region had to relocate their settlements often due to the landscape changes brought about by the rivers, but they rarely moved far. There is considerable value in remaining in a region as well endowed as this one (Christine Padoch, personal communication, 1990; see also Hiraoka 1986, 1989). In addition, people in the upper floodplain have maintained regular economic exchange relations with populations in the Andean region that further stabilized them over time and in space. Studies in this region have been numerous and are sometimes better known by their reference to the *montaña*, or montane rain forests, which I will discuss later in this chapter. Rainfall in these areas is very high and agriculture has variable potential—but overall, soils have higher levels of nutrients than in areas of the lower Amazon. Many notable studies have been carried out in these areas in recent years, among them those by Vickers (1976), Johnson (1975, 1982, 1989), Behrens (1986, 1989), Johnson and Behrens (1982), Bergman (1980), Hern (1976, 1988), and Ross (1978).

By contrast, the *lower floodplain* conforms better to our current image of the floodplain: it is characterized more by oportunities than by constraints. The lower floodplain is enriched by alluvium from the high Andes, and its nutrient-rich rivers support large fish populations that account for 90 percent of the fish biomass in Amazonia (Junk 1984:215). The major constraints in this ecosystem are the variability and unpredictability of water levels and flooding. This unpredictability tends to require complex ethnoecological knowledge for predicting water levels in order to produce the large crop surpluses that potentially are possible.

The lower floodplain area seems to have supported both large populations and complex cultural systems with stratification (Myers 1989; Porro 1989; Roosevelt 1980, 1987, 1989). The complexity of managing this area is evident in the nonreemergence of intensive systems of agriculture in the lower floodplain since the depopulation events at the time of European contact (Sweet 1974). The ability to predict floods, build raised fields, and develop fast-growing varieties of crops is an essential component of várzea agriculture. Our best opportunity to understand the use of this region lies in the intensive study of *caboclo* and *ribereño* populations who have lived in this region since the demographic disaster of the seventeenth and eighteenth centuries (Denevan and Padoch 1988; Hemr 1978, 1987; Hiraoka 1986, 1989; Padoch and deJong 1989).

The *estuary* extends from the mouth of the Xingu River to Marajo Island at the mouth of the Amazon. The estuary differs from the lower floodplain in that it is filled by oceanic tides twice daily rather than only once a year for several months as is the case farther upriver. This regular inflow leads to very different adaptive strategies and a very different ecology. The estuary is not particularly rich in plant biodiversity but is characterized instead by species dominance, and many of the dominant species are palms of economic value. This pattern is probably the result of long-term manipulation by human populations who realized long ago the advantages of this region for net yield and for its location near riverine and oceanic aquatic resources. Fisheries in this area take advantage of both types of resources, and extractive activities are both high yielding and sustainable.

Intensive systems of management have been documented in the estuary (Anderson and Ioris 1989; Anderson et al. 1985), notably in agroforestry management supporting up to 48 persons per square kilometer and giving a rate of return higher than that documented for any other region of Amazonia (although this may be due to proximity to the large market of the city of Belém). Intensive management has been possible without any apparent deforestation. Agriculture in the estuary is more difficult and less productive than is plant extraction (Anderson and Ioris 1989). The estuarine ecosystem resembles a system in perpetual secondary succession owing to the frequent fall of trees and the dynamic impact of the aquatic environment on the landscape.

Terra Firme Ecosystems

At least five distinct ecosystems can be defined for the terra firme, given our current knowledge of environmental constraints: the well-drained savannas, the black-water basins, the vine forests, the montaña, and the poorly drained savannas (see Table 3.2 for a list of constraints and opportunities offered by these ecosystems). It is to be hoped that other distinctive ecosystems will emerge as further research highlights the environments and adaptive responses of populations.

Well-drained savannas are characterized by periods of high rainfall followed by marked droughts during the dry seasons. Agriculture in these areas is constrained by extremely acid, low phosphorus soils that, when combined with excellent drainage and low rainfall during the growing season, make agriculture very uncertain and, in the absence of irrigation,

Table 3.2 Amazonian Terra Firme Ecosystems: Constraints and Opportunities

Black-Water Basins	Terra Firme Forests	Montane Forests	Savannas
Extremely low levels of nutrients or oligotrophy	Very high species diversity	Lower plant and animal biomass than terra firme forests	Acid, low phosphorous soils
Hydrologic stress of flooding/ drought cycles	Few individuals of a species per unit area	Variable soils, extremely patchy	Great diversity of ecotones
Poor optical resolution of rivers	High incidence of acid, nutrient-poor soils	High erosion potential due to steep gradient	Lesser importance of fishing
Tendency toward dominance in flora	High incidence of leguminous species	Frost potential in some areas	Greater animal biomass productivity
Low plant and animal biomass productivity	Environmental patchiness		Some soils with impeded drainage drained
Nearly closed nutrient cycle	High incidence of superior soils		
Fish resources concentrated in flooded forest and cataracts	Patches of forest with concentration of plants of economic value		
Low above-bround biomass			
High frequency of plants with toxic secondary compounds			

Source: Moran 1990.

of relatively low productivity in the open savannas. The well-drained savannas, like most parts of Amazonia, are crosscut by rivers. Gallery forests, often growing on outcrops of nutrient-rich basaltic soils, hug the banks of permanent rivers. Indigenous populations practice a diverse and relatively productive horticulture in these forests—in many cases based on corn rather than manioc. They also follow a seasonal pattern of trekking across the dry savannas to take advantage of the ease of visibility that these open areas lend to hunting. Fishing is generally less productive in these areas and less attention is devoted to it, except when a population happens to locate next to some particularly productive section of a river. In addition, they take advantage of the great diversity of ecotones lying within short distances for gathering wild food resources.

Human populations on the savannas are not as dense as they are on the floodplain or in the vine forests. Their social organization is often dualistic, an effective response to the cycles of social fission and fusion (Gross 1979; Zarur 1979) that result from their need to fission for trekking and to fuse for horticulture. Because the savannas lie midway between the rich coastal regions and the rich floodplain, their human societies sometimes developed substantial warfare capabilities in an effort either to defend themselves from the more powerful Tupian chiefdoms of the coast or to overthrow them and take control of those better-endowed regions. They have proven persistent because of their flexible social organization. Today they are among the most numerous populations of native Amazonians and among the most savvy in dealing with outsiders (Anderson and Posey 1985; Gross et al. 1979; Posey 1985; Werner 1979).

Black-water basins have long attracted the attention of limnologists and other scientists (see Sioli 1950; Spruce 1908). These so-called "rivers of hunger" have a distinct vegetation (e.g., *campina*, *caatinga*, or xeromorphic vegetation) that reminds one of the spiny scrub forests of northeast Brazil. From the point of view of constraints, black-water basins are probably the most fragile and constrained ecosystems of Amazonia (Jordan and Herrera 1981). Rainfall is high, with a relatively short dry season— but because of the dominant white sandy soils (spodosols), even this short dry season is enough to cause severe drought stress in the vegetation, which has responded by developing many of the morphological characteristics of arid plants.

This ecosystem has been described by biologists as oligotrophic—as a nutrient-limited habitat that structurally and functionally has become an exemplar of the closed nutrient cycling that many people mistakenly generalize for the entire Amazon region (Jordan 1982; Jordan and Uhl 1978). However, the completeness of the array of nutrient-cycling mechanisms seen in the black-water basins is probably not found anywhere else in the Amazon. Loss of nutrients is minimized by a deep above-ground root mat (ca. 20 cm) that intercepts leaf fall and facilitates its breakdown through the interaction of fungi and mycorrhiza, thereby preventing loss of nutrients (Herrera et al. 1978; Stark and Jordan 1978). Herbivory is reduced by the high phenol content of the leaves and the presence of many toxic secondary compounds. Although total biomass is comparable in this white-sand–black-water ecosystem to that of other areas in Amazonia, in the black-water basins as much as two-thirds of it may be below ground.

The low above-ground biomass and extremely acid and nutrient-poor soils translate into very low biomass productivity of game and fish. Sioli (1950) described the rivers as being of "distilled water purity" from the point of view of dissolved minerals. The inkiness of the rivers, caused by undecomposed organic matter and dissolved phenols, makes fishing with traditional arrows and lances less effective than it is in clearer rivers. The spodosols found over much of this region experience fluctuating drought and flood (Herrera 1979). Because of an impermeable B-horizon in the soils, rainfall does not drain rapidly, causing vegetation to experience stress due to lack of oxygen at the roots (perhaps explaining the above-ground root layer), followed by severe drought stress (explaining the xeromorphic response of plants).

Agriculture in these areas has been practiced primarily along small levees near river banks (Hill and Moran 1983) and in small patches of terra firme forest growing on oxisols (Clark and Uhl 1987). In the levees there is sufficient organic matter due to the slow decomposition resulting from high phenol content, but the underlying soils are extremely acid—sometimes in the 3.5 to 4.0 range—which limits agriculture to a few plants such as manioc that are adapted to such low pH and to otherwise toxic levels of aluminum saturation. Human populations living along black-water rivers tend to be widely scattered and to hold hierarchically structured claims to points along the river in order to control the limited areas of fish concentration in flooded forests and cataracts (Chernela 1982; Goldman 1963; Hill and Moran 1983; Jackson 1983; Moran 1990, 1991; Uhl 1980). Secondary succession is much slower than in other areas of Amazonia, necessitating much longer fallow periods before swidden cultivation can be practiced again (Uhl et al. 1982).

The upland vine forest ecosystems of terra firme are found throughout the Amazon basin, covering nearly 100,000 km^2 in the Brazilian Amazon alone. Recently it has been suggested that these forests are the product of intentional manipulation by prehistoric populations (Balée 1989). This interpretation is based not only on the presence of many species associated with secondary growth and their frequent association with ceramics and other prehistoric archaeological material, but also on their patchy occurrence in areas of high relief in the south and southeast portions of the basin—Rondônia, Roraima, Amapa, and areas between the Xingu and Tocantins rivers (Pires and Prance 1985). These areas have sizable outcroppings of high base-status parent material, resulting in soils of medium to high fertility (alfisols), and rainfall regimes with a distinctive dry season of two to four months. In these forests there are a surprisingly large number of patches of both eutrophic soils (alfisols) and anthropogenic black soils—*terra preta do indio* or *terra preta arqueologica* (Kern 1988; Kern and Kampf 1989; Smith 1980).

The rivers drain watersheds that carry clear water with moderate loads of minerals and have small but productive levees. Fishing is rewarding because of the water's optical clarity. When turbidity reduces the effectiveness of fishing during the rainy season, the surrounding forests are relatively rich in animal biomass because of their relatively high aboveground plant biomass and productivity and because of the creation of "edges" by the human population—areas with greater biotic diversity as a result of their successional quality (Balée and Gely 1989). These are the forests referred to by Herrera (1985) as eutrophic, compared with the oligotrophic rain forests of black-water watersheds. The above-ground root mat noted in black-water basins is almost nowhere visible here, nor are many other nutrient-conservation mechanisms referred to earlier.

The marked dry period and the prevalence of woody vines and trees with modest diameters (ca. 25 to 35 cm dbh) makes the clearing of these forests easier and their drying more effective (Moran 1981). The result is not only richer initial soil fertility through effective burning from year to year, but also longer periods of cultivation per unit of land cleared, owing to higher initial soil fertility and pH values closer to 5.5 to 6.0. Cultivation periods as long as 10 to 15 years are technically possible before yields decline to 50 percent of the first-year yield (Sanchez 1976). Indigenous people in these areas cultivated a great variety of crops, but it should be noted that a surprisingly high incidence of corn-based horticulturalists is found in these areas, in contrast to the more commonly found maniocbased horticulturalists that most anthropologists and geographers have studied (Coimbra 1989; Galvão 1963; Moran 1990). The superior soils found here probably promoted a greater degree of circular settlement relocation to ensure continued access, and perhaps even claims, to these areas and to secure benefits from forest-patch management often associated with these areas. When fields are abandoned, secondary succession is much quicker in these areas—approximating 90 percent of total above-ground biomass within 10 years after the end of cultivation (Sanchez 1976).

Poorly drained savannas are quite distinct from the well-drained savannas. In particular, poorly drained savannas are found in sizable areas of Bolivia's high, flat plateaus with rich soils and moderate climate and in areas like Marajó Island at the mouth of the Amazon. They are believed to be important pre-Columbian sites with intensive agricultural systems. Denevan (1966) studied the Llanos de Mojos and found ridging and mounding, drainage canals, and other forms of intensive management that probably supported relatively high populations. Today, these areas are the objects of mechanized agriculture by Japanese and Mennonite populations who successfully produce for the market as well as for their own subsistence. This type of ecosystem is still poorly understood by cultural anthropologists and geographers, despite its likely importance in pre-Columbian times. This lack of understanding may be due to the decline in intensive systems of production following the loss of population during the first century of contact and the difficulty of finding contemporary populations practicing intensive management. Archaeology remains one important hope for understanding these systems (Zucchi and Denevan 1979).

By the second millenium B.P. there is evidence for prehistoric population in these areas, which seem to have had complex polities, perhaps even chiefdoms. These people made sophisticated polychrome pottery, used funerary urns, and gave greater emphasis to anthropomorphic figures in their art and symbolism (Roosevelt 1987). Some, like the Marajoaras, declined even before the arrival of the Europeans in the sixteenth century, while other populations higher up the river maintained chiefdoms as late as the seventeenth century before they too disappeared through warfare and disease. The Omagua, for example, experienced a loss of population of 70 percent in the first century of contact (Porro 1989:8).

The *montane forest*, or *montaña*, has been the focus of many ecological studies in anthropology (Behrens 1986, 1989; Johnson 1975, 1989; Ross 1978; Vickers 1976, 1984). It is a very distinctive forest from those discussed heretofore. It has lower tree biomass but more epiphytes. It has noticeably lower animal biomass, evident in lower hunting yields (Vickers 1984). Its soils are quite variable in acidity, minerals, and nutrient status. Human populations in these areas are constrained by the lower animal biomass and productivity, but the slightly higher frequency of soils of moderate acidity and fertility makes agriculture somewhat more productive and certain than in the lowland forests. These populations seem to have had long-standing economic relations with the complex chiefdoms of the high Andes from prehistoric times to the present. This area still has large and well-organized native populations whose expertise in dealing with variability along an altitudinal gradient deserves particular attention.

Native Strategies and Political Ecology

Paying attention to the adaptations of human populations to habitat constraints should not lead us to overlook the variability in the responses of local populations or the impact of local social systems and external political economic forces upon the adaptability of local populations. Contemporary ecological anthropology seeks to move away from a traditional emphasis on local, isolated populations removed from market forces and toward a process-oriented ecological approach that incorporates political economy and historical trajectory in its assessments of adaptive change (Ellen 1982; Lizarralde and Beckerman 1982; Moran 1984; Orlove 1980; Posey 1985).

For each of the ecosystems I have disaggregated above, it is important to delve into local history, to understand the transformations in ecology and society that have been brought about through time. This is a task for the individual investigator and is as detailed in nature as is ecological data collection. Generalizations about local history are not useful even if they are possible. On the other hand, there are significant patterns in regional histories that may serve to explain, at a different level of analysis, patterns of contemporary resource use. In what remains of this chapter, I will offer some indications of the sorts of evidence that serve to give historical grounding to environmental analyses of human adaptive behavior in Amazonian ecosystems.

In the lower floodplain and estuary, one finds the earliest and most notable impact of colonial contact, for the various and numerous populations of the region experienced the brunt of warfare, slave raiding, and epidemic disease (Hemming 1978). Myers (1989) notes that the land of the Omagua in the sixteenth century included 23 to 34 villages strung along 700 km of river front from the mouth of the lower Napo to the mouths of the Javarí and Içá rivers. Some of these villages had up to 8,000 inhabitants (Porro 1989). These large populations, like many others, were reduced by more than 70 percent within the first hundred years of contact, leading to a loss in capacity to sustain complex polities and, no less important to us, the complex systems of resource management that made those large populations possible.

In order to understand the potentials of the lower floodplain and the estuary, it will be increasingly necessary to delve into the colonial archives and to undertake more detailed archaeology than has been attempted so far, in the hope of finding suggestions as to how native people of Amazonia managed to maintain systems of sustainable resource use (Sweet 1974). In addition, greater attention will have to be paid to the caboclos and ribereños who replaced the indigenous populations along the major rivers and floodplains following depopulation. In some areas, these populations today practice sustainable systems of agroforestry and forest extraction that merit attention from contemporary societies in the Amazon. It should be remembered that intensive systems of management will neither occur nor be sustainable unless there is significant *demand* for floodplain products. This is clearly shown by the sustainable systems present in the estuary islands near Belém and by the long-term extraction practiced in the forested portions of Marajó for Belém's market and export markets.

Exploitation of the upper floodplain has been most influenced by the development of fisheries, both in their artisanal form and through modernized systems of aquaculture (Goulding 1980). Paddy rice cultivation has increased in importance in recent years, especially in Peru, due to favorable price supports. Native peoples have shown considerable talent in managing this crop, but it is unclear whether this development is entirely positive (Behrens 1989; Hern 1988). One favorable development is the emergence of regional industries, such as beer production based upon rice, that are likely to be able to absorb production and ensure price levels over time. The paddies, on the other hand, could become serious health hazards unless care is taken to prevent the entry of vectors of schistosomiasis and the further creation of breeding areas for malarial mosquitoes. The economy of this area has the advantage of better articulation with local and regional markets (Padoch and deJong 1989) than Brazil's floodplain areas and a sophisticated understanding of systems of diverse agroforestry among its ribereño and indigenous populations (Padoch and deJong 1989). People in this region seem to have maintained greater contact with their precolonial past, and native communities have greater developed unity, as is evident in groups like the Shuar Federation.

Turning to the black-water basins, it can be said that despite the impacts of disease, the rubber era, and other forms of colonial pressure, the Rio Negro basin has, on the whole, experienced a lesser degree of assimilation and extinction that many others in Amazonia. Perhaps the biggest reason has been the lesser economic interest of Europeans in this area, which is so evidently poor in resources of interest (Galvão 1959:9). Here one finds a remarkably strong sense of ethnic identity, especially along the Vaupés and Içana rivers (Chernela 1983; Jackson 1976, 1983).

This region offers a glimpse into what may have been a much wider pattern of relations between people and land. Clans hold territorial controls over specific areas, controls that are justified by ancient clan myths and are understood *regionally*. Although this does not mean that the clans that currently control given areas of the river always had such control, it does suggest that the process was highly structured and required legitimation in regional mythology. Thus, as the Makú today approach riverine areas currently occupied by Tukanoans, their gradual population movement is preceded by a growing number of marriages between Makús and Tukanoans that may permit, at some future date, the transformation of clan membership and rights to territories currently withheld from the Makú (Reid 1979).

In this region, people manage the environment through an extremely dispersed pattern of settlement, very low population densities, and highly specialized resource exploitation in which some ethnic groups focus upon riverine resources and others upon terrestrial resources. The poverty of this region for any form of intensive resource use provides strong grounds for protecting it. Such protection should include some insurance to its native people against the common tendency to disfranchise them from the land. Their lives might be bettered considerably if greater attention were given to their knowledge of toxic plants with potential for medicine. This knowledge could become an important source of income for local populations if appropriate forms of compensation were found and if sustainable, in situ production of such plants were undertaken.

The terra firme forests together make up nearly 50 percent of the Amazon basin. The diversity of species found in them deserves special attention, and, at least in the short term, they should be protected from deforestation. Many of these areas have soils that can be made productive only with considerable addition of fertilizers and careful selection of cultivars preadapted to conditions of high acidity and aluminum saturation and low levels of essential nutrients. Although nutrient poverty is less extreme than in black-water watersheds, it is enough to limit agricultural production without fertilization to the first year after forest removal.

Until infrastructural development and other economic conditions permit, the terra firme forests are unlikely to be made productive for contemporary urban societies. They can be managed less intensively by local indigenous people whose systems of extensive, low-impact resource use are likely to maintain biodiversity while ensuring human biological and cultural survival. There is discussion now of First World countries' paying for maintaining areas safe from deforestation in compensation for the role forests play in clearing the air of urban pollutants and in stabilizing climate, especially in the hydrologic cycle. Advocates of "debt-for-nature" swaps have suggested that indigenous people might be paid to manage the forests as further insurance against the destruction of vegetation.

What I said above about terra firme forests does not apply to the areas of terra firme covered by upland vine forests. These areas show evidence of previous occupation, often have soils of medium to high quality, and support a greater density of plants of economic interest. These areas, especially those with alfisols, should become the special objects of intensive agricultural management. Under no circumstances should they be put into pasture or into production that is not of high food and commercial value. Patches of alfisols could be managed with annual crops alongside the agroforestry management of patches of oxisols and ultisols in close proximity. Doing so would allow for both diversity of production and a better fit between resources and their use. This is clearly the case in areas of Rondônia managed by the Suruí Indians, who cultivated corn on the alfisols while developing groves of *babaçú* palm on the poorer soils near settlements (Carlos Coimbra, personal communication, 1989).

Additional Trends and Research Priorities

In addition to these dimensions of ecosystem use, one must perforce explore the impact of demography. The demographic changes experienced by native Amazonians are influenced by external ideologies. The ideology of Christian missionaries, for example, often emphasizes the noncontrol of fertility. Such an emphasis may not be entirely negative, considering the high rates of mortality that accompany the first one or two generations of permanent contact between indigenous people and Westerners. A policy emphasizing maximization of births would in all likelihood allow the population to regain its original size faster than a policy aimed at reducing fertility. But in time a policy that encourages reproduction will lead to rates of growth beyond the carrying capacity of native landholdings and, accordingly, to outmigration and merging with the urban poor. The sometimes conflicting relationship between missionaries and anthropologists has limited the controlled study of the impact of particular religious ideologies on the biological survival and adjustment of native Amazonians—and of whether the population, after biological adjustment, begins to modify the ideologies promoted by missionaries.

What all this suggests about research on human adaptability is that understanding demographic change, particularly at the level of households and villages, is a sine qua non for understanding how populations respond to epidemiological changes at the level of the social group—in addition to the already mentioned concern with epidemiology per se, that is, changes in disease prevalence. Disease, depopulation, and missionization affect the entire village population, as well as household units and individuals.

In addition, a number of external forces affect the very existence of social groups as distinct territorial units—especially control over land, monetization, and the incorporation of Amazonia into the world economic system. What has perhaps been missing in anthropological studies has been an effective way of linking these considerations of political economy and political ecology to issues of ecosystem structure, function, and management.

For example, very little research has been done that might help us understand the appropriate size of reservations if they are to provide sufficient land to permit both biological and cultural survival. This lack of research has been a serious deficiency in designing reserves for the Yanomami (e.g., Ramos and Taylor 1979). The oversight is all the more remarkable given that research is currently under way to establish the "minimum critical size of ecosystems" in the Amazon (Lovejoy et al. 1983), but unfortunately, this research, or its equivalent, fails to consider the role of human communities in ecosystems. The knowledge possessed by native peoples could very well inform scientists not only about how to preserve the environment but also about how to exploit it—at a time when the protective functions of the forest in the carbon cycle need to be understood and incorporated into our responses to the dangers of global warming.

The impact of monetization has been noted frequently, but rarely has it been studied as a central focus. The transformation of relatively autonomous societies engaged in long-distance exchange into societies trading on the basis of a common currency is a major readjustment. Monetization has been associated with the demise of work parties, with the individualization of work effort, and with changes in rules of reciprocity and marriage. Such changes are not necessarily negative, but they lead to a transformation of societies sensitive to local environmental change into societies sensitive to terms of trade. Moreover, indigenous people often find themselves in unfavorable positions in exchanges due to their peripheral positions in national economies.

During periods of change there is enormous potential for environmental destruction. The current period of change may take several generations and can be seen throughout most countries of the world today as people pay greater attention to the generation of foreign exchange, to capital accumulation, and to international markets than to the stability and long-term productivity of their renewable resources.

Anthropology needs to engage the problems of contemporary societies and assist in sustainable development. Anthropologists need to join native Amazonians in legalizing their claims to land and alerting the population to the complexities of a money-based economy. A direct intervention in the educational process that is sensitive to the cultural values of native Amazonians and that makes them knowledgeable about the imperfections of the world economic system should provide them with the ability to adjust to monetization in their own reflexive terms, rather than naively join the trend without recognizing the costs that it implies in autonomy and the quality of social relations.

The incorporation of previously autonomous populations into larger systems requires major adjustments. When such incorporation occurs quickly and when states are themselves dependent on world economic forces, the ability of local systems to maintain stable characteristics has proven time and again to be very limited. Herein lies one of the great challenges for research in anthropology and development in contemporary Amazonia. Can systems of social relations be conceived that permit a degree of local autonomy over production, consumption, distribution, and ethnic identity, yet allow local populations to participate in the health, education, and economic gains made possible by "development"? On the whole, it is evident that a vast number of the peoples of the Third World have shared inequitably in the aggregate gains of development. Of these, native Amazonians have been among those benefiting the least. Changing the terms of exchange and the degree of participation in such a way that greater work leads to greater social benefit remains a challenge to the imagination of each and every one of us. It is a challenge that we must meet: in the balance hangs the fate of one of the richest biological regions on earth, the fate of hundreds of distinct societies, and perhaps our own future.

Acknowledgments

I thank Leslie Sponsel for very useful and detailed comments on an earlier draft of this chapter. Earlier versions were presented as papers at an international workshop on "Origins, Adaptations, and Biological Diversity of Native Amazonians" in Belém, Pará, Brazil, on May 24–27, 1988, and at a symposium at the annual meeting of the American Anthropological Association in November 1987 in Chicago, Illinois. Revisions were undertaken while I was a John Simon Guggenheim Memorial Foundation Fellow and a Fellow of the Institute for Advanced Study at Indiana University (1989–90). I thank these organizations for the time they gave me to develop my ideas. They should not be held responsible for the views expressed herein.

References Cited

Anderson, A., and E. M. Ioris
1989   The Logic of Extraction: Resource Management and Income Generation by Extractive Producers in the Amazon Estuary. Paper presented at a conference on "Traditional Resource Use in Neotropical Forests," Gainesville, Florida.

Anderson, A., and D. Posey
1985   Manejo de cerrado pelos indios Kayapó. *Boletim do Museu Paraense Emílio Goeldi*, Botánica 2(1):77–98.

Anderson, A., et al.
1985   Um sistema agroflorestal na várzea do estuario amazonico. *Acta Amazônica* 15(1–2, suppl.):195–224.

Balée, W.
1989   The Culture of Amazonian Forests. *Advances in Economic Botany* 7:1–21.

Balée, W., and A. Gely
1989   Managed Forest Succession in Amazonia: The Ka'apor Case. *Advances in Economic Botany* 7:129–58.

Barbira-Scazzocchio, F.
1979   *Land, People and Planning in Contemporary Amazonia*. Cambridge University, Centre for Latin American Studies.

Beckerman, S.
1979   The Abundance of Protein in Amazonia: A Reply to Gross. *American Anthropologist* 81:533–60.

Behrens, C.
1986   The Cultural Ecology of Dietary Change Accompanying Changing Activity Patterns Among the Shipibo. *Human Ecology* 14:367–95.
1989   The Scientific Basis for Shipibo Soil Classification and Land Use. *American Anthropologist* 91:83–100.

Bergman, R. W.
1980   *Amazon Economics: The Simplicity of Shipibo Indian Wealth*. Dell Plain Latin American Studies, no. 6. Syracuse University, Department of Geography.

Chagnon, N.
1968   *Yanomamo: The Fierce People*. New York: Holt, Rinehart and Winston.

Chernela, J.
1982   Indigenous Forest and Fish Management in the Vaupés Basin of Brazil. *Cultural Survival Quarterly* 6(2):17–18.

1983   Hierarchy and Economy of the Uanano Speaking Peoples of the Middle Vaupés Basin. Ph.D. dissertation, Department of Anthropology, Columbia University.

Clark, K., and C. Uhl
1987   Farming, Fishing, and Fire in the History of the Upper Rio Negro Region of Venezuela. *Human Ecology* 15:1–26.

Coimbra, C., Jr.
1989   From Shifting Cultivation to Coffee Farming: The Impact of Change on the Health and Ecology of the Surui Indians of the Brazilian Amazon. Ph.D. dissertation, Department of Anthropology, Indiana University.

Denevan, W.
1966   The Aboriginal Cultural Geography of the Llanos de Mojos. Berkeley: University of California Publications.
1976   The Aboriginal Population of Amazonia. In *The Native Population of the Americas Before 1492*, edited by W. Denevan. Madison: University of Wisconsin Press.

Denevan, W., and C. Padoch, eds.
1988   *Swidden-Fallow Agroforestry in the Peruvian Amazon*. Monograph no. 5. New York: New York Botanical Garden.

Ellen, R.
1982   *Environment, Subsistence and System*. Cambridge: Cambridge University Press.

Furley, P.
1979   Development Planning in Rondônia based on Naturally-Renewable Surveys. In *Land, People and Planning in Contemporary Amazonia*, edited by F. Barbira-Scazzocchio, pp. 37–45. Cambridge University, Centre for Latin American Studies.

Galvão, E.
1959   Aculturação indígena no Rio Negro. *Boletim do Museu Paraense Emilio Goeldi*, Antropologia 7:1–60.
1963   Elementos basicos da horticultura de subsistencia indígena. *Revista do Museu Paulista* 14:120–44.

Goldman, I.
1963   *The Cubeo*. Urbana: University of Illinois Press.

Goulding, M.
1980   *The Fishes and the Forest*. Berkeley: University of California Press.

Gross, D.
1975   Protein Capture and Cultural Development in the Amazon Basin. *American Anthropologist* 77(3):526–49.
1979   A New Approach to Central Brazilian Social Organization. In *Brazil: Anthropological Perspectives*, edited by M. Margolis and W. Carter, pp. 321–42. New York: Columbia University Press.

Gross, D., et al.
1979   Ecology and Acculturation Among Native Peoples of Central Brazil. *Science* 206:1043–50.

Hames, R., and W. Vickers, eds.
1983   *Adaptive Responses of Native Amazonians.* New York: Academic Press.

Harris, M.
1977   *Cannibals and Kings.* New York: Vintage Books.

Hemming, J.
1978   *Red Gold: The Conquest of the Brazilian Indians.* Cambridge, Mass.: Harvard University Press.
1987   *Amazon Frontier: The Defeat of the Brazilian Indians.* Cambridge, Mass.: Harvard University Press.

Hemming, J., ed.
1985   *Change in the Amazon Basin.* 2 vols. Manchester: Manchester University Press.

Hern, W.
1976   Knowledge and Use of Herbal Contraceptives in a Peruvian Amazon Village. *Human Organization* 35:9–19.
1988   Polygyny and Fertility Among the Shipibo: An Epidemiologic Test of an Ethnographic Hypothesis. Ph.D. dissertation, Department of Epidemiology, University of North Carolina.

Herrera, R.
1979   Nutrient Distribution and Cycling in an Amazonian Caatinga Forest on Spodosols in Southern Venezuela. Ph.D. dissertation, University of Reading.
1985   Nutrient Cycling in Amazonian Forests. In *Key Environments: Amazonia,* edited by G. Prance and T. Lovejoy, pp. 95–105. Oxford: Pergamon Press.

Herrera, R., and E. Moran, eds.
1984   Human Ecology in the Amazon. *Interciencia* 9(6):321–424.

Herrera, R., et al.
1978   Amazon Ecosystems: Their Structure and Functioning with Particular Emphasis on Nutrients. *Interciencia* 3:223–32.

Hill, J., and E. Moran
1983   Adaptive Strategies of Wakuenai People to the Oligotrophic Rain Forest of the Rio Negro Basin. In *Adaptive Responses of Native Amazonians,* edited by R. Hames and W. Vickers. New York: Academic Press.

Hiraoka, M.
1986   Zonation of Mestizo Farming Systems in Northeast Peru. *National Geographic Research* 2:354–71.
1989   Agricultural Systems on the Floodplains of the Peruvian Amazon. In *Fragile Lands of Latin America,* edited by J. Browder. Boulder, Colo.: Westview Press.

Hoag, R., et al.
1987   Alluvial Soils of the Amazon Basin. In *Tropsoils: Technical Report 1985–86*, edited by N. Caudle and C. McCants, pp. 78–79. Raleigh, N.C.: Tropsoils Management Entity.

Jackson, J.
1976   Vaupés Marriage: A Network System in the Northwest Amazon. In *Regional Analysis*, vol. 2, edited by C. Smith. New York: Academic Press.
1983   *The Fish People: Linguistic Exogamy and Tukanoan Identity in Northwest Amazonia.* Cambridge: Cambridge University Press.

Johnson, A.
1975   Time Allocation in a Machigenga Community. *Ethnology* 14(3): 301–10.
1982   Reductionism in Cultural Ecology: The Amazon Case. *Current Anthropology* 23(4):413–28.
1989   How the Machigenga Manage Resources: Conservation or Exploitation of Nature? *Advances in Economic Botany* 7:213–22.

Johnson, A., and C. Behrens
1982   Nutritional Criteria in Machigenga Food Production Decisions. *Human Ecology* 10:167–189.

Jordan, C.
1982   Amazonian Rain Forests. *American Scientist* 70:394–401.

Jordan C., and R. Herrera
1981   Tropical Rain Forests: Are Nutrients Really Critical? *American Naturalist* 117:167–80.

Jordan, C., and C. Uhl
1978   Biomass of a "Tierra Firme" Forest of the Amazon Basin. *Oecologia Plantarum* 13:387–400.

Junk, W. J.
1984   Ecology of the Várzea, Floodplain, of Amazonian Whitewater Rivers. In *The Amazon: Limnology and Landscape Ecology of a Mighty Tropical River and Its Basin*, edited by H. Sioli, pp. 215–44. Dordrecht: W. Junk Publisher.

Kern, D. C.
1988   Caracterização pedológica de solos com terra preta arqueológica na região de Oriximiná, Pará. Master's thesis, Department of Agronomy, University Federal de Rio Grande do Sul (Brazil).

Kern, D. C., and N. Kampf
1989   Antigos assentamentos indígenas na formação de solos com terra preta arqueológica na região de Oriximiná, Pará. *Revista Brasileira de Ciencia do Solo* 13:219–25.

Lizarralde, R., and S. Beckerman
1982   História contemporánea de los Barí. *Antropológica* 58:3–52.

Lovejoy, T., et al.
1983   *Ecological Dynamics of Tropical Forest Fragments.* London: Blackwell.

Meggers, B.
1971   *Amazonia.* Chicago: Aldine.

Ministerio da Agricultura
1972   *Altamira I.* Brasilia: Ministerio da Agricultura.

Moran, E. F.
1979   *Human Adaptability: An Introduction to Ecological Anthropology.* North
        Scituate, N.J.: Duxbury Press. Reprinted by Westview Press, Boulder,
        Colorado, 1982.
1981   *Developing the Amazon.* Bloomington: Indiana University Press
1982   Ecological, Anthropological, and Agronomic Research in the Amazon
        Basin. *Latin American Research Review* 17:3–41.
1990   *A ecologia humana das populacoes da Amazonia.* Petropolis, Rio de
        Janeiro: Editora Vozes.
1991   Human Adaptive Strategies in Amazonian Blackwater Ecosystems.
        American Anthropologist 93(2):361–82.

Moran, E. F., ed.
1983   *The Dilemma of Amazonian Development.* Boulder, Colo.: Westview
        Press.
1984   *The Ecosystem Concept in Anthropology.* Washington, D.C.: American
        Association for the Advancement of Science.

Myers, T.
1989   The Expansion and Collapse of the Omagua. Paper presented at a
        Wenner-Gren Foundation conference on "Amazon Synthesis," Nova
        Friburgo, Brazil.

Orlove, B.
1980   Ecological Anthropology. *Annual Review of Anthropology* 9:235–73.

Padoch, C., and N. deJong
1989   Production and Profit in Agroforestry: An Example from the Peruvian
        Amazon. In *Fragile Lands of Latin America*, edited by J. Browder. Boul-
        der, Colo.: Westview Press.

Pires, J. M., and G. Prance
1985   The Vegetation Types of the Brazilian Amazon. In *Key Environments:
        Amazonia*, edited by G. Prance and T. Lovejoy, pp. 109–145. New York:
        Pergamon Press.

Porro, A.
1989   Social Organization and Power in the Amazon Floodplain: The
        Ethnohistorical Sources. Paper presented at a Wenner-Gren Foundation
        conference on "Amazon Synthesis," Nova Friburgo, Brazil.

Posey, D.
1985   Indigenous Management of Tropical Forest Ecosystems: The Case of the
        Kayapó Indians of the Brazilian Amazon. *Agroforestry Systems* 3:139–58.

Prance, G., and T. Lovejoy, eds.
1985   *Key Environments: Amazonia.* New York: Pergamon.

Ramos, A., and K. Taylor
1979   *The Yanomama in Brazil.* Document no. 37. Copenhagen: International Workgroup for Indigenous Affairs.

Reid, H.
1979   Some Aspects of Movement, Growth and Change Among the Hupdu Maku Indians of Brazil. Ph.D. dissertation, Faculty of Archaeology and Anthropology, University of Cambridge.

Roosevelt, A. C.
1980   *Parmana: Prehistoric Maize and Manioc Subsistence Along the Amazon and Orinoco.* New York: Academic Press.
1987   Chiefdoms in the Amazon and Orinoco. In *Chiefdoms of the Americas,* edited by R. Drennan and C. Uribe. Washington, D.C.: University Press of America.
1989   Resource Management in Amazonia Before the Conquest: Beyond Ethnographic Projection. *Advances in Economic Botany* 7:30–62.

Ross, E.
1978   Food Taboos, Diet and Hunting Strategy: The Adaptation to Animals in Amazon Cultural Ecology. *Current Anthropology* 19:1–36.

Salati, E., et al.
1984   *Amazonia.* Brasilia: CNPq (National Research Council of Brazil).

Sanchez, P.
1976   *Properties and Management of Soils in the Tropics.* New York: Wiley.

Schmink, M., and C. Wood, eds.
1984   Frontier Expansion in Amazonia. Gainesville: University of Florida Press.

Schubart, H. O. R., and E. Salati
1982   Natural Resources for Land Use in the Amazon Region: The Natural Systems. In *Amazonia: Agriculture and Land Use Research,* edited by S. Hecht. Cali, Colombia: Centro Internacional de Agricultura Tropical.

Sheridan, T.
1988   *Where the Dove Calls: The Political Ecology of a Peasant Corporate Community in Northwestern Mexico.* Tucson: University of Arizona Press.

Sioli, H.
1950   Das Wasser im Amazonasgebiet. *Forschungen und Fortschritte* 26:274–80.

Sioli, H., ed.
1984   *The Amazon: Limnology and Landscape Ecology of a Mighty Tropical River and Its Basin.* Dordrecht: W. Junk Publisher.

Smith, N.
1980   Anthrosols and Human Carrying Capacity in Amazonia. *Annals of the Association of American Geographers* 70:553–66.

Sponsel, L.
1986   Amazon Ecology and Adaptation. *Annual Review of Anthropology*
        15:67–97.

Spruce, R.
1908   *A Botanist on the Amazon and Andes.* 2 vols. Edited by A. R. Wallace.
        London: Macmillan.

Stark, N., and C. Jordan
1978   Nutrient Retention by the Root Mat of an Amazonian Rain Forest. *Ecology* 59:434–37.

Sweet, D.
1974   A Rich Realm of Nature Destroyed: The Middle Amazon Valley,
        1640–1750. Ph.D. dissertation, Department of History, University of
        Wisconsin.

Uhl, C.
1980   Studies of Forest, Agricultural, and Successional Environments in the
        Upper Rio Negro Region of the Amazon Basin. Ph.D. dissertation,
        Department of Botany, Michigan State University.

Uhl, C., et al.
1982   Successional Patterns Associated with Slash-and-Burn Agriculture in
        the Upper Rio Negro Region of the Amazon Basin. *Biotropica* 14:
        249–54.

Vickers, W.
1976   Cultural Ecology of the Siona Secoya Indians of Ecuador. Ph.D. dissertation, Department of Anthropology, University of Florida.
1984   The Faunal Components of Lowland South American Hunting Skills.
        Interciencia 9:366–76.

Wagley, C., ed.
1974   *Man in the Amazon.* Gainesville: University of Florida Press.

Werner, D.
1979   Subsistence Productivity and Hunting Effort in Native South America.
        Human Ecology 7:303–15.

Wolf, E.
1982   *Europe and the People Without History.* Berkeley: University of California
        Press.

Zarur, G.
1979   Ecological Need and Cultural Choice in Central Brazil. *Current Anthropology* 20(3):649–53.

Zucchi, A., and W. Denevan
1979   *Campos elevados e história cultural prehispánica en los llanos occidentales
        de Venezuela.* Caracas: University Católica Andrés Bello.

4

Historical Ecology of Amazonia

William Balée

A historical ecology of Amazonia begins with the premise that historical, not evolutionary, events are responsible for the principal changes in relationships between human societies and their immediate environments. The central axiom of historical ecology is that the essence of the relationship between human societies and given environments is dialectical and interactive (Crumley 1994). Historical ecology does not deny process in the unfolding of the changes in such relationships. Rather, like the concept of "punctuated equilibrium" in biology, it assumes that certain essentially historical events may alter, arrest, efface, or even reverse prior trajectories of development. As with the theory that asteroid impacts may have resulted in the "pulse extinctions" inferred from the fossil record (Raup 1991), so the European conquest of Amazonia may have led to fundamental changes in the use of biological resources by the indigenous sociocultural systems that somehow survived it.

The conquest, as a watershed event, set in motion certain intelligible processes. It effected immediate, interactive environmental and historical changes in Amazonia as it did elsewhere. Through the mutual causation of these variables, new societies with novel relationships to the flora and fauna of particular regions came into being.

Similar processual changes in the use of botanical resources that several widely separated contemporary foraging societies seem to have experienced are especially intriguing. I refer specifically to the Guajá, Héta, Šeta, Aché, Avá-Canoeiro, and Yuquí, all of whom are affiliated with the Tupí-Guaraní family of languages.[1] By classifying these peoples as "foraging societies," I mean that across multiple generations they did not trans-

form natural forests for swidden cultivation even if long ago their antecedent society was certainly horticultural. Comparison of these groups
reveals that what is most unusual is not so much that both societies of
foragers and cultivators may exist in the same language family (the co-
affiliation of Aztec and Shoshone in the Uto-Aztecan family, for example,
is a familiar precedent), even though this itself requires some explanation.
Rather, the historical paths that these diverse peoples have taken and the
botanical resources that they now exploit, despite their wide separation
in space and the apparent lack of cultural and linguistic borrowing among
them, manifest remarkable convergences. These convergences, in turn,
require nothing less than a general theory in order to be made comprehen-
sible. Such a general theory derives from historical ecology.

Agricultural Regression

Although Guajá informants claim no prior knowledge of agriculture, say-
ing *nə tum awá* ("people do not cultivate crops"), shreds of written records indicate that the Guajá would have lived near the lower Tocantins
River of Brazil in villages—a settlement pattern incompatible with
Amazonian foraging—during the 1700s (Balée 1992b:39; Gomes 1988:
140–141; Noronha 1856:8–9). The Héta of Paraná state, some 1,400
miles to the south, appear to have "practiced some plant cultivation"
prior to becoming nomadic foragers (Kozák et al. 1979:366). Both the
Aché of eastern Paraguay and the Avá-Canoeiro of the middle Tocantins
basin probably cultivated maize in the past (Clastres 1972:143, 1973:271;
Métraux and Baldus 1946:436; Rivet 1924:177; Toral 1986). And the
Yuquí of eastern Bolivia have been described as "remnants" of a formerly
horticultural people (Stearman 1989:22), perhaps a subgroup of the
aboriginal Guaraní themselves. All these groups share certain similarities
in terms of the botanical resources (which may be defined in cultural
terms as domesticates, semidomesticates, and nondomesticates) that in
modern times they utilize.

A historical-ecological approach to lowland South America reveals
that the transition from horticulture to foraging was usually processual,
not abrupt. Donald Lathrap, who was one of the pioneers of Amazonian
historical ecology even though he was not completely free of the influences of environmental determinism, argued that some societies of the
upper Amazon had undergone "degradation" (Lathrap 1968:25). For example, compared to the horticultural Shipibo of the Ucayali River, the
linguistically related Amahuaca of the Peruvian *montaña* constituted "de-
graded descendants of peoples who at one time maintained an advanced

form of tropical forest culture" (Lathrap 1968:25). The Shipibo were once a densely populated, sedentary chiefdom; the Amahuaca, on the other hand, had a very low population density and lived as seminomadic trekkers. The Amahuaca regressed, in Lathrap's view, because the new environment into which they were shoved imposed more stringent exigencies on their meager technological means.

Lathrap's arguments are useful for comparing the similarities and differences between floodplain and interfluvial societies of the pre-Columbian past. On the other hand, an understanding of the biotic and productive potentials that divide the white-water floodplains and the black-water *terra firme* lands into two opposed environmental zones ignores the prehistoric and historic transformations that took place in both. It also cannot further help to elucidate the profound differences to be noted among peoples whose principal economic activities were confined to one or the other zone.

The focus in this chapter is on comprehending the historical ecology of terra firme societies, who are by far the most numerous remaining indigenous peoples of today. This necessarily involves addressing why some contemporary societies have remained horticultural while others did not. Another pioneer of Amazonian historical ecology, Pierre Clastres, sought to illuminate what could be "learned from the movement of the greatest number of societies from hunting to agriculture, and the reverse movement, of a few others, from agriculture to hunting" (Clastres 1989: 201). Although Clastres was chiefly engaged in describing the possible sociopolitical effects of each type of transition, his question has profound relevance for understanding the historical ecology of Amazonia. Both movements took place there. Understanding the "reverse movement," which has occurred far more often than had been heretofore realized in Amazonia, entails investigating whether any convergence in cultural experience, aside from hunting and gathering in the abstract, may exist among contemporary, diverse groups of foragers.

The importance of historical ecology in achieving a truly comparative understanding of terra firme peoples may be further illustrated by examining very different societies that co-inhabit the same region. (A region, as one of the central analytical concepts of historical ecology, constitutes "a unit that can be recognized at a certain scale in its distinctiveness from and interrelations with other such units, both spatially and temporally" [Crumley 1993a:378]). The Ka'apor and Guajá pairing represent one of the few Amazonian cases in point. The Ka'apor and Guajá speak mutually unintelligible Tupí-Guaraní languages. Both live in the region of the pre-Amazonian forests of northern Maranhão state, Brazil (which are today threatened with total destruction by invading loggers, ranchers, and landless settlers). Beyond these similarities, sociocultural and linguistic differences between the two peoples are striking. The Ka'apor are heavily dependent on the cultivation of domesticated plants, especially bitter manioc, whereas the Guajá until quite recently cultivated no plants.

Although the Guajá language does not lexically distinguish between sweet and bitter manioc plants, both of which are called *tãrãmã*, Ka'apor has three nonsynonymous folk generic names (*mani'i, makaser,* and *maniaka*) and a total of twenty-four nonsynonymous folk specific names designating *Manihot esculenta* alone (Balée 1994). Underdifferentiation of generic domesticates may be expected from a foraging society that only quite recently has begun to adopt (or readopt) a horticultural way of life (e.g., Berlin 1992:285–88; Brown 1985). In addition, the Guajá language has no more than twenty folk specific plant names, whereas Ka'apor possesses several hundred such names. Perhaps most significant, the number of generic plant names in Ka'apor is about 479, whereas the corresponding number in Guajá (for the same flora) appears to be only 353 (Balée 1994). This reduction of plant vocabulary in Guajá is associated with other features of the abandonment of a sedentary and agricultural existence (probably in part because of introduced epidemic diseases and depopulation), such as a very low population density (less than 0.1 person/km^2) when compared to surrounding horticultural peoples (who are at 0.2 persons/km^2 and above).

Lévi-Strauss (1966:66–67) astutely noted that "the structural features of a language will probably change if the population using it, which was once numerous, becomes progressively smaller." In other words, given that both the Ka'apor and Guajá shared a horticultural antecedent (Proto-Tupí-Guaraní, the mother language of both), it may be argued that some total process has abbreviated severely the plant vocabulary of Guajá. I call this process "agricultural regression" (Balée 1992b). For reasons of history, the Guajá experienced it fully, but the Ka'apor did not.

Perhaps most compelling is the linguistic evidence for prior horticulture. The mother language of Guajá, Šeta, Héta, Avá-Canoeiro, Aché, and Yuquí was Proto-Tupí-Guaraní, which was spoken about the same time as Latin. Linguistic research suggests that several terms for domesticates, including manioc, maize, yams, and sweet potatoes, existed in the lexicon of Proto-Tupí-Guaraní (Balée and Moore 1991; Lemle 1971; Rodrigues 1988). In addition, several of these terms have survived in daughter languages associated with contemporary foragers (Gomes 1988: 140; Stearman 1989:73). For example, Guajá names for domesticated plants that indicate descent from a language associated with a horticultural society include *wači* (or *ᵏwači*), "maize," *kará*, "yams," and *paku*, "bananas." The reconstructed proto-Tupí-Guaraní terms for these plants, respectively, would be **aßatí*, **kará*, and *pakóßa*.

Cognate terms for maize appear at least in the Guajá, Avá-Canoeiro, Šeta, Aché, and Yuquí languages (Héta is insufficiently described to make this assertion possible), whereas terms for manioc and other important domesticates of the past have survived less consistently, if at all, in these languages. This is because maize may be one of the last domesticates to be eliminated from a horticultural group's repertoire. Cognate terms for manioc were lost because manioc as a crop was abandoned earlier than maize (Balée 1992b, 1994).

I would argue that the generic, indigenous terms for bitter manioc vanish before the loss of terms for maize during the transition from horticulture to foraging. The Guajá language (and Aché language [Clastres 1968:53; Vellard 1939:90–91]) has retained a cognate term for maize (*awači* or *ᵏwači*), but not one for manioc (*tǝrǝmǝ*). Yet manioc is probably older than maize in the domesticated plant inventory of Tupian peoples (Rodrigues 1988) and it has usually been the more significant food crop (Brochado 1977). The focal referent of the Guajá word for manioc is the edible mesocarp of the babaçu palm, which was probably the main carbohydrate source in the aboriginal diet (Balée 1988, 1992b). Even though in their own historical memory the Guajá have not cultivated maize (nor any other plant, according to Ricardo Nassif [1993]), the Guajá language itself suggests that their ancestors cultivated maize more recently than manioc, before they jettisoned plant cultivation entirely.

I have elsewhere suggested that bitter manioc is probably abandoned before sweet manioc in the process of agricultural regression (Balée 1992b, 1994). Although I do not wish to belabor the argument, it is worth repeating that many trekking societies cultivated both maize and sweet manioc but not bitter manioc. These societies included the Hotí, Yanomama, Campa, Amahuaca, Waorani, and Uru-eu-wau-wau. As for the Uru-eu-wau-wau, whom I visitied in 1992, informants claimed that only eight species of domesticates were grown. Only three of these domesticates, moreover, included more than one named variety. These were sweet manioc (two varieties), sweet potato (two varieties), and maize (three varieties). Maize appears to have been the most important crop, judging by the greater space devoted to its cultivation today. The Uru-eu-wau-wau, moreover, grew no bitter manioc. Although the Araweté may have retained as many as three varieties of bitter manioc (Eduardo Viveiros de Castro, personal communication, 1993; Viveiros de Castro 1992:40), a point of which I was unaware before (Balée 1992b), it was certainly an unimportant crop and seems to have been nearly "lost" by the time of contact in the mid-1970s. Maize, of which the Araweté discriminate four varieties, is far more important than manioc by any measure (Viveiros de Castro 1992:40–41).

It is extremely important to consider, moreover, that the ancestral tongue of Araweté and Uru-eu-wau-wau was Proto-Tupí-Guaraní, which almost certainly was associated with the cultivation of bitter as well as sweet manioc, given that the generic term for bitter manioc reconstructs in the protolanguage and that the generic term for sweet manioc was different (Lemle 1971; Rodrigues 1988). The association of sweet manioc with maize in the seminomadic horticulture of trekkers is probably based on the fact that bitter manioc, to be a successful staple, requires greater energetic investments and installations than do sweet manioc and maize, both of which mature quickly and are easier to process. For a mobile people, maize also shows advantages over sweet manioc as a staple.

Fallows and Foragers

The transport and processing costs of maize are probably less than those of sweet manioc, which, like the bitter varieties, is planted from cuttings, not seeds. This helps explain why a society undergoing agricultural regression tends to abandon manioc in all its forms prior to abandoning maize. Given proper edaphic conditions, maize may even assume a dominant position in a trekking society's suite of domesticated crops, as it has with the Araweté (Balée 1989:11; Viveiros de Castro 1992:40–41) and probably the precontact Uru-eu-wau-wau.

The Araweté lived in a village of 168 inhabitants as of 1988 (Viveiros de Castro 1992:30). They traditionally cultivated maize, sweet manioc, sweet potato, yam, cotton, tobacco, a fibrous bromeliad (*Neoglaziovia variegata*) used for rope and bowstring, papaya, banana, pineapple, calabash, and the annatto tree, among others (Viveiros de Castro 1992:40). A group of seven Araweté who had become accidentally separated from their kinsmen several years ago recently came to the attention of the Fundação Nacional do Índio (FUNAI), or National Indian Foundation of Brazil. The swidden clearing of these seven Araweté contained only one crop, maize (Balée 1992b).

Maize seems to be the one crop that a trekking society cannot lose lest it become a foraging society. It is not spurious, therefore, to refer to agricultural regression as a process, just as many others have referred to the reverse phenomenon of domestication and sedentarization. The end result of the process of agricultural regression is a foraging, if not an extinct, society.

The term *regression* suggests a processual degradation of society's means of producing food as well as textiles, tools, and utensils derived from domesticates. This process is set in motion by historical and demographic forces that did not act equally on human populations. For example, the conquest eliminated only some, not all, indigenous societies, probably because of variable demographic and sociopolitical conditions among those societies themselves (Newson 1992). Some societies that partially survived disease, depopulation, warfare, and slave raids could not maintain sedentary horticultural lifestyles. These people first became trekkers, and later they became foragers.

What is most remarkable is the convergence of these historically determined foragers in terms of the plant resources they exploit. They are dependent not so much on the swidden crops of neighboring horticultural peoples (but see Araújo Brusque 1862; Stearman 1989; Vellard 1939) as on plants that typically occur in the advanced successional stages of old fallows. In a sense, these foragers became dependent on horticultural practices of the past. This may be the general case with foraging peoples associated with tropical forests (Bailey n.d.; Bailey and Headland 1992).

In particular, several palms that are indicative of fallow land in lowland South America are more important economically to hunter-gatherers than they are to horticultural peoples. *Acrocomia* palms are said to "follow the plow"—their occurrence typically marks sites of prior agriculture (Markley 1956). They were a food source for both the Héta and the Aché (Hill et al. 1984; Kozák et al. 1979:379; Loureiro Fernandes 1964:40–41). Both groups also used the jerivá palm (*Syagrus romanzoffiana*), an indicator of disturbance. The Héta ate the mesocarp, kernel, and palm heart; they made receptacles from the spathes; and they made basketry, rope, infant-carrying straps, sleeping mats, and fishing line from the fibers (Kozák et al. 1979:395; Loureiro Fernandes 1959:25, 1964:41–43). The Aché obtained edible buds, flour, and weevil larvae in addition to bow wood, bowstring, roofing thatch, matting, fans, and cases for keeping feather art from the jerivá palm (Clastres 1972:162; Métraux and Baldus 1946:436; Vellard 1934:232, 240). These palms, *Acrocomia* and *Syagrus*, are found in forests that also harbor feral oranges, much bamboo, and patches of liana forests (Hill et al. 1984:125; Kaplan and Hill 1985:229; Kozák et al. 1979:367; Maack 1968:217; Métraux and Baldus 1946:436; Vellard 1934:240). These factors taken together indicate that the Aché and Héta relied on plant resources from old fallows of other horticultural populations.

The Guajá also did so. They used the palms growing on old fallows for many ends. For example, until quite recently they obtained fiber for bow-strings, hammocks, women's skirts, foreskin string, infant-carrying straps, rope, and string for beads exclusively from *Astrocaryum vulgare*, which, according to a neotropical palm specialist (Wessels-Boer 1965:132) "never" grows in undisturbed forest. They also consumed the fruits of *Maximili-ana* and *Orbignya* palms; prior to their ongoing process of sedentarization and "re"-agriculturalization, these were probably the most significant plant foods in the diet. They also camped in *Orbignya* palm groves, which are strongly indicative of past villages and fields of surrounding horticul-tural peoples, including the Ka'apor. (I should mention another parallel: like the Sirionó and the Yuquí [Stearman 1989:52], the Guajá lost the technology of fire making [Balée 1992a] during the process of agricultural regression.) In other words, in addition to having undergone what appears to be a highly convergent process of agricultural regression, these contem-porary foragers also intensified their use of very similar plants, especially palms of old fallows.

The Tupí-Guaraní–speaking Sirionó and Yuquí of Beni Province in eastern Bolivia also inhabit a region that is noteworthy for its anthropo-genic landscapes, in particular the mounds, raised fields, causeways, and drainage ditches of aboriginal chiefdoms that have been extinct for more than 500 years (Denevan 1966; Erickson n.d.; Erickson et al. 1991; Roose-velt 1992). Before they became sedentary in the 1940s and 1950s, the Sirionó constituted a trekking society; the Yuquí until quite recently were a foraging people (Stearman 1987, 1989). Both societies probably ulti-mately derived from a pre-Columbian Guaraní migration from Paraguay into Bolivia (Stearman 1989:22).

Sirionó informants with whom I spoke in 1993 claimed that their an-cestors camped exclusively on prehistoric mounds that were flood free, the prehistoric "habitation mounds" discussed by Denevan (1966:130–132). Preliminary analysis of a forest inventory I directed in 1993 on one of these mounds (called *ibi-báte*, "land-high," in the Sirionó language), which was formerly the site of Sirionó camps, shows a high frequency of palms with edible and other useful parts in the genera *Attalea* (as reported also in Denevan 1966:104) and *Astrocaryum*. Stearman (1989:69) has noted, in addition, that "palm fruits are probably the most consistently available and prolific fruits gathered by the Yuquí."

Although the status of these palms as disturbance indicators (or semidomesticates) remains unknown, certain other species in the inventoried forest of the mound near the Sirionó do indicate past horticultural influences. These include feral orange (*Citrus* sp.), *Inga* spp., hog plum (*Spondias mombim*), pau d'arco (*Tabebuia* spp.), *Cecropia* spp., and kapok tree (*Ceiba pentandra*), all of which have been collected and identified. Several of these same genera and species are found far to the south and east in fallows that characterized the habitats of the Aché and Héta of Paraguay and Brazil (Balée 1992b).

A middle-aged Sirionó man named Chiro (who was also one of Allyn Stearman's principal informants [Stearman 1987]) indicated to me that the Sirionó of the past made their camps exclusively on such flood-free mounds for several reasons, including (1) to be able to detect the movements of their enemies with greater ease and lead time; (2) to plant calabash trees (*Crescentia cujete*), bamboo (for arrow points), annatto trees (*Bixa orellana*), and maize (they did not cut and burn forest, incidentally, when planting these groups); and (3) to be near a perennial source of drinking water (although these mounds do not flood, they are strategically located near perennial creeks and springs, whereas much of the seasonally inundated forest and grasslands that surround the mounds dry up entirely during July and August).

Regardless of the overriding importance of meat from wild game animals in the Sirionó diet (Stearman 1987), the people appear to have been more dependent economically on plants of old fallows (mound sites in this instance) than on plants from pristine forests, which indeed may not even exist in their habitat. In other words, the Sirionó depended on the horticultural activities of past peoples, given their historical and continuing association with anthropogenic landscapes (also see Roosevelt 1992). This is not unlike the dependence on fallow species and anthropogenic landscapes exhibited by other trekking peoples elsewhere in Amazonia (Balée 1992b).

Many of the same uses that contemporary foragers derive from the semidomesticates in old fallows, horticultural peoples obtain from the domesticates in swiddens. For example, whereas the horticultural Ka'apor and Araweté both utilized cotton for infant-carrying straps, the Aché, Héta, and Guajá employed semidomesticated palm fibers for the same end. For making the infant-carrying strap, the foraging Yuquí used the bast fibers from (more than one?) species of *Cecropia* (Stearman 1989: 46–47), a genus that is very often associated with habitats that have been disturbed by horticulture in Amazonia. This suggests that for many foragers, some old fallow plants "substitute" for domesticates (see May et al.

1985:125). The double irony is that these foragers depended on horticulture, if not on domesticates themselves.

Process in Historical Ecology

These convergences are intelligible within the framework of historical ecology. The specific explanation begins with the variable susceptibility of precontact Indian populations to disease and severe depopulation. Next came the asteroid impact of conquest. This was followed by a seemingly convergent process of agricultural regression on the part of some depopulated societies that nevertheless survived in attenuated form. Some of these societies went sequentially from horticultural sedentarism to trekking and finally to foraging, losing domesticates in a fairly predictable order. In the end, some of these foraging societies did not become completely estranged from horticulture. The plant resources of old fallows, more so than those of high forests, constituted superior substitutes for domesticates lost long before, a point which may hold universally for the world's tropical forests (Bailey and Headland 1992).

Based on inventories of four hectares of fallow forest in the habitat of the Guajá and Ka'apor Indians, 14 of the 30 ecologically most important plant species are significant food plants, whereas in inventories of four hectares of primary forest in the same region, only 6 of the 30 ecologically most important plant species are significant food plants (Balée 1994). Some of the significant food plants of the fallows include babaçu palm, hog plum, tucumã palm, inajá palm, bacuri fruit trees, and copal trees (Balée 1994). (Several of these species, moreover, occur in fallows throughout Amazonia, suggesting certain constants with respect to the horticultural human factor of the past.) Fallows, in other words, constitute indigenous orchards, the result of unconscious yet highly rational forest management.

In conclusion, the historical ecology of Amazonia can be grasped most readily in terms of the biocultural sites called old fallows, which are artifacts of human social processes. Carole Crumley (1993:378) has aptly defined *landscape* as "the material manifestation of the relation between humans and the environment." Using this definition, old fallows constitute landscapes par excellence. Old fallows and their associated species represent, moreover, a substantive economic link between foragers and surrounding horticulturalists. Under conditions of historical and demographic duress, such as those of the conquest and some of its long-term effects, fallows became the meeting ground of history and ecology in Amazonia.

Acknowledgments

I would like to thank the Biodiversity Support Program of the World Wildlife Fund, the Jessie Smith Noyes Foundation, the Wenner-Gren Foundation, and Tulane University for financial support for most of the fieldwork on which this chapter is based. I am also grateful to Leslie Sponsel and two anonymous reviewers for helpful suggestions on improving the original manuscript. An earlier version was presented at the 91st annual meeting of the American Anthropological Association in San Francisco.

Note

1. I would like to clarify an earlier statement. I wrote that all these societies "lead exclusively foraging existences" (Balée 1992b:38). What I meant to say is that up *until quite recently* these societies appear to have led exclusively foraging existences. This is because the Héta and Šeta are recently extinct as societies; many of the Aché practice some horticulture as of late (e.g., Kaplan and Kopischke 1992); and some of the Guajá are becoming increasingly dependent on horticulture, which has been reintroduced by the National Indian Foundation only in the last few years, a point discussed more fully in Balée (1994). This clarification changes none of the substantive findings of Balée (1992b).

References Cited

Araújo Brusque, F. C. de.
1862   *Relatório apresentado à assemblea legislativa da província do Pará na primeira sessão da XIII Legislatura.* Belém: Typographia Frederico Carlos Rhossard.

Bailey, R. C.
n.d.   Promoting Biodiversity and Empowering Local People in Central African Forests. Manuscript.

Bailey, R. C., and T. N. Headland
1992   The Tropical Rain Forest: Is It a Productive Environment for Human Foragers? *Human Ecology* 19(2):261–85.

Balée, W.
1988   Indigenous Adaptation to Amazonian Palm Forests. *Principes* 32(2): 47–54.
1989   The Culture of Amazonian Forests. *Advances in Economic Botany* 7:1–21.
1992a   Indigenous History and Amazonian Biodiversity. In *Changing Tropical Forests: Historical Perspectives on Today's Challenges in Central and South America,* edited by H. K. Steen and R. P. Tucker, pp. 185–97. Durham, N.C.: Forest History Society.

1992b   People of the Fallow. In *Conservation of Neotropical Forests*, edited by
        K. H. Redford and C. Padoch, pp. 35–57. New York: Columbia Univer-
        sity Press.
1994   *Footprints of the Forest: Ka'apor Ethnobotany.* New York: Columbia
        University Press.

Balée, W., and D. Moore.
1991   Similarity and Variation in Plant Names in Five Tupí-Guaraní Languages
        (Eastern Amazonia). *Bulletin of the Florida Museum of Natural History,
        Biological Sciences* 35(4):209–62.

Berlin, B.
1992   *Ethnobiological Classification.* Princeton, N.J.: Princeton University
        Press.

Brochado, J. P.
1977   *Alimentação na floresta tropical.* Caderno no. 2. Porto Alegre: Univer-
        sidade Federal do Rio Grande do Sul.

Brown, C. H.
1985   Mode of Subsistence and Folk Biological Taxonomy. *Current Anthropol-
        ogy* 26:43–62.

Clastres, P.
1968   Ethnographie des indiens Guayaki (Paraguay-Brésil). *Journal de la
        Société des Americanistes* 57:9–61.
1972   The Guayaki. In *Hunters and Gatherers Today*, edited by M. G. Bicchieri,
        pp. 138–74. New York: Holt, Rinehart, and Winston.
1973   Eléments de demographie amérindienne. *L'Homme* 13(1–2):23–36.
1989   *Society Against the State: Essays in Political Anthropology.* Translated by
        R. Hurley and A. Stein. New York: Zone Books.

Crumley, C. L.
1993   Analyzing Historic Ecotonal Shifts. *Ecological Applications* 3(3):377–84.
1994   Introduction. In *Historical Ecology*, edited by C. L. Crumley, pp. 1–16.
        Santa Fe, N.M.: School of American Research Press.

Denevan, W. M.
1966   *The Aboriginal Cultural Geography of the Llanos de Mojos of Bolivia.*
        Ibero-Americana: 48. Berkeley: University of California Press.

Erickson, C. L.
n.d.   Archaeological Methods for the Study of Ancient Landscapes of the
        Llanos de Mojos in the Bolivian Amazon. Manuscript.

Erickson, C. L., J. Esteves, W. Winkler, and M. Michel
n.d.   Estudio preliminar de los sistemas agrícolas precolombinos en el depar-
        tamento del Beni. University of Pennsylvania and Instituto Nacional de
        Arqueología. Manuscript.

Gomes, M. P.
1988   *Os índios e o Brasil.* Petrópolis: Editora Vozes.

Hill, K., K. Hawkes, M. Hurtado, and H. Kaplan
1984   Seasonal Variance in the Diet of Aché Hunter-Gatherers of Eastern Paraguay. *Human Ecology* 12(2):101–36.

Kaplan, H., and K. Hill
1985   Food Sharing Among Aché Foragers: Tests of Explanatory Hypotheses. *Current Anthropology* 26(2):223–46.

Kaplan, H., and K. Kopischke
1992   Resource Use, Traditional Technology, and Change Among Native Peoples of Lowland South America. In *Conservation of Neotropical Forests*, edited by K. H. Redford and C. Padoch, pp. 83–107. New York: Columbia University Press.

Kozák, V., D. Baxter, L. Williamson, and R. L. Carneiro
1979   *The Héta Indians: Fish in a Dry Pond*. Anthropological Papers of the American Museum of Natural History, vol. 55, part 6. New York: American Museum of Natural History.

Lathrap, D.
1968   The "Hunting" Economies of the Tropical Forest Zone of South America: An Attempt at Historical Perspective. In *Man the Hunter*, edited by R. B. Lee and I. DeVore, pp. 23–29. Chicago: Aldine.

Lemle, M.
1971   Internal Classification of the Tupí-Guaraní Linguistic Family. In *Tupi Studies*, edited by I. D. Bendor-Samuel, pp. 107–29. Norman, Okla.: Summer Institute of Linguistics Publications in Linguistics and Related Fields, Publication no. 29.

Lévi-Strauss, C.
1966   *The Savage Mind*. Chicago: University of Chicago Press. (Originally published in French, 1962.)

Loureiro Fernandes, L.
1959   The Xetá: A Dying People of Brazil. *Bulletin of the International Committee on Urgent Anthropological and Ethnological Research* 2:22–26.
1964   Les Xetá et les Palmiers de la foret de Dourados. In *VI Congrès International des Sciences Anthropologiques et Ethnologiques, Tome II*, pp. 39–43. Paris: Musée de L'Homme.

Maack, R.
1968   *Geografia física do estado do Paraná*. Curitiba: Banco de Desenvolvimento do Paraná, Universidade Federal do Paraná e Instituto de Biologia e Pesquisas Tecnológicas.

Markley, K. S.
1956   Mbocayá or Paraguay Cocopalm: An Important Source of Oil. *Economic Botany* 10(1):3–32.

May, P. H., A. B. Anderson, M. M. Balick, and J. M. F. Frazão
1985   Subsistence Benefits from the Babassu Palm (*Orbignya martiana*). *Economic Botany* 39:113–29.

Métraux, A., and H. Baldus
1946   The Guayaki. In *Handbook of South American Indians*, vol. 2, edited by
        J. H. Steward, pp. 435–44. Washington, D.C.: Smithsonian Institution.

Nassif, R. C.
1993   Interim Report to the Biodiversity Support Program/World Wildlife
        Fund. Manuscript.

Newson, L. A.
1992   Cultural Influences on the Impact of Old World Diseases in Colonial
        Latin America. Paper presented at the annual meeting of the American
        Anthropological Association, San Francisco.

Noronha, J. M. de
1856   Roteiro da viagem da cidade do Pará até as ultimas colonias dos
        dominios portuguezes em os rios Amazonas e Negro. In *Notícias para a
        história e geographia das nações ultramarinas*, vol. 6. Lisbon.

Raup, D. M.
1991   *Extinction: Bad Genes or Bad Luck*. New York: W. W. Norton.

Rivet, P.
1924   Les indiens Canoeiros. *Journal de la Société des Americanistes*, n.s.
        16:169–81.

Rodrigues, A. D.
1988   Proto-Tupi Evidence for Agriculture. Paper read at the First Interna-
        tional Congress of Ethnobiology, Belém.

Roosevelt, A. C.
1992   Secrets of the Forest. *The Sciences* 32(6):22–28.

Stearman, A. M.
1987   *No Longer Nomads: The Sirionó Revisited*. Lanham, Md.: Hamilton Press.
1989   *Yuquí: Forest Nomads in a Changing World*. New York: Holt, Rinehart
        and Winston.

Toral, A.
1986   Situação e perspectivas de sobrevivência dos Avá-Canoeiro. Unpub-
        lished manuscript. Centro Ecumênico do Documentação e Informação
        (CEDI), São Paulo.

Vellard, J.
1934   Les indiens Guayaki. *Journal de la Société des Americanistes* 26:223–92.
1939   *Une civilisation du miel*. Paris: Gallimard.

Viveiros de Castro, E.
1992   *From the Enemy's Point of View*. Chicago: University of Chicago Press.

Wessels-Boer, J. G.
1965   *Palmae, Flora of Suriname*, vol. 5. Leiden: E. J. Brill.

PART II

FORAGING, NUTRITION, AND HEALTH

Ultimately, subsistence and economy are important in providing adequate nutrition, which in turn facilitates good health. Nutritional and medical anthropology need to be more closely linked to research on human ecology in Amazonia. Under Western influence, indigenous nutrition and health often deteriorate, and this can endanger survival and welfare.

In chapter 5, Kenneth Good argues that extensive trekking is the primary characteristic of the subsistence economy of traditional Yanomami in Venezuela. They spend not just weeks but even months subsisting by hunting game and gathering wild plants in their interfluvial, rain forest, and mountain habitat, and during these extended treks they may consume few if any crops. The Yanomami are primarily foragers and only secondarily farmers, yet they adapt quite successfully in a tropical rain forest ecosystem. Accordingly, the Yanomami are one of the challenges to the controversial hypothesis advanced by Thomas Headland and Robert Bailey that humans cannot survive by foraging alone in a tropical forest but depend on farming or trade with farmers.

In chapter 6, Rebecca Holmes presents data from her research with Yanomami in Venezuela that bear on the controversial issue of whether small stature is adaptive or maladaptive. Holmes explores small stature as a reflection of the interplay of genetic and environmental factors. She argues that the Yanomami may be short because they have successfully adapted to their highland forest ecosystems, where protein is probably a limiting factor. Smaller body size is adaptive rather than maladaptive or pathological in this ecological context because food requirements are lower. Holmes goes on to draw some of the policy implications of her research. For instance, she asserts that Venezuelan and Western growth standards, which would indicate that the Yanomami are maladaptive in their nutritional status, may be inappropriate for indigenous populations in tropical forest ecosystems.

In chapter 7, Darna Dufour describes the process that the Tucanoans use to eliminate the toxicity of bitter manioc in the Vaupés region of Colombia. Dufour also critically reviews some common ideas about the disadvantages of manioc, indicating that it is not as poor a source of protein and minerals as previously assumed. She points out that the nutritional value of manioc is in part a function of the specific methods employed in processing. Dufour also cautions that with sociocultural change women may not have as much time to adequately process manioc, and the toxic residue that remains could lead to health problems.

In chapter 8, Carlos Coimbra suggests that the precontact period was not necessarily a utopia for health; rather, traditional indigenous populations also faced the adaptive challenges of various diseases and parasites, even though the situation certainly became much worse with contact. Coimbra also outlines some of the agenda for future research on the much neglected but extremely important topic of the medical anthropology of Amazonia.

5

Yanomami of Venezuela

Foragers or Farmers—Which Came First?

Kenneth Good

The major thrust of my research has been to demonstrate the requirements of maintaining adequate meat consumption among the Yanomami
of Venezuela and the sociocultural implications of those requirements,
particularly for community size and degree of sedentariness (Good 1987,
1989). These questions have been debated intensely for almost two decades (Gross 1975; Harris 1974, 1984; Ross 1980; Sponsel 1983, 1986).
Much research has been carried out, and our knowledge of Amazonian
subsistence practices has grown enormously. Despite the great increase
in our knowledge of Amazonian societies, there are still issues that have
yet to be resolved. By now some have grown weary of the "protein debate"
and have moved on to other problems. Nevertheless, this issue remains
relevant, and useful data are still coming in.

Recently, a number of papers have been presented claiming the unlike-
lihood or impossibility of a hunting and gathering existence in tropical
forest regions without some influence from domesticated crops (Bailey et
al. 1989; Headland 1987). This is a relatively new question and an important one. But my research has addressed the converse question: Can Yanomami be horticulturalists without the significant influence of hunting
and gathering? Or more precisely, can the interfluvial Yanomami (and
this includes 95 percent of Venezuelan Yanomami today) remain sedentary without the direct or indirect influence of alternate sources of animal
foods? Just as the former question asks whether humans could have lived
in the tropical forest as hunters and gatherers before the invention of agriculture, my question is, Could they have lived as agriculturalists before
the invention of animal husbandry?

Tropical forest cultigens generally provide minimal amounts of protein. This leaves forest animals as the only significant source of this essential nutrient. My data from nonriverine communities demonstrate that in relatively short periods (1–3 years' residence at a new garden), hunting yields decline, indicating a depletion of local game animals (Table 5.1). Without domesticated food animals, adequate protein consumption would be difficult, if not impossible, for sedentary agricultural communities. As villages grow large in numbers of inhabitants, this problem becomes even more acute (Table 5.2). Not only biological needs are affected. Village harmony and cohesion are severely strained as distribution of meat to all inhabitants becomes impossible in large villages (Good 1987).

In carrying out field measurements I found that the challenge is similar, but not identical, to that of demonstrating the impossibility of a pure hunting and gathering existence in tropical forests—that is, the challenge of proving a negative. Just as we have no pure hunters and gatherers today

Table 5.1   Yields for *Rami* (One-Day) Hunts of the Hasupiwët^heri at Home Base, New Garden, and on *Wayumi* Treks

	Home Base	New Garden		Wayumi Trek
		Year 1	Year 2	
Number of hunts	523	348	474	512
Number hunters per day	7.20	6.10	6.90	8.60
Number hours per hunt	6.51	6.38	6.55	5.84
Dressed game per hunt (kg)	1.62	2.83	2.04	2.64
Dressed game per hunter-hour (kg)[a]	0.25	0.44	0.31	0.45
Dressed game per capita per day (kg)	0.11	0.16	0.13	0.21
Meat per capita per day (kg)	0.09	0.13	0.10	0.17
Protein per capita per day (g)	17.28	25.57	20.85	33.64
Success rates (%)	40.93	47.25	42.20	52.60

Notes: Data are derived from 1,857 hunts from 1975 to 1983. Periods when data were recorded can be seen in Good (1989:Table 9). Mean population: 108.

[a]All hunts, successful and unsuccessful, were included for the calculation of productivity. The calculations in my previous article (1987:Table 16.1) included only the successful hunts. The percentages of these are indicated on the bottom line of that table. Although these rates indicate the average quantity of meat procured on a *rami* hunt when there were one or more kills, the rates in this table indicate overall productivity for all hunts regardless of outcome.

Table 5.2 Yields and Frequencies of *Rami* (One-Day) Hunts from the
Home Bases of Four Villages

	Village Size			
	42	67	92	127
Number of hunts	326	485	323	246
Number hunters per day	3.88	4.80	6.59	8.78
Total dressed game per day (kg)	7.28	10.95	10.25	12.80
Dressed game per hunter (kg)	1.88	2.28	1.56	1.46
Number hours per hunt	6.65	6.79	6.60	7.10
Dressed game per hunter-hour (kg)	0.28	0.34	0.24	0.21
Dressed game per capita per day (kg)	0.17	0.16	0.11	0.10
Meat per capita per day (kg)	0.14	0.13	0.09	0.08
Protein per capita per day (g)	27.73	26.15	17.83	16.13

Note: Exact periods when data were recorded can be seen in Good (1989:Table 11).

to scrutinize, there are no interfluvial *sedentary* Yanomami groups to
evaluate. It is important to realize that just because today there are no
hunters and gatherers without some kind of horticultural influence does
not necessarily mean that there never were any. There are no "stone age"
tribes living today without technological influence from outside. This
does not mean such groups never existed. In eleven communities that I
was the first non-Yanomami to reach, I found no clay pots. The craft has
become extinct.

The Yanomami never remain sedentary long enough to demonstrate
empirically a long-term decline in hunting yields. They react before depressed yields occur. They abandon their house and gardens to set off on
a trek, subsisting primarily by hunting and gathering. Trekking is carried
out for as much as 60 percent of the yearly round but most often for
about 40 percent of the time. When Yanomami are at their communal
gardens, approximately two-thirds of their diet consists of cultivated
foods (primarily plantains), while the rest is gathered and hunted. While
they are trekking in the forest, only about 10 percent of their food consists
of cultivated crops. This 10 percent is an average for the duration of a
trek, and it is noteworthy that there are periods during which virtually no
cultivated crops are eaten.

As I have stated elsewhere, the principal reason for initiating a trek is the depletion of crops at the home base (Good 1987, 1989). But a number of other factors also come into play. Yields of gathered foods drop, often to almost zero. Hunting yields show declines, although not precipitous ones. Firewood is exhausted, resulting in drastic increases in the cost of providing heat and cooking fuel for the family. The environs of the house become fouled with excrement and garbage. Bugs infest the house, attracted by waste matter. In the context of all this, community social relations become tenser, quarrels increase, complaints of meat-hunger are frequent, and dissatisfaction arises over proportions of meat in the village-wide distribution of peccary (meat being the only item distributed to the entire village). All these changes occur after only a few months' (2–4) residence at the gardens.

While on trek the community travels as a single group unless it is above average in size. Yanomami communities range from 40 to 150 people with an average of about 60. A village of 80 or more will split up into two or three groups for part or all of the trek. All personal possessions are carried. If there are any cumbersome or heavy objects they are stored (hidden) in the forest. These are most often Western goods, but in former times large clay pots were stored. At each encampment a new provisional shelter is made. Leaves are carried from site to site for the quickly made roof. The amount of time spent on hunting and gathering dramatically increases. These activities are carried out enthusiastically. On the trek it is rare that anyone stays home to pass the day in his or her hammock, as about 10 percent of the village do at the home garden. Variety and quantity of wild foods increase over those of the home base. Hunting yields increase by 91 percent (Table 5.2). This can be attributed to fresh hunting areas and more time spent hunting.

Another approach to assessing the possibility or impossibility of people's living as pure hunters and gatherers is to define the available foods, speculatively determine the degree of difficulty of exploiting them, and measure the energetic requirements of doing so. Those who suggest that subsistence based solely on hunting and gathering was impossible before influences from gardening appeared accept that the tropical forest is highly productive but difficult for *human* exploitation. Robert Bailey and Thomas Headland say that most foods are high up in trees and costly to reach, and that they are very dispersed, requiring high cost in travel time (Bailey and Headland 1991:4). These foods also have a very pronounced seasonality. Bailey and Headland add that seeds, fruits, and tubers require digging, pounding, scraping, soaking, and cooking. For these reasons they conclude that there are not, and probably never were, any "true" hunters and gatherers in tropical rain forest ecosystems (Bailey and Headland 1991).

I would answer that Yanomami—and I would think full-time hunters and gatherers even more—are quite adept at scaling trees. Amazonian foods are indeed seasonal, but trees do not all produce in the same season. The enormous variety of wild foods and the sequence of production ensure that one kind of food or another is available throughout the year. The fact that they are highly dispersed does not burden foragers. Their group size and mobility are designed to exploit dispersed foods and different microenvironments during the various seasons. Dispersed foods present problems only for sedentary or semisedentary horticulturalists like the Yanomami.

In terms of the costs of harvesting and processing, many wild foods actually require nothing more than being picked off the ground. For other foods, I do not think that the tasks of digging, scraping, soaking, and certainly cooking can be considered energetically costly activities. It would be useful to quantify this. Hunting and gathering groups are small. Gathering trips are outings, not hard days of labor from which people look forward to completion, relaxation, and leisure. High costs of intensive energy outlays can be better associated with the hunt. Gathering wild foods is at once a social and a pleasurable event. Foragers have been described as the original affluent society because they have to spend only two to three hours a day to get their food (Sahlins 1968).

If anything has influenced the subsistence of modern-day hunters and gatherers it is the introduction of manufactured tools. The machete and the ax greatly alter the time and energy costs of procuring wild foods (Carneiro 1979). It is this difference that should be considered in relation to precontact, prehorticultural hunters and gatherers, rather than ethnocentric or ecocentric notions about the availability of edible plants for carbohydrates.

After 14 years of living with the Yanomami, I am convinced that hunters and gatherers could have subsisted in Amazonia, at least in the part of it I know, without domesticated plants. But to do so, they would have had to live in certain ways. That is, they would have had to live like hunters and gatherers as they are typically defined: few in numbers, migratory, keenly aware of a wide variety of food resources, and expert in exploiting a diversity of microenvironments. There is plenty of wild food in Amazonia, but not for sedentary villages. Mobility and knowledge are among the more important factors in the successful foraging adaptation of the Yanomami.

Discussion

The most salient and distinctive characteristic of the Yanomami subsistence system is the community trek (Good 1989:ch. 2). Relatively few tribes practice trekking (notwithstanding Werner 1983:225). This is particularly so if we restrict the definition of trekking to expeditions by an entire community over periods of time ranging from several weeks to several months. It is noteworthy that trekking has another important advantage beyond exploiting diverse resources and microenvironments: evading enemies in warfare—but that is another issue to be considered elsewhere.

That the Yanomami still engage in trekking very likely sheds some light on their historical background. It has been hypothesized that the Yanomami, who probably originated in the Parima Highlands, probably were hunters and gatherers and did not practice agriculture to any significant degree until the introduction of plantains and bananas in post-Columbian times (Harris 1974:101–102). Although the inception of plantain gardening enabled a more sedentary village life and a more abundant source of calories for the Yanomami, it has not incorporated them into a fully stable agricultural system. The seminomadic subsistence pattern of farming interspersed with community treks has advantages over full-scale farming for the Yanomami. The fact that the Yanomami live away from rivers and today have little technology for exploiting aquatic resources suggests a prior emphasis on hunting and only a minor reliance on fishing. Furthermore, even today the Yanomami represent a foraging culture that has not made maximum use of horticulture and has not entirely given up the nomadic behavior of the past. When planted in limited amounts and not throughout the year, plantains do not provide a steady source of food. Moreover, unlike manioc, they cannot be stored or left unharvested until needed. This is part of the reason for Yanomami trekking.

Decades ago Robert Carneiro (1960) demonstrated that there is no environmental limitation on growing enough crops to assure a reliable supply and enable a village to remain sedentary. It appears that one reason the Yanomami plant fewer crops then they might is because they expect to go on treks. During treks, meat consumption almost doubles, and many new sources of wild foods are exploited. Thus, the hunting and gathering ways are used to tide the community over when crops are exhausted or when they are not yet ready to harvest. Treks also provide a change from the routine of village life, and they do not involve the kind of struggle for existence that Bailey and Headland imply. In this regard the Yanomami are similar to the Sirionó hunters and gatherers observed by Allan Holmberg:

Although agriculture has been practiced for many years by the Sirionó (they may originally have been a strictly nomadic people), it has never reached a sufficient degree of development to prevent their remaining a fairly mobile people. On the whole, its practice is subsidiary in the total economy to both hunting and collecting. One of the reasons for this may be that the game supply of an area becomes scarce before the rewards of agriculture can be reaped, thus entailing a migration of the band to other areas to search for game. (1969:67)

Conclusion

As already mentioned, Yanomami communities still living in the interfluvial regions today spend about 40 percent of their time away from their gardens, camped in the forest, hunting and gathering for survival. But this subsistence pattern is being increasingly influenced as each year passes and will change even more in coming years as outside contact increases. Communities that have access to machetes and axes clear larger gardens, remain more stationary or completely so, and participate in fewer and shorter treks or in none at all. Villages that have been attracted to Western settlements on the major rivers and have acquired the technology to exploit the vast aquatic resources of rivers like the Orinoco and its tributaries have virtually abandoned traditional trekking patterns.

For the many communities that still live in the hinterland on the slopes and crests of the rolling hills, foraging and trekking have remained crucial components of the Yanomami adaptive strategy for consuming adequate calories and protein.

References

Bailey, Robert, et al.
1989   Hunting and Gathering in Tropical Rain Forest: Is It Possible? *American Anthropologist* 91:59–82.
Bailey, Robert, and Thomas Headland
1991   Introduction: Have Hunter-Gatherers Ever Lived in Tropical Rain Forest Independently of Agriculture? *Human Ecology* 19(2):115–286.
Carneiro, Robert
1960   Slash-and-Burn Agriculture: A Closer Look at Its Implications for Settlement Patterns. In *Men and Cultures: Selected Papers of the International Congress of Anthropological and Ethnological Sciences*, edited by A. Wallace, pp. 229–34. Philadelphia: University of Pennsylvania Press.

1979   Tree Felling with the Stone Ax: An Experiment Carried Out Among the Yanomamö Indians of Southern Venezuela. In *Ethnoarchaeology: Implications of Ethnography for Archaeology*, edited by Carol Kramer, pp. 21–58. New York: Columbia University Press.

Good, Kenneth
1987   Limiting Factors in Amazonian Ecology. In *Food and Evolution: Toward a Theory of Human Food Habits*, edited by Marvin Harris and Eric Ross, pp. 407–21. Philadelphia: Temple University Press.
1989   Yanomami Hunting Patterns: Trekking and Garden Relocation as an Adaptation to Game Availability in Amazonia, Venezuela. Ph.D. dissertation, Department of Anthropology, University of Florida.

Gross, Daniel
1975   Protein Capture and Cultural Development in the Amazon Basin. *American Anthropologist* 77:526–49.

Harris, Marvin
1974   *Cows, Pigs, Wars and Witches: The Riddles of Culture*. New York: Random House.
1984   A Cultural Materialist Theory of Band and Village Warfare: The Yanomamo Test. In *Warfare, Culture, and Environment*, edited by R. Brian Ferguson, pp. 111–40. New York: Academic Press.

Headland, Thomas
1987   The Wild Yam Question: How Well Could Independent Hunter-Gatherers Live in a Tropical Rain Forest Ecosystem? *Human Ecology* 15:463–91.

Holmberg, Allan
1969   *Nomads of the Long Bow*. New York: The Natural History Press.

Ross, Jane Bennett
1980   Ecology and the Problem of the Tribe: A Critique of the Hobbesian Model of Preindustrial Warfare. In *Beyond the Myths of Culture: Essays in Cultural Materialism*, pp. 33–60. New York: Academic Press.

Sahlins, Marshall
1968   Notes on the Original Affluent Society. In *Man the Hunter*, edited by Richard B. Lee and Irven Devore, pp. 85–95. Chicago: Aldine Atherton.

Sponsel, Leslie
1983   Yanomami Warfare, Protein Capture, and Cultural Ecology: A Critical Analysis of the Arguments of the Opponents. *Interciencia* 8(4):204–10.
1986   Amazon Ecology and Adaptation. *Annual Review of Anthropology* 15:67–97.

Werner, Dennis
1983   Why Do the Mekranoti Trek? In *Adaptive Responses of Native Amazonians*, edited by R. Hames and W. Vickers. New York: Academic Press.

6

Small Is Adaptive

Nutritional Anthropometry of Native Amazonians

Rebecca Holmes

Amazonian indigenes, like all human populations, have developed strategies for coping with environmental stress. In the past these strategies, or cultural responses, have been successful. Pre-Columbian populations were higher than they are today (Meggers, this volume), and certain groups, including the Yanomami of this study, have gone through periods of population and territorial expansion. The current pace and nature of environmental change, however, have upset the delicate balance between stress and cultural response, thereby threatening the health and survival of many groups (Coimbra, this volume). It is important to examine the biological as well as the cultural adaptations of native Amazonians in order to determine when and whether these indigenes need outside intervention to alleviate the problems associated with rapid environmental change.

In Amazonia, one of the most important physical adaptations to environmental stress has been small body size. By the yardstick of the developed world, smallness is usually regarded as pathological. Classification of indigenous groups as malnourished is common and may lead to the conclusion that they are unable to care for themselves and need to be rescued by the "more civilized" national culture. It is important, then, to distinguish between a population of undernourished individuals who need aid and a population of small but generally healthy individuals who should, on the contrary, be protected from outside intervention. In this context it is especially important to be able to accurately assess nutritional status, which is one of the best indicators of the health of a population.

Anthropometry is a convenient and low-cost method for evaluating the nutritional status of a community because it can be employed by para-medical personnel and does not involve time-consuming dietary studies or the taking of blood, urine, or fecal samples, all of which may be considered objectionable by the indigenes. However, the lack of appropriate standards with which to compare populations can lead to errors. In order to recognize real nutritional crises when they occur, the special anthropometric characteristics of native Amazonians must be taken into account. It is the purpose of this paper (1) to present a profile of anthropometric characteristics of the Venezuelan Yanomami, as well as those of certain other Amazonian indigenes, (2) to analyze possible genetic and environmental origins of these characteristics, and (3) to propose that "small is adaptive" under the environmental conditions prevailing in Amazonia.

Study Population, Materials, and Methods

The Yanomama occupy the border area between southern Venezuela and northern Brazil. They number some 20,000 individuals divided about evenly between the two countries. In Venezuela they form two dialect groups, the Yanomami of the upper Orinoco and Parima mountain range (studied here) and the Sanemá, who inhabit the headwaters of the Caura River (fig. 6.1). Part of the study population comes from the high savanna land in the Sierra Parima (1,000 m above sea level); it consists of several hundred individuals in more than ten *shabonos* (village complexes). Eight shabonos, from both Parima A and B, are included in the study sample.[1] The other group, Coyoweteri shabono (population 150), is found in a lowland tropical rain forest in the upper Orinoco, about 20 minutes by plane, or two days' walk by jungle trail, from Parima B.

These indigenous communities have remained largely unacculturated, continuing to practice their traditional subsistence activities: hunting, gathering, and gardening (fishing is minimal). They consume plantains and bananas as their staple starch, on occasion with cassava bread (a relatively recent introduction from their Ye'kuana neighbors). Their diet is supplemented with small game as well as crabs, spiders, frogs, and insects. At the time of the fieldwork, Protestant missionaries had been living among these Yanomami for eight to fifteen years. Owing to this contact, some Yanomami had changed their religious practices, and some modifications had also been made in social structure and settlement patterns. Village diet, however, was not much affected because the missionaries did not sell or trade food, and groups of Yanomami left on long expeditions (lasting several weeks or months) to hunt, attend forest gardens, and meet with other groups. Rivalries were still expressed in raids, warfare,

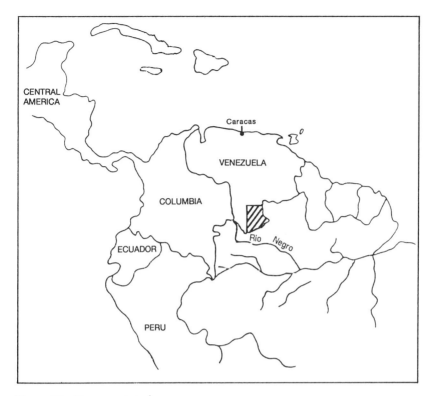

Figure 6.1. Yanomami study area.

and physical challenges, but infanticide had been strongly discouraged. Gold miners had not penetrated these areas. Contact with missionaries and other outsiders had not caused depopulation, probably owing to the introduction of modern medicine and the elimination of infanticide. (See Schkolnik [1983] for a demographic analysis of Parima.)

Anthropometric measurements were taken on groups of 145 to 242 individuals, depending on the field visit. Repeat measurements were made on many individuals, allowing for the calculation of growth velocities in the children. Between 50 and 60 percent of the study population consisted of children 18 years or younger. Measurements for height, weight, left arm circumference, and triceps and subscapular skinfolds were made according to World Health Organization (WHO) methods (Jelliffe 1966).[2] Anthropometric data were compared with both international and Venezuelan reference populations, as noted on each graph (figs. 6.2–6.6).[3]

Human height, weight, and other physical characteristics are influenced by the interaction of a complex set of genetic and environmental factors that are difficult, if not impossible, to separate due to their synergistic relationships. In order to make a case for nutritional intervention, however, the separation is often attempted. To do this, health evaluators study a given population or racial group under optimal environmental conditions (that is, where growth is thought to reach its full genetic potential) and compare the results with those of genetically distinct groups enjoying the same advantaged conditions. Differences in anthropometric measurements among distinct racial groups living in advantaged environments would point to genetic origins, whereas different measurements from a single genetic group under advantaged and disadvantaged conditions would point to environmental origins.

Ideal environmental conditions for human growth, however, are a recent phenonomen confined largely to developed countries and found rarely in Third World or Fourth World (indigenous) populations. Martorell and Habicht (1986:242) go so far as to state that "to date, studies of samples of well-nourished native Amerindian children are not available." Therefore it is impossible to separate genetic from environmental influences on the growth of these groups using conventional methodology. By default we are left only with the standards developed for the privileged members of the country in which the indigenous people reside, or with international standards derived almost exclusively from persons of northern European ancestry.

One could argue that environmental, rather than genetic, differences account for the greatest share of variation in measurements, and thus the errors caused by ignoring genetic differences will be small. This is the position of the World Health Organization, which encourages use of uniform international standards or standards derived from the privileged groups of a given country, for studies in both the developed and the developing world. The appropriateness of this methodology for assessing the nutritional status of the Yanomami and, by extension, other Amazonian groups is challenged here.

Results

Height and Weight

The Yanomami are pygmoid in size (average adult male height 150 cm or less): the men from Parima averaged 146.9 cm in height and the women 136.9 cm, with average weights of 43.7 kg and 37.9 kg, respectively. Yanomami children characteristically exhibit very low ratios of height for age and weight for age, which, according to international standards, classifies them as suffering from first or second degree malnutrition. More than half the boys between 6 and 14 years of age were classified as severely, or third degree, malnourished in terms of height for age (Holmes 1983:130). Results for girls were similar.

Arm Circumference

The left arm circumferences of all children were compared with Venezuelan standards (derived from measurements of healthy, well-fed, Caracas private school students [Méndez Castellano et al. 1981]). Virtually none of the Yanomami boys reached the fiftieth percentile and most of the younger boys fell below the third percentile. The girls fared somewhat better, with five individuals falling above the fiftieth percentile; all of these were postpubertal girls. As with the boys, a considerable number of younger girls fell below the fiftieth percentile (Holmes 1983:132, 1985:251).

Skinfolds

Triceps and subscapular skinfold measurements again showed the Yanomami children to be well below the Caracas standards, with most falling below the tenth percentile (Holmes 1983:133, 1985:252). Since adults as well as children were found to have very low skinfold measurements, a study of upper arm muscle circumference (in individuals eight years old to adult) was undertaken to see whether increased muscularity was evident in the population. This measure again confirmed the very small size of the Yanomami (Holmes 1983:134). Even the low fat stores of the upper arm did not bring muscle circumferences up to the lower levels of the North American reference population (Stini 1972b:347), since the upper arm circumference itself was very small. The average muscle circumference for Yanomami men was lower than that for North American women. Sexual dimorphism (difference between the sexes) was the same for the Yanomami as for the reference population. Compared with arm muscle circumferences obtained for Tucanoans by Darna Dufour (personal communication, June 1983)—measurements of 265 and 228 mm for men and women, respectively—the Yanomami values of 220 and 190 mm are low for northwest Amazonian tropical forest peoples.

Weight for Height

In contrast to the markedly substandard results mentioned above was the pattern of weight for height as it evolved through the growth years. Figure 6.2 (for girls; results for boys were similar) compares the mean of the Yanomami girls with the fiftieth percentile of the Caracas reference population. Prepubertal children of both sexes (under 130 cm in height) were thinner on the average than the reference populations, but surprisingly, all postpubertal children (above 130 cm in height) were heavier. Recall that by the age of 18 years, neither height nor weight for age of the Yanomami reached standard levels. Yet when the effect of average size difference is eliminated by using the ratio of weight for height, we find Yanomami teenagers stockier than the reference group.

Growth Velocity

Growth in height was calculated for 24 boys and 17 girls over two years old and compared with standards for English children (Tanner 1976).[4] The mean for Yanomami boys (fig. 6.3) fluctuated between the tenth and fiftieth percentiles of the reference population. With the exception of three individuals, all fell within the range of normally developing children. The girls' height increases were within the range of the English chil-

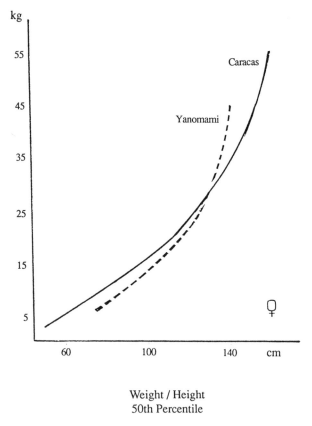

Weight / Height
50th Percentile

Figure 6.2. Body proportions, Yanomami versus Caracas children.

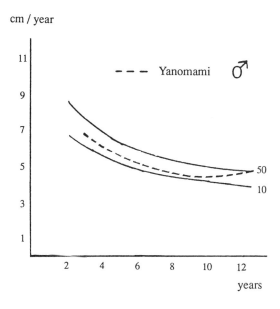

Height Velocity

Figure 6.3. Growth in height, Yanomami boys. Reference population Tanner 1978:177.

dren; four of them gained height between 15 and 18 years of age, indicating late maturation.

Yearly increase in weight for 46 boys (fig. 6.4) showed them to have a low-normal trajectory and a delayed adolescent growth spurt. Results were similar for the 19 girls studied.[5]

Yanomami children between the ages of 2 and 18 show low-normal growth. Considering this result, the question remains: Why are these children so small, and why is the adult population pygmoid in stature? In order to maintain growth velocity within the normal range and yet produce children and adults of extremely small size, children must be either unusually small before the age of two or of exceedingly low birth weight and length. A cross-sectional analysis of the Yanomami infant from birth to 24 months sheds some light on the dynamics of this process.

Infant Height and Weight

Heights were obtained for 24 Yanomami infants of both sexes in the high savanna and lowland jungle sites. In figure 6.5, the mean heights of these

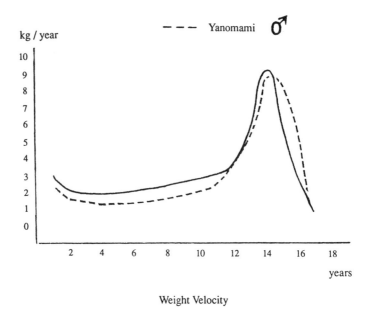

Weight Velocity

Figure 6.4. Growth in weight, Yanomami boys. Reference population Tanner 1978:182.

babies are plotted against the growth curves for well-fed Caracas infants.[6] Of the seven babies under one year of age, only two fell within the boundaries of the reference population; the rest, all seven months old or younger, fell below the tenth percentile. Yanomami babies are smaller at birth than the reference infants and continue to increase in height, with the group's mean lying near the fifth percentile of the reference population.

Mean weight for age was plotted for 37 Yanomami infants (fig. 6.6), again with sexes combined. This parameter shows an interesting pattern: 9 of the 12 infants under one year old were actually within the range of the well-fed Caracas population. From 12 to 24 months of age, however, none of the babies reached even the lower tenth percentile of the reference population. If one can draw a longitudinal conclusion from these cross-sectional data, apparently the normal weight increases of the Yanomami children under one year old are not maintained as the child enters the 12- to 24-month-old period. The babies from one to two years old actually stagnate, that is, they become thin, as weights do not keep pace with heights. Seven of the 17 infants between one and two years old are within the normal height for age range, but none of the children in this age group is within the normal range in weight for age.

The extreme smallness of Yanomami children and adults seems to originate both from a small birth size and from the dynamics of the growth process during the 12- to 24-month-old period. Infants entering the next age cohort are very small. This smallness combines with the slightly lower than normal childhood growth velocities (figs. 6.3 and 6.4) to produce small adults at the end of the growth process.

Traditional or Baseline Height

To determine more precisely whether the smallness of Yanomami children is due to a recent, detrimental environmental condition related to contact with outsiders (e.g., change in availability of food, introduction of exogenous diseases), I compared their predicted adult heights with those of their parents and with a sample of Parima adults (James Neel expedition, January 1969) at the time of the first medical and missionary

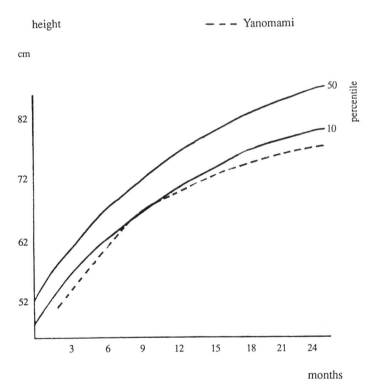

Figure 6.5. Growth in height, Yanomami infants. Reference population Méndez Castellano et al., 1981.

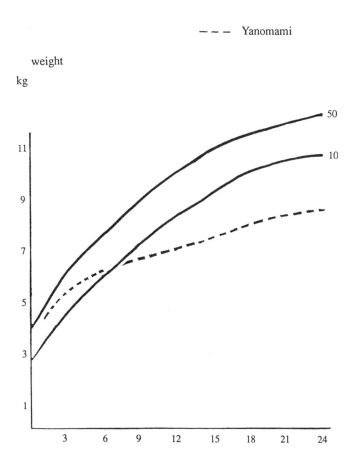

Figure 6.6. Growth in weight, Yanomami infants. Reference population Méndez Castellano et al., 1981.

contacts.[7] The comparison of predicted heights with the actual heights of the adult Parima population of 160 individuals (82 men, 78 women) appears in Table 6.1.

The mean predicted height for boys of 145.16 cm was not significantly different from the actual mean height for Parima men of 146.96 cm or the mean height (144.3 cm) of 31 men from Niyayoweteri (Parima B) measured in 1969. Likewise, the mean predicted height for girls (135.11 cm) was not statistically different from that of Parima women (136.85 cm) or of the 37 women from Parima B (134.7 cm) measured at first contact. The question of whether or not to lump all adults together was an important one. Since missionary and direct outside contact with these Yanomami began approximately 15 years before the study, it could have been that those adults who reached maturation after contact (individuals between 18 and 30 years old at the time of the study) would differ in height from adults over 30 years old, who had reached their full height before contact. Table 6.1 shows a breakdown of mean adult heights in these two groups. Mean heights and standard deviations in the pre- and postcontact adults are virtually identical, showing no statistically significant difference.

From the similarity between mean projected heights and actual heights, it appears that the study children are replicating the growth of their parents—that is, this is not an aberration caused by contact.

Average adult male height among 391 Yanomami studied shortly after direct contact with outsiders was 153.1 cm (Neel, Layrisse, and Salzano 1977).

Although direct contact with the Yanomami in Parima was relatively recent, missionaries were living with Yanomami in adjacent areas in the 1950s, and indirect contact had gone on sporadically for many decades before that. I do not believe that Yanomami stature was significantly affected by these contacts. However, there is archaeological evidence that

Table 6.1 Predicted and Actual Heights of Parima
          Population

	X̄ (cm)	s	n
Predicted height, children 2–12 years[a]			
Boys	145.16	6.50	63
Girls	135.11	7.05	61
Actual height, adults 18 years and over			
Men	146.96	4.77	82
Men 18–29	146.97	4.59	36
Men 30 and over	146.96	4.95	46
Women	136.85	4.24	78
Women 18–29	136.65	4.31	31
Women 30 and over	136.98	4.23	47

Note: The means were not different at the $\alpha = 0.05$ level of
       significance using a two-tailed test.
[a]Calculated from Tanner (1978:203).

other South American Indians were taller in pre-Columbian times than are their present day descendents (Anna Roosevelt, personal communication; Jelliffe and Jelliffe 1979:150).

Discussion

Are the Yanomami and other Amazonian Indians small because of long-term evolutionary processes or are they stunted because of present-day hardships? Both factors seem to be at work. Although genetic and environmental influences interact and are difficult to separate, it is useful to attempt the separation because it may help to identify the special characteristics of Amazonian indigenes, especially their Mongoloid ancestry.

Genetic Evidence

Height and Weight / It is well known that stature, both during the growth period and at adulthood, has a strong genetic component in human populations.[8] Within and among human racial groups, growth and adult stature vary under similar environmental conditions. Well-to-do persons of Asian heritage are shorter on average than either Europeans or Africans of privileged groups (Ashcroft 1971:295; Davies 1988:80; Eveleth and Tanner 1976:226; Martorell, Mendoza, and Castillo 1988:63; Tanner 1978:137). Weight is also lower for Asiatics, which is in part a result of their lower height; characteristically they are smaller people. Amazonian Indians share a common Mongoloid ancestry with other South American Indians; their small body size (Table 6.2) is consistent with this genetic heritage. The Yanomami are the shortest population of Asiatics in the Americas listed in *Worldwide Variation in Human Growth* (Eveleth and Tanner 1976:144).

The Yanomami may be a special case.[9] Neel, Layrisse, and Salzano (1977:116) propose "the hypothesis that the ancestors of the Yanomama — probably a relatively small group — found their way into the Parima Mountain Range several thousand years ago and have remained in virtual isolation ever since. If this hypothesis . . . is correct, then the Yanomama are most unusual among human populations." In reply to the suggestion that the Yanomama were small due to long-term environmental (nutritional) stress, to which they had adapted through reduced body size (Holmes 1985), Neel (personal communication) answered that he felt that their stature owed more to the characteristics of the original group of migrants to Parima, who were probably a splinter group of small-stature individuals, than to malnutrition.

Table 6.2 Mean Weights and Heights for Native South Americans

	Height (cm)		Weight (kg)	
	Men	Women	Men	Women
Caracas elite[a]	172.9	161.1	61.4	52.8
Xikrin[b]	168.7	155.9	63.6	56.0
Mekranoti[b]	166.4	153.1	66.6	56.4
Yaruro[c]	165.6	—	58.8	—
Warao: Jobure[d]	160.7	—	57.5	—
Sacopana	154.6	—	50.8	—
Winikina	156.6	—	57.0	—
Pemón: Camaracoto[e]	160.0	146.9	—	—
Jaurepan	156.0	146.0	—	—
Guajiro[c]	159.2	—	60.5	—
Curripaco[f]	157.3	144.4	59.2	50.2
Kariña[g]	156.6	146.7	56.5	—
Yecuana[e]	156.0	146.0	62.0	53.0
Tucano[h]	156.0	146.0	—	—
Mundurucu[i]	155.6	145.4	—	—
Guahibo[c]	155.4	—	54.1	—
Bari[c]	154.5	—	—	—
Apalai-Waiana[i]	154.2	142.8	—	—
Auca[j]	154.0	144.0	—	—
Yanomami: Coyoweteri	152.3	139.6	44.3	38.2
Parima	146.9	136.9	43.7	37.9
Motilón[c]	146.2	138.1	—	—

[a] Méndez Castellano et al. 1981.
[b] Black et al. 1977:144.
[c] Comas 1971:366, 367, 375.
[d] Gardner, Egstrom, and Wilbert 1968:22.
[e] Layrisse and Wilbert 1966.
[f] Holmes 1981:81.
[g] Kohn de Brief and Méndez de Pérez 1972:17.
[h] Dufour, personal communication, 1983.
[i] Black, personal communication, 1988.
[j] Broennimann 1981:11.

There is little doubt that the Yanomami, and probably other Amazonian indigenes, have a genetically determined small stature. South and Central American Indians are shorter and lighter than North American Indians and "differ considerably in physique and craniofacial structure. These differences probably relate to the early migration and settlement patterns of man in the new world" (Eveleth and Tanner 1976:127). Martorell, Mendoza, and Castillo (1990) found Mexican American adolescents to be shorter than non-Hispanic whites, even when the poverty variable was controlled for.

Arm Circumference /   In general, Asiatic boys and girls have smaller arm circumferences than either European or African individuals of the same social status (Eveleth and Tanner 1976:152). Although information on this variable is not abundant, Amazonian studies by Berlin and Markell (1977) and Holmes (1981), for Peru and Venezuela, respectively, indicate that arm circumferences in children from birth to five years are within normal ranges of the WHO reference population (Jelliffe 1966) in three out of four individuals. However, the older children and adults fare less well, and in the case of the Aguaruna Jívaro adults, only one in five individuals falls in the normal range.

Skinfolds /   The thickness of the skinfolds, a reflection of the amount of subcutaneous fat deposited over the triceps muscle or the shoulder blade, has been found to be inferior to international standards in Guatemalan Ladinos, Quechuas, and other Amerindians (Eveleth and Tanner 1976:153), although the subscapular skinfolds are higher than those of the triceps. Johnson (1984) confirms this finding for both privileged and disadvantaged youths living in Guatemala City. López Contreras-Blanco et al. (1986:177–78) found consistently lower skinfold measurements among Caracas mestizos, even among children of high socioeconomic class, than among a British reference population, and this in spite of the fact that these same individuals attained heights and weights equal to or superior to the British children. I have found lower than normal skinfolds for all Amazonian indigenous groups (Curripaco, Piapoco, Piaroa) measured in Venezuela (unpublished work).

Weight for Height /   This measure reflects body proportions in terms of both thinness-fatness and the trunk or leg length compared to stature. Amerindians in general have higher weight for height ratios than do Europeans (Eveleth and Tanner 1976:143). This was also found to be the case for Mexican Americans (Martorell, Mendoza, and Castillo 1990). Frisch and Revelle (1967:7), working with large data bases in making a comparison of Asian and Latin American populations, found that "men and women in the Asian countries do not differ significantly in mean height from the Latin American, but they weigh significantly less, even though both groups of people apparently consume about the same mean quantity of calories." They suggest that this difference may have a genetic origin. The Cormic index (sitting height/stature) for Venezuelan indigenes in the upper Río Negro (Holmes 1981:105) is much higher (0.550 for men, 0.554 for women) than that for a North American population (0.525 men, 0.526 women). Sitting heights were not obtained, however, for the Yanomami population of the present study.

Growth Velocity /   The rate of growth and maturation of different racial groups is determined in part by genetics. Individuals of Asian origin mature more rapidly than do those of either European or African origin. However, the pace of growth varies depending on age (Eveleth and Tanner 1976). Early maturation was reported by López Contreras-Blanco et al. (1986:183) for Caracas private school children. In this study, girls matured fifteen months and boys four months earlier than individuals from the English standards.

Infant Height and Weight /   Davies (1988:figs. 3, 4, 5) found a definite downward shift in length among Asiatic children who were brought up in favorable socioeconomic conditions. When compared with the non-Asiatic reference population, the magnitude of this shift, taking place between the ages of six months and two years, was approximately two standard deviations. Davies (1988:83) concludes that "this downward shift after birth in Asiatic babies makes a sizable contribution to the eventual smaller adult size of Asiatic peoples." A similar shift in height progression among Yanomami babies in this age range may take place. At present, sufficient data on birth weights are lacking for this determination.

Genetic control of infant length was shown by Smith et al. (1976) in a classic study of shifting linear growth. They found that full-term, environmentally privileged babies shifted their growth upward or downward depending on the mean stature of their parents. Lagging or downward growth was exhibited in mid-infancy (mean age 13 months) by babies whose parents were short. "Given an adequate environment, the postnatal linear growth rate becomes ever more related to the infant's genetic background, as indicated by mean stature of his parents. The genetic influences on growth tend to be self-stabilizing and target seeking, and to become channelized" (Smith et al. 1976:229). Infant length in our cross section of Yanomami babies shows falling off of height growth between one and two years (fig. 6.5).

In summary, there is considerable indirect support in the literature for the hypothesis that genetic factors play a part in the anthropometric profile of the Yanomami and other native Amazonians, producing the following characteristics: small size (short stature), small arm circumference, low skinfolds (especially triceps), normal or high weight for height (especially adults), normal growth velocity and maturation, and a falling off of infant growth during the period from 12 to 24 months old.

Environmental Influences and Adaptation

Height and Weight / The evidence for genetic influence on human stature notwithstanding, environment probably accounts for the greater share of the variation among populations (Habicht et al. 1974; Martorell and Habicht 1986:244, fig. 2). The finding of a worldwide positive secular trend in heights as health and nutritional conditions have improved cannot be ignored. Many investigators have shown the close correlation of socioeconomic level with growth (Waterlow 1988).

It is not hard to find reasons for placing the Yanomami environment in the underprivileged category. Food supply is not always constant. Hunting and gardening tasks are accomplished with a relatively low level of technology and under the threat of attack from neighboring Yanomami. The introduction of exogenous diseases, the endemicity of infectious and parasitic diseases (malaria, onchocerciasis, and intestinal parasitism), and poor sanitation are potentially important environmental factors adversely affecting health and growth. These problems affect all Yanomami to a greater or lesser degree, and many other Amazonian indigenes as well, whether they live in isolated and traditional communities or are in close contact with missionaries, miners, and other outsiders.

Nevertheless, far from dying out in the face of numerous adversities, historically the Yanomami population has often increased to the point of challenging the carrying capacity of the environment, necessitating the evolution of cultural controls on population growth such as village fissioning, warfare, and child spacing through postpartum sex taboos and infanticide (Neel, Layrisse, and Salzano 1977; Neel et al. 1972). Neel et al. (1972:100) note that in the last 100 years "the Yanomama have been numerically as well as geographically an expanding population."[10]

Good nutritional status has been found among several groups of South American indigenes of short stature (Black 1977; Broennimann 1981; Holmes 1981). Barker (1954:441), a missionary and one of the first outsiders to live with the Venezuelan Yanomami, found them to be "well-fed, but generally not muscular or fat." Two anthropologists (Jacques Kenneth Good) and a medical doctor–anthropologist (Jean Chiapp. would not classify the Yanomami groups with whom they have lived for many years as malnourished, although they admit that certain individuals, especially young children, have been undernourished at some point in their lives as the result of illness (personal communications). In a review of the nutritional status of Amazonian Indians, Dufour (personal communication) found that most groups were reported to be nutritionally healthy upon first contact, but of small stature, especially those from northern Amazonia. Stature was greater in some populations south of the Amazon, particularly those from the Alto Xingu and the Xavante area.[11]

Small body size has been hypothesized to be adaptive in populations with low food availability in southern Peru (Frisancho et al. 1973),[12] as well as in India (Stini 1972a:6), where smaller infants actually have a higher survival rate than larger ones. Small infant size in these studies was positively correlated with small parent stature. Stini has suggested that reduced body size results in less pressure on food resources due to the decreased nutritional needs of small bodies. Thus, more individuals can exist with a "given" food supply; and more individuals mean greater genetic variability in the population, which is advantageous for survival. Goldstein and Tanner (1980) have acknowledged that "in a poor environment, a child who is small may have an advantage over faster-growing children in terms of morbidity and mortality *in that poor environment.*"

High protein intake is known to stimulate growth factors (Waterlow 1988). Could the limited availability of animal protein in the Yanomami (and Sanemá) rain forest (Sponsel 1981, 1986) have brought about reduced body size as an adaptive response?

Muscle Circumference / Reductions in lean body mass, as represented by the low Yanomami muscle circumferences, imply a lower metabolic demand, which also would be an advantage with limited food resources. Although low muscle circumference is not necessarily associated with malnutrition in the individual, the degree of sexual dimorphism for this characteristic is. Stini (1972b) suggests that decreased sexual dimorphism is associated with a protein-deficient diet. Even though the Yanomami males and females have much lower muscle circumferences than the U.S. population studied, and appear to have less sexual dimorphism at all ages for this trait, if the figures are corrected for the smaller total circumference of the muscles, there is virtually no difference between the relative male-female muscle circumferences of the Yanomami and the well-fed U.S. individuals. In both cases the mean adult male circumference is 117 percent of the adult female mean, indicating that the Yanomami do not have decreased sexual dimorphism relative to the U.S. subjects. Although Yanomami population and body size may be limited by protein scarcity, this does not necessarily indicate a protein deficient diet.

Weight for Height /   In general, Yanomami adults and older children do not show signs of thinness (or wasting). They are well proportioned, and many are even stockier than the norms in weight for height. This is most likely an adaptation to mild and chronic malnutrition, where the body responds by reducing linear growth. Several investigators have found this pattern in Latin America (Martorell and Habicht 1986:246). Stini (1972b:5) has called this phenomenon "normal dwarfism." More recently, Seckler (1982a) has termed this type of adaptation "small but healthy."

Although prepubertal children of both sexes are thinner on the average than the reference populations, the mean postpubertal weight-for-height measures, again for both sexes, show these teenagers to be stockier than the references. The degree of thinness of many young children may indicate that this segment of the population is undernourished. The teenage survivors of this rigorous childhood, however, do not appear to be undernourished, especially in view of the fact that their stocky or heavy proportions are maintained in spite of low fat stores (Holmes 1985). There may be a selective process at work, either culturally or biologically, that produces healthy, well-nourished young adults entering the reproductive period.

Growth Velocity /   Growth is one of the surest indicators of individual and community health and nutritional status (Eveleth 1981). Most Yanomami children of Parima between the ages of two and eighteen have growth velocities within the normal range (figs. 6.3–6.6). The adolescent growth spurt is delayed in some individuals, which may be associated with a less than adequate nutritional status. Since adolescents are clearly the best off of the Yanomami children, however, genetic determinants of the timing and intensity of this delayed growth spurt cannot be ruled out. Dietz et al. (1989:510) have suggested that "consistently low weights and heights without an associated decline in growth velocity would support the hypothesis of genetic short stature." This could well apply to the Yanomami.

Infant Height and Weight /   International infant growth standards are based on measurements from bottle-fed babies who are larger in later infancy than are babies who consume exclusively mother's milk. Bottle-fed babies on a skim milk, rather than whole milk, diet (high protein, low energy) grow well in height but not in weight in the same proportion (Waterlow 1988). Because they are breast fed, Yanomami infants, small at birth, may continue to be small and to fall off from the standard trajectory in weight faster than in height, due to the type and composition of the milk they consume.

Yanomami babies under nine months old are very short compared to international standards, but their weights are relatively higher, leading to a chubby look. Thus there is evidence that they are not environmentally stunted at this stage in their development. This fat storage may be a natural mechanism preparing them for later infancy, when they will be subjected to weaning stress. A similar pattern was found among Thai infants (Dorothy Jackson, personal communication, 1989).

Although Yanomami infants show some indications of adaptation to a difficult environment, it is at the crucial period of six months to two years that these indigenes suffer high losses through infant mortality. There may be a selective process at this stage that allows only the most immunologically competent individuals to survive. Malnutrition, documented by the failure to gain weight in the 12- to 24-month-old age cohort, is probably the most important underlying cause of this high infant mortality. A similar pattern is observed in other populations (Martorell 1989:170). One would expect Yanomami growth to favor chubby babies in the first months of life, in preparation for weaning stress, and then to favor small body size to compensate for environmental food scarcity.

In summary, small body size among the Yanomami and other Amazonian indigenes cannot in itself be considered pathological. Indeed, there is evidence that being small in Amazonia is adaptive due to the many stresses that humans face in the tropical forest, among them low availability of protein and endemic infectious diseases.

Small Is Adaptive

Height, weight, and growth velocities are measurements of the adaptation of the human body to a combination of interacting genetic and environmental influences. I suspect that because of genetic factors (selection in favor of smaller individuals with lower food requirements), the range of heights of the Yanomami and probably other Amazonians is lower than that of the WHO reference populations, so that their mean height, even under optimal conditions of food intake and freedom from disease, would still not be on a par with international standards. Nevertheless, it is likely that the Yanomami are in the lower range of their possible heights.

It has been proposed that most of the populations that are now classi-fied as malnourished because their measurements do not meet interna-tional standards are actually "small but healthy," having adjusted to low food availability by reducing body size (Seckler 1982a, 1982b). According to Seckler, this is a nonpathological adaptive response that adjusts food demand to food supply. He refers to this group as "World 2": "people who are not properly nourished, but who are also not functionally impaired" (Seckler 1982b:146). (World 1 includes the well-fed, and World 3, the pathologically malnourished.) I would place the Yanomami in World 2, but rather than call them "small but healthy," I prefer "small and adaptive."

In opposition to Seckler, Martorell (1989) argues that the marginally undernourished cannot be classified as healthy because (1) small body size is the consequence of unhealthy conditions, poor diet, and infection, and (2) growth retardation is a warning signal of future health problems. He states that "to acclaim small body sizes as a desirable attribute for popula-tions is also to affirm that its causes are desirable" (Martorell 1989:15).

The "small but healthy" debate cannot help but spill over into the policy arena. A review of the many facets of this problem is presented by Messer (1986) in relation to recommended daily allowance food stan-dards, and not to anthropometric standards. Smallness as an adaptation to nutritional stress is seen throughout the Third and Fourth (indigenous) worlds. It is generally found to be the result of retarded child growth associated with poor nutrition and infection (Martorell 1989; Waterlow 1988). Indeed, so strong is the association that height and growth are used as measures of the well-being of a population. Even within devel-oped countries, small body size is linked to low socioeconomic status, and risk of disease is correlated with height. Barker (1990:1) found that in England, "counties with taller populations have lower mortality from chronic bronchitis, rheumatic heart disease, ischaemic heart disease and stroke." These diseases of adulthood have their roots in childhood, so, on average, the better nourished the child, the taller and healthier he or she will be and the less likely to develop certain diseases later in life.

A few examples can be found of small infants having lower mortality than larger ones (Ashcroft 1971), or of marginally malnourished children having the same mortality (not morbidity) risk as normal ones (Chen, Chowdhury, and Huffman 1982). Kielmann et al. (1976) report "normal or quasi-normal muscular development and immune response" in non-hospitalized, stunted rural children in India. In part, these contradictory findings may be due to population comparisons between racial groups (Ashcroft 1971) or within populations where infection rates are high in all children, whether they are malnourished or not. However, the ability of the human body to adapt to adverse conditions and survive at an acceptable level of health is often disregarded by nutritionists who are looking for the optimum environment.

Recently, experts in the field of epidemiology and auxology have questioned the "bigger is better" hypothesis. Barker (1990:1), who found a strong positive correlation between height and some diseases of the lungs and circulatory system, also found that English counties with taller people had "higher mortality from three hormone-related cancers, of the breast, prostate and ovary . . . [which] could suggest that promotion of child growth has disadvantages as well as benefits." Certainly the diets that have allowed many populations in the developed world to reach the upper limits of their growth potential may not be the healthiest in the long run. As Goldstein and Tanner state (1980:583), "growth is indeed a fine yardstick of the health of individuals and populations, perhaps the best there is. But it remains so only for as long as we view our standards as a sensitive balance to be adjusted if conditions change, and not an immutable ceiling to which we should all eat our way." The best criterion for nutritional evaluation, then, should be greater health, rather than greater size. Goldstein and Tanner (1980:583) suggest that "a better definition of optimal would be the level of nutrition and medical care which is associated with the greatest amount of health . . . based on the lowest mortality and morbidity rates."

How, then, does my study population fit into this picture of nutritional evaluation? My proposal of separate growth standards for the Yanomami, adjusted to their special genetic and environmental limitations, met with strong objections from Martorell: "Unless you can show that diet and infection are not problems, your call for 'standards' is unjustified" (personal communication, September 1989). This, of course, is an impossible task. Even if the Yanomami diet could be shown to be adequate (I know of no long-term, quantitative dietary studies of the Yanomami), there are no groups in Venezuela who are free from infection. Disease is, no doubt, an important constraint on Yanomami growth, and probably always has been. The Yanomami of this study have an infant mortality rate 10 times as high as that of the Venezuelan population (200 vs. 20 per 1,000 live births), and onchocerciasis affects at least 90 percent of Venezuelan Yanomami (CAICET records). Recently, malaria has caused numerous deaths in the upper Orinoco River basin (the malaria mosquito does not live in the Parima mountains).

Despite these severe health problems, the demographic results reported by Schkolnik (1983), whose fieldwork coincided with mine, indicate that the Yanomami of Parima had a high crude birth rate, 55.2. Neel reports a similar figure, 57.3, for the Yanomami studied between 1966 and 1970. These figures are higher than those for the Hutterites, 45.9, known for their high fertility (see Schkolnik 1983:124 for a comparison with other groups). The gross reproduction rate (number of daughters reaching reproductive age) for the Parima Yanomami (3.78) was virtually as high as that for the Yanomami in Neel's study (4.0), and for the Hutterites (4.0). The Yanomami of my study are a population of high reproductive capacity and high infant mortality. They are also a population of high morbidity, suffering from respiratory, intestinal, eye, and skin infections (CAICET and author's records).

Is smallness, then, a symptom of adversity portending grave future health problems for the Yanomami and other Amazonians, as Martorell would argue, or is it a strategy, evolved by nature, to favor the continued survival of these populations in rather hostile environments? At the very least we can conclude that nutritional assessments that do not make allowance for the characteristic smallness of the Yanomami and other Amazonians will tend to exaggerate existing problems or create problems where none really existed.

Those considering how best to help Amazonian indigenes face difficult choices. Greater availability of modern medicine and health care (without birth control programs) will surely result in more rapid population growth, which cannot be dealt with through traditional subsistence strategies. However, to withhold medical help in response to periodic epidemics caused by the introduction of exogenous pathogens against which the native population has little defense would be unconscionable.[13] Nutritional supplementation programs may do more harm than good, as they may encourage dependence on imported foods, discourage breast feeding, and, if given to women of reproductive age, accelerate population growth. The choice, unfortunately, is between the lesser of two evils: preservation of the status quo, with all its seemingly repugnant features, which will favor Yanomami independence and cultural integrity, or serious intervention, which may pay off in the short run in terms of improved health status but which will surely hasten cultural extinction. The academic debate about the advantages and disadvantages of smallness should not be allowed to obscure this more fundamental issue of cultural survival.

Acknowledgments

Fieldwork for this investigation was carried out with the support of the medical team from the Amazon Center for the Investigation and Control of Tropical Diseases (CAICET) in Venezuela, under the direction of Luis Yarzábal. Fruitful discussions on the origins of Yanomami smallness were held with James Neel, Frank Black, Mercedes de Blanco, Zulay Layrisse, Daniel Gross, and Steve Beckerman. I am grateful to Kathleen Clark and William Dietz for editing the text in its early stages, and to comments from J. M. Tanner, John Waterlow, William Dietz, Reynaldo Martorell, David Holmes, and Gustavo Eskildsen on later versions.

Notes

1. Parima A includes Jolajolamobateri, Jocoobateri, and Cobaliwateri; Parima B includes Wainamateri, Pabloteri, Ishawareteri, Ijilubateri, and Niyayobateri. Data presented here were collected during three visits (March 1982, October 1982, and March 1983) to Parima and Coyoweteri by the author, and during a preliminary visit in May 1981 by Venezuelan doctors from the Amazon Center for Investigation and Control of Tropical Diseases (CAICET).

2. Medical identification cards with photographs were made for each person. These were used by the CAICET team in its onchocerciasis (river blindness) research and treatment program as well as for the anthropometric study. The cards helped to identify individuals on return field trips and served as a convenient medical history for recording and comparing data. Resident missionaries provided invaluable help in identifying individuals and acting as translators. Accurate ages for children from birth to 15 years old were obtained from birth records kept by the resident missionary, Diana Shaylor, and her predecessors. Details on anthropometric measurement methods and calculation of growth velocities and predicted heights may be obtained from the author.

3. Some data from this study have been published previously in Spanish (Holmes 1983) and English (Holmes 1985).

4. Many boys, but few girls, returned to our field clinic to be weighed and measured. More weight than height data are analyzed, because heights recorded on the first field trip by the CAICET doctors had to be discarded due to the inaccuracy of the method used.

5. Notable weight gains for three girls between the ages of 16 and 18 may again be a reflection of late maturation, although a pregnancy in its early stages cannot be ruled out.

6. Since there is little variation between the sexes at these ages, the data from the reference population (Méndez Castellano et al. 1981) has been elaborated into a combined male-female growth chart.

7. The calculation of predicted heights based on actual heights was obtained for 124 individuals (63 boys, 61 girls) following Tanner (1978:202).

8. Adult males are taller than females; heights for monozygotic twins are more closely correlated than for dizygotic twins; a child's height tends toward the mean height of the parents; persons with genetic abnormalities such as achondroplastic dwarfism or Down's or Turner syndrome are shorter than unaffected persons.

9. James V. Neel and others who have conducted numerous biodemographic and genetic studies of the Yanomami describe their long relative physical isolation from neighboring tribes, inbreeding, unique language, and unusual dental morphology, among the many characteristics that set them apart from other Amerindians. They possess a uniform blood group, O, Kell (–), and Gm(ag) or (axg), which strongly suggests a complete lack of admixture with Caucasoids or Negroids.

10. The 1990 Venezuelan Indian census should reveal whether the population is stabilizing or decreasing due to recent malaria mortality.

11. See Stewart (1973:123) for an anthropometric chart of early contact data from the Xingu and other southern South American Indian groups.

12. Specifically related to conditions of hypoxia (Frisancho, personal communication).

13. Certainly intervention is justified and required in cases of new environmental threats (epidemics of malaria, tuberculosis, measles, and onchocerciasis, or deforestation and occupation of native lands for mining and agriculture) to which Amazonians have not adapted.

References Cited

Ashcroft, M. T.
1971   Some Aspects of Growth and Development in Different Ethnic Groups in the Commonwealth West Indies. In *The Ongoing Evolution of Latin American Populations*, edited by Francisco M. Salzano, pp. 281–309. Springfield, Ill.: Charles C. Thomas.

Barker, D.
1990   Height and Mortality in the Counties of England and Wales. *Annals of Human Biology* 17(1):1–6.

Barker, J.
1954   Memoria sobre la cultura de los Guaika. *Boletín Indigenista Venezolano* 1:433–89.

Berlin, E. A., and E. K. Markell
1977   An Assessment of the Nutritional and Health Status of an Aguaruna Jívaro Community, Amazonas, Peru. *Ecology of Food and Nutrition* 6:69–81.

Black, F. L., W. J. Hierhoizer, D. P. Black, S. H. Lamm, and L. Lucas
1977   Nutritional Status of Brazilian Kayapó Indians. *Human Biology* 49(2): 139–53.

Broennimann, P.
1981   *Auca on the Cononaco: Indians of the Ecuadorian Rainforest*. Basel: Birkhauser.

Comas, J.
1971   Anthropometric Studies in Latin American Indian Populations. In *The*

Ongoing Evolution of Latin American Population, edited by F. M. Salzano. Springfield, Ill.: Thomas.

Chen, L. C., A. K. Chowdhury, and S. L. Huffman
1982   Anthropometric Assessment of Energy-Protein Malnutrition and Subsequent Risk of Mortality Among Preschool Aged Children. In *Newer Concepts in Nutrition and Their Implications for Policy*. Pune, India: Maharashtra Association for the Cultivation of Science Research Institute.

Davies, D. P.
1988   The Importance of Genetic Influences on Growth in Early Childhood with Particular Reference to Children of Asiatic Origin. In *Linear Growth Retardation in Less Developed Countries*, edited by J. C. Waterlow. New York: Raven Press.

Deitz, W. H., B. Marino, N. R. Peacock, and R. C. Bailey
1989   Nutritional Status of Efe Pygmies and Lese Horticulturists. *American Journal of Physical Anthropology* 78:509–18.

Eveleth, P. B.
1981   Growth and Development of the Infant and Young Child. In *Maternal and Child Health Around the World*, edited by H. M. Wallace and G. J. Ebrahim. London: Macmillan.

Eveleth, P. B., and J. M. Tanner
1976   *Worldwide Variation in Human Growth*. Cambridge: Cambridge University Press.

Frisancho, A. R., J. Sánchez, D. Pallardel, and L. Yánez
1973   Adaptive Significance of Small Body Size Under Poor Socio-economic Conditions in Southern Peru. *American Journal of Physical Anthropology* 39:255–62.

Frish, R., and R. Revelle
1967   *Variations in Body Weights Among Different Populations*. Cambridge, Mass.: Center for Population Studies, Harvard University.

Gardner, G. W., G. H. Egstrom, and J. Wilbert
1968   Physical Working Capacity of the Warao Indians of Venezuela. *Antropológica* 23:19–34.

Goldstein, H., and J. M. Tanner
1980   Ecological Considerations in the Creation and Use of Child Growth Standards. *Lancet*, March 15, pp. 582–85.

Habicht, J-P., R. Martorell, C. Yarbrough, R. M. Malilna, and R. E. Klein
1974   Height and Weight Standards for Preschool Children. How Relevant Are Ethnic Differences in Growth Potential? *Lancet*, April 6, pp. 611–14.

Holmes, R.
1981   Estado nutricional en cuatro aldeas de la selva amazonica, Venezuela: Un estudio de adaptación y aculturación. Master's thesis, Instituto Venezolano de Investigaciones Cientificas, Caracas.

1983   Estado nutricional en la población Yanomami de la sierra Parima, Venezuela. In *Filariasis humanas en el territorio federal Amazonas (Venezuela)*, edited by L. Yarzábal, R. Holmes, M. G. Basáñez, I. Petralanda, C. Botto, M. Arango, and S. Schkolnik. Caracas: Proicet Amazonas.

1985   Nutritional Status and Cultural Change in Venezuela's Amazon Territory. In *The Frontier After a Decade of Colonisation*, edited by J. Hemming. Manchester: Manchester University Press.

Jelliffe, D. B.
1966   The Assessment of the Nutritional Status of the Community. Geneva: World Health Organization.

Jelliffe, D. B., and E. F. P. Jelliffe
1979   Growth and Nutrition (editorial). *Tropical Pediatrics and Environmental Health* 25(6):149–50.

Johnson, F. E.
1984   A Comparison of International Standards versus Local Reference Data for the Triceps and Subscapular Skinfolds of Guatemalan Children and Youth. *Human Biology* 56(1):57–171.

Kielmann, A. A., I. S. Uberoi, R. K. Chandra, and V. L. Mehra
1976   The Effect of Nutritional Status on Immune Capacity and Immune Responses in Preschool Children in a Rural Community in India. *Bulletin of the World Health Organization* 54:477–83.

Kohn de Brief, F., and B. Méndez de Pérez
1972   *Antropometría de los indios Cariña.* Caracas: Universidad Central de Venezuela.

Layrisse, M., and J. Wilbert
1966   *Indian Societies of Venezuela: Their Blood Group Types.* Caracas: Fundación La Salle de Ciencias Naturales.

López Contreras-Blanco, M., M. Landaeta-Jiménez, I. Espinoza, C. Tomei, and H. Méndez Castellano
1986   Estudios de crecimiento y desarrollo en Venezuela: Comparación con las normas de referencia británicas. *Archivos Venezolanos de Puericultura y Pediatría* 49(3, 4):172–85.

Martorell, R.
1989   Body Size, Adaptation and Function. *Human Organization* 48(1): 15–20.

Martorell, R., and J-P. Habicht
1986   Growth in Early Childhood in Developing Countries. In *Human Growth: A Comprehensive Treatise*, vol. 3, edited by F. Falkner and J. M. Tanner. New York: Plenum Press.

Martorell, R., F. Mendoza, and R. Castillo
1988   Poverty and Stature in Children. In *Linear Growth Retardation in Less Developed Countries*, edited by J. C. Waterlow. New York: Raven Press.

1990 Genetic and Environmental Determinants of Growth in Mexican-Americans. *Pediatrics.*

Méndez Castellano, H., M. López Contreras, A. de Tineo, and I. de Limongi
1981 *Estudio transversal—area metropolitana de Caracas 1981: Patrones de referencia.* Caracas: Fundacredesa.

Messer, E.
1986 The "Small but Healthy" Hypothesis: Historical, Political, and Ecological Influences on Nutritional Standards. *Human Ecology* 14(1):57–75.

Neel, J., T. Arends, C. Brewer, N. Chagnon, H. Gershowitz, M. Layrisse, Z. Layrisse, J. MacCluer, E. Migliazza, W. Oliver, F. Salzano, R. Spielman, R. Ward, and L. Weitkamp
1972 Studies on the Yanomama Indians. *Human Genetics.* Proceedings of the Fourth International Congress of Human Genetics, Paris. Amsterdam: *Excerpta Medica.*

Neel, J., M. Layrisse, and F. Salzano
1977 Man in the Tropics: The Yanomama Indians. In *Population Structure and Human Variation*, vol.2, edited by J. A. Harrison. Cambridge: Cambridge University Press.

Seckler, D.
1982a "Small but Healthy": A Basic Hypothesis in the Theory, Measurement and Policy of Malnutrition. In *Newer Concepts in Nutrition and Their Implications for Policy.* Pune, India: Maharashtra Association for the Cultivation of Science Research Institute.
1982b "Malnutrition": An Intellectual Odyssey. In *Newer Concepts in Nutrition and Their Implications for Policy.* Pune, India: Maharashtra Association for the Cultivation of Science Research Institute.

Schkolnik, S.
1983 Aspectos demográficos de la población Yanomami de sierra Parima, territorio federal Amazonas, Venezuela. In *Filariasis humanas en el territorio federal Amazonas, Venezuela*, edited by L. Yarzábal, R. Holmes, M. G. Basáñez, I. Petralanda, C. Botto, M. Arango, and S. Schkolnik. Caracas: Proicet Amazonas.

Smith, D. W., W. Truog, J. E. Rogers, L. J. Greitzer, A. L. Skinner, J. J. McCann, and M. A. Harvey
1976 Shifting Linear Growth During Infancy: Illustration of Genetic Factors in Growth from Fetal Life Through Infancy. *Journal of Pediatrics* 89:225–30.

Sponsel, L. E.
1981 The Hunter and the Hunted in the Amazon: An Integrated Biological and Cultural Approach to the Behavioral Ecology of Human Predation. Ph.D. dissertation, Cornell University.
1986 Amazon Ecology and Adaptation. *Annual Review of Anthropology* 15:67–97.

Stewart, T. D.
1973   *The People of America*. London: Weidenfeld and Nicolson.

Stini, W. A.
1972a   Malnutrition, Body Size, and Proportion. *Ecology of Food and Nutrition* 1:1–6.
1972b   Reduced Sexual Dimorphism in Upper Arm Muscle Circumference Associated with Protein Deficient Diet in a South American Population. *American Journal of Physical Anthropology* 36:341–52.

Tanner, J. M.
1978   *Foetus into Man: Physical Growth from Conception to Maturity*. Cambridge, Mass.: Harvard University Press.

Waterlow, J. C.
1988   Observations on the Natural History of Stunting. In *Linear Growth Retardation in Less Developed Countries*. New York: Raven Press.

7

A Closer Look at the Nutritional Implications of Bitter Cassava Use

Darna L. Dufour

Cassava, or manioc (*Manihot esculenta* Crantz), is the traditional dietary staple of many native Amazonians. Although it is very productive on the *tierra firme* soils of Amazonia, it is one of the few food crops in which the content of cyanide can create problems of toxicity, and therefore its use is a potential source of nutritional stress.

In the last 20 years there has been a tremendous increase in the research on cassava (for reviews, see Cock 1985; Okezie and Kosikowski 1982). This research has been stimulated by the growing importance of cassava in both human and animal diets. Cassava is now the fourth most important source of food energy in the tropics worldwide (Cock 1982), and its use is expected to double before the year 2000 (Okezie and Kosikowski 1982). The potential toxicity of cassava is considered one of the major limiting factors in its use for both culinary purposes and animal feed (Okezie and Kosikowski 1982), and some researchers consider the "bitter," or high-cyanide, cultivars unsuitable for human food (Gomez et al. 1984). Cyanide toxicity associated with cassava consumption has been linked to a number of health problems in Africa (Nestel and MacIntyre 1973; Ermans et al. 1980; Osuntokun 1981; Rosling 1987).

Among indigenous peoples in Amazonia, the high-cyanide, or so-called "bitter," cassava appears to have been the staple crop in the Amazon basin, northeastern South America, and the Antilles (Nordenskiold 1924; Steward and Faron 1959). Low-cyanide, or "sweet," cassava was more widely distributed (Nordenskiold 1924) but tended to be part of a crop complex dominated by either maize or bitter cassava (Renvoize 1972). The exception to this is on the eastern slopes of the Andes where sweet cassava was the staple crop (Steward 1959). The elaborate processing systems associated with "bitter" varieties have long attracted the attention of anthropologists and other observers, but their actual effectiveness in reducing toxicity has received little attention. Other important questions regarding the toxicity of the cultivars used, the distribution of bitter and sweet cultivars, and the roles of bitter and sweet cassava in the adaptation of native peoples have gone unanswered.

The purpose of this chapter is to report the results of recent research on the use of bitter cassava by Tukanoan Indians in northwest Amazonia, and in doing so to focus attention on the use of cassava by native Amazonians. In addition I would like to reconsider some of the commonly cited disadvantages of cassava use. These disadvantages are, first, that it is a crop with low nutrient density and hence is a relatively poor source of dietary protein and minerals. Second, the "bitter" varieties of cassava require extensive processing, which further reduces protein and mineral content. The third disadvantage, proposed by Spath (1981), is that the residual toxicity, i.e., cyanide, in a cassava-based diet increases the need for the amino acids methionine and cystine, which are generally more abundant in animal than in plant proteins. This last disadvantage is part of the broader question of the toxicity of cassava.

The fieldwork reported here was done in 1984–86 with Tukanoan Indians in the Colombian Vaupés, primarily in the village of Yapu on the Papuri River.[1] The characteristics of this group have been discussed previously (Dufour 1983). Ecologically the Vaupés is an area of low elevation covered with dense tropical rain forest broken with patches of *caatinga* (a type of low forest occurring on white sand) and drained by black-water rivers. In climatic terms the area is humid to very humid. Precipitation averages 3,500 mm a year, and temperatures average 26°C. During the long "dry" season from about November to February, precipitation averages between 150 and 200 mm per month (PRORADAM 1979:13).

Yapu is a village settlement of Tatuyo-speaking Tukanoan Indians. Like other traditional Tukanoans, those at Yapu are swidden horticulturalists whose principal crop is cassava. Secondary crops include plants such as taro (*Colocasia* spp.), sweet potato (*Ipomoea* sp.), arrowroot (*Maranta ruiziana*), bananas, plantains, and a number of fruits. Animal foods are obtained from fishing, hunting, and gathering (Dufour 1983).

Cassava

Cassava is a perennial woody shrub belonging to the family Euphorbiaceae. It is native to the Neotropics and well adapted to the low fertility, highly acid soils that are common in Amazonia (Rogers 1965; Moran 1973; Cock 1985; Howeler 1985). It is tolerant of drought as well as high rainfall, so long as drainage is good (Cock 1985:18). It is grown primarily for its starchy storage roots, but the leaves are also used as food.

The plant and the edible roots are referred to as both cassava and manioc. Cassava is now the more widely used term in English, and it is the one I will use here. It is probably derived from *casabe*, *cazabe*, or *kasabi*, the Taino (Arawak) word for cassava bread (Carrizales 1984; Jones 1959:29). Manioc is from the Tupí-Guaraní *mandioca* (Sauer 1950), and is also the word for the plant in French.[2]

The toxicity of cassava results from the presence of cyanogenic glucosides that break down into glucose and hydrogen cyanide (prussic acid) upon hydrolysis. Hydrolysis results from contact between the glucosides and the endogenous enzyme linamarase; it occurs when plant tissues lose their physiological integrity or are damaged by processes such as harvesting, peeling, or grating. All cassava cultivars contain cyanogenic glucosides, but the concentrations vary greatly between cultivars and with season, climate, and edaphic conditions (Coursey 1973; Bourdoux et al. 1980). The distinction between sweet and bitter cassava is common throughout Amazonia, and indeed throughout the world. In general it refers to roots that can simply be peeled, boiled, and eaten, as opposed to those that are considered bitter or toxic and require additional processing before being consumed. In a more precise way, *sweet* is used to refer to cassava roots with cyanide concentrations of less than 100 ppm, and *bitter* is used for those with concentrations of greater than 100 ppm fresh weight (FW). This is the sense in which the terms are used here.

Cassava in Northwest Amazonia

Tukanoans at Yapu maintain about 100 named cassava cultivars, all but two of which they classify as *kii* and consider "bitter." These are the dietary staples. The remaining two are referred to by the Geral term *makasera* and are considered "sweet." A sample of common kii cultivars from Yapu had cyanide concentrations ranging from 280 to 531 ppm FW, with a mean of 454 ppm FW. Hence, they are properly considered "very bitter," or high-cyanide containing (Dufour 1988a). There is no information on the cyanide content of the cultivars used by other native Amazonians, but in comparison to those of other areas of the world, the average cyanide concentration of the Yapu cultivars is the highest of any reported.

In the northwest Amazon, cassava appears in the diet in a number of forms, the most important of which are *casabe*, a bread, and *fariña*, a

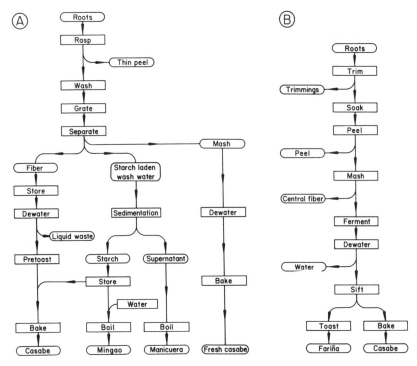

Figure 7.1. Flow diagram of Tukanoan-style cassava processing for (a) casabe and related products and (b) fariña.

toasted meal. Casabe is a uniquely Amazonian use of cassava and traditionally was the most widespread mode of preparation (Schwerin 1971: 12). Among Tukanoans, casabe is a thick, soft bread made fresh daily from white-fleshed roots. It is the preferred accompaniment to fish, game, and insects, and when those are not available, it is eaten after being dipped in a "pepper pot." Fariña is the basis of meals when people are traveling or working away from the village, and it is most commonly consumed as a drink—a small amount swirled in water.

The Tukanoan processing technique for casabe is elaborate and has been described previously (Dufour 1985, 1989; Hugh-Jones 1979). It is shown schematically in figure 7.1. First, the roots are rasped to remove the outermost layer of peel, and then they are washed and grated. Grating reduces the roots to a fine, watery mash, which is then separated into three fractions: liquids, starch, and fiber. The separation is accomplished by washing (with water and extracted juices) and squeezing the mash in a basketry strainer to remove the starch and liquids from the more fibrous portion, and then allowing the starch to settle out of the wash water. Once the starch has settled, the supernatant is decanted off and boiled immediately to make the beverage *manicuera*. The other two products, starch and fiber, are stored at least overnight but preferably for 48 hours, and then are recombined and baked as a casabe. To prepare casabe, the fiber is dewatered in a *tipiti* (basketry sleeve press), lightly toasted, and then mixed with the starch. The starch is also used to thicken beverages (*mingao*) and fish porridges (*puné*).

Casabe can also be prepared by simply dewatering and baking the freshly grated mash. This type of casabe is not very commonly consumed in Yapu and is referred to here as "fresh casabe." It is a denser bread and lacks the fermented taste of ordinary casabe. When baked as a cracker-thin cake it is used as an ingredient in beer. Other types of casabe include those made from plain starch, in either a thick or a thin form, and those made from the raw, fermented mash destined for fariña.

Fariña is prepared from yellow-fleshed roots that are trimmed of the stem end and soaked in stream water until softened (two to four days), then peeled, grated, allowed to ferment for a minimum of three days, dewatered with a tipiti, sifted to produce an even texture, and toasted (see fig. 7.1). The type of fariña prepared by Tukanoans is called *farinha d'agua* in Brazil.

Effectiveness of Processing Techniques

The effectiveness of the processing techniques used to prepare casabe and fariña in detoxifying roots was assessed in a series of experiments conducted at the Centro Internacional de Agricultura Tropical (CIAT) in Cali, Colombia, and is discussed in detail in Dufour (1989). In these experiments we measured the loss of free cyanide, or HCN, and total cyanide, which includes both HCN and cyanogenic glucosides. Cyanide in the form of cyanogenic glucosides is also referred to as bound cyanide, i.e., cyanide bound to glucose.

The changes in total and free cyanide that occurred during processing for casabe are shown in Table 7.1. There was only a modest reduction in total cyanide with rasping and grating. The grated mash, however, showed a dramatic increase in free cyanide, indicating that the grating resulted in the conversion of cyanogenic glucosides to the free form. Since free cyanide is water soluble, most of the remainder was concentrated in the wash water and then volatilized with cooking. The boiled juice, manicuera, contained only 0.8 percent (FW basis) of the initial concentration of total cyanide.

Table 7.1 Changes in Total and Free Cyanide in Cassava Roots Processed for
Casabe. Values are the average of three processing runs with MCOL1684
and three with MVEN25 on a fresh weight basis (FW). Dry matter
values in parentheses.

Day	Process Stage	Moisture %	Cyanide, ppm FW Total	Free	F/T %	Total Cyanide % Initial
Day 1	Whole roots	64	528 (1,441)	76 (211)	14	100.0
	Rasped roots	65	411 (1,158)	72 (227)	18	77.8
	Mash (grated roots)	64	416 (1,136)	289 (789)	69	78.8
	Fiber, fresh	74	103 (396)	54 (215)	52	19.5
	Starch, fresh	49	91 (182)	75 (148)	82	17.2
	Wash water[a]	92	153 (3,229)	130 (3,138)	85	29.0
	Manicuera	82	4 (19)	3 (10)	75	0.8
	Mash, dewatered	50	236 (451)	173 (330)	73	44.7
	Casabe, fresh	29	40 (58)	10 (15)	25	7.6
Day 2	Fiber, sour	73	80 (290)	56 (206)	70	15.1
	Fiber, sour, dewatered	56	68 (153)	44 (96)	65	12.9
	Starch, sour	48	62 (120)	50 (99)	81	11.7
	Casabe, ordinary	26	39 (55)	25 (35)	64	7.4
Day 3	Fiber, sour	72	60 (209)	37 (129)	62	11.4
	Fiber, sour, dewatered	58	40 (96)	28 (68)	70	7.6
	Starch, sour	45	39 (72)	35 (64)	90	7.4
	Casabe, ordinary	25	17 (22)	7 (10)	41	3.2

[a]Dry matter values are for a single processing run.

The cyanide levels in the starch and fiber continued to decline slowly during storage and with cooking. The casabes made with starch and fiber that had been stored for 48 hours contained less than 4 percent of the initial total cyanide. Those made with starch and fiber stored 24 hours contained more than twice as much, as did the fresh casabes.

The effectiveness of the Tukanoan technique in reducing cyanide levels in cassava is due to several factors. First, grating causes extensive disintegration of the plant tissues, and the subsequent mixing ensures maximal contact between the enzyme and the glucosides, a process that maximizes the conversion of bound to free cyanide. Second, the inner peel is grated along with the pulp. This facilitates hydrolysis because enzymatic activity in the peel is higher than in the pulp (Bruijn 1973; Nambisan and Sundaresan 1985). This practice of including the inner peel has been reported only for Tukanoans and Karinya (Karl Schwerin, personal communication). Third, the washing of the mash concentrates most of the free cyanide in the wash water, where it can be effectively volatilized by boiling.

Cyanide losses during the processing of fariña are shown in Table 7.2. The roots showed a gradual decline in total cyanide with trimming and soaking, and when softened (day 6), contained only 21 percent of the initial total cyanide. The loss of cyanide can be attributed to enzyme hydrolysis and volatilization of HCN, as well as to fermentation (Ayernor 1985:94). The roots showed additional small decreases in cyanide content with peeling and mashing, and in the first days of fermentation. The fermented mash on day 10 contained only 2.4 percent of the initial total cyanide. Total and free cyanide content was further reduced by toasting (see values on a dry matter basis).

The values for total and free cyanide obtained in the processing experiment are comparable to those found in fariña samples collected in the

Table 7.2 Changes in Total and Free Cyanide in Cassava Roots Processed for Fariña. Values are for one processing run with MCOL1684 on a fresh weight basis (FW). Dry matter values in parentheses.

Day	Stage	Moisture %	Cyanide, ppm FW		F/T %	Total Cyanide % Initial
			Total	Free		
Day 1	Whole roots	67	328 (972)	42 (124)	13	100.0
Day 2	Soaked roots	67	247 (758)	18 (56)	7	75.3
Day 3	Soaked roots	70	222 (744)	34 (113)	15	67.7
Day 4	Soaked roots	73	175 (642)	63 (232)	36	53.3
Day 5	Soaked roots	73	104 (338)	40 (149)	38	31.7
Day 6	Soaked roots	69	68 (251)	36 (116)	53	20.7
	Peeled-grated	68	35 (109)	18 (55)	51	10.6
Day 7	Fermented mash	66	11 (32)	10 (29)	92	3.4
Day 8	Fermented mash	66	10 (30)	8 (23)	80	3.0
Day 9	Fermented mash	66	8 (22)	7 (20)	75	2.4
Day 10	Fermented mash	66	6 (16)	4 (11)	67	1.8
	Fariña	3	8 (8)	4 (4)	50	2.4

Colombian Vaupés region. These had concentrations of 8.3 ± 2.59 ppm total cyanide and 6.2 ± 0.48 ppm free cyanide on a fresh weight basis (n = 24).

Role of Processing Steps in Detoxification

The results of these processing experiments challenge some of the assumptions held by anthropologists regarding the role of Amazonian processing techniques in detoxification. Three common assumptions are that the peeling, the use of the tipiti, and the application of heat are the important steps in detoxification. A fourth assumption is that processing significantly reduces the nutritional value of cassava (Sponsel 1986).

First, peeling, which was assumed to remove a large portion of the cyanide (Dole 1978) does not really achieve that in the "bitter" varieties, although it certainly does in the "sweet." Rather, when very bitter cultivars are used, leaving the inner peel intact when the roots are grated facilitates hydrolysis.

Second, the tipiti, that famous and unique basketry sleeve press, has been assumed to play a key role in detoxification (Carrizales 1984). However, as Dole (1978) pointed out, the tipiti's principal function is dewatering. It can function in detoxification because both the glucosides and free cyanide are water soluble, but its role depends on when in the processing sequence it is used. In the Tukanoan processing sequence used for casabe, dewatering is done after there has been adequate time for hydrolysis and volatilization of free cyanide; hence it plays a very minimal role in detoxification. The use of the tipiti would be most important when freshly grated roots were used for casabe and when cooking was done shortly after grating. This method of preparing casabe, however, does not appear to be very common. Other groups that make casabe without extracting the starch typically let the mash set overnight before baking it (Lancaster et al. 1982; Seigler and Pereira 1981). This should allow adequate time for both hydrolysis and volatilization of HCN, even if the mash is dewatered before it is stored.

The key tool in detoxification is the one that precedes the tipiti in the processing sequence—the grating board. This instrument macerates the plant material and in doing so allows hydrolysis to proceed rapidly. In the preparation of fariña, the long period of soaking is the most effective part of the process in detoxifying the roots. Again the tipiti is not very important because the total cyanide content has already been reduced more than 98 percent before it is used.

A third assumption is that because heat volatilizes free cyanide, the application of heat results in detoxification (Schwerin 1985). A corollary of this is that simple methods of processing, such as boiling and baking, are adequate for detoxification (Roosevelt 1980:129). But in elaborate processing systems such as that of the Tukanoans, the application of heat is of only minimal importance because most of the glucosides have been converted to free cyanide and released before heat is applied. The application of heat in this type of processing system is probably most important in gelatinizing the starches and producing the desired texture in foods. Further, although the application of heat will volatilize HCN, it usually stops hydrolysis because the enzyme linamarase is deactivated at 72°C. Therefore, if heat is applied before hydrolysis has been completed, the food can retain significant amounts of bound cyanide, which is thermally stable up to 150°C (Nambisan and Sundaresan 1985).

It follows that simple cooking techniques such as boiling and roasting can eliminate free cyanide but will not be as effective in removing cyanogenic glucosides (Cooke and Maduagwu 1978). In boiling, free cyanide is lost to the air through volatilization, but bound cyanide goes into solution and can be found in the cooking water. Thus, cooked dishes, such as stews, in which the cooking water is consumed retain as much as 88 percent of the total cyanide (Bruijn 1971, cited in Cooke and Maduagwu 1978; Cooke and Maduagwu 1978). In areas such as India, where bitter cultivars are boiled, the cooking water is not consumed and is actually changed two or three times during cooking (Nambisan and Sundaresan 1985). This practice of changing the cooking water has not been reported for indigenous groups in Amazonia.

The roasting of whole cassava roots by burying them in hot ashes is done in the northwest Amazon with sweet cultivars and has been reported for a number of groups in Amazonia (Schwerin 1971). Cyanide loss under these kinds of conditions has not been studied, but it is probably similar to that observed during the baking of cassava chips in ovens, which has been shown to be a relatively ineffective method of reducing cyanide levels, again because the enzyme linamarase is inactivated at 72°C and linamarin is heat stable to 150°C (Cooke and Maduagwu 1978). It is doubtful that in normal roasting, as done by indigenous peoples, the root tissues reach 150°C, since they are thoroughly cooked at less than 100°C. Thus the roasting of whole tubers in ashes would probably remove little of the total cyanide.

In summary, the simpler methods of processing such as boiling and roasting are not very effective in reducing cyanide concentration and are only suitable for use with low-cyanide roots. This finding suggests that the exclusive use of these techniques will be confined to populations using low-cyanide cultivars. It does not follow, however, that groups using more complex processing techniques are necessarily using high-cyanide cultivars.

The fourth common assumption is that processing significantly reduces the nutritional value of cassava (Sponsel 1986). This is not a valid generalization; nutritional loss depends on the type of processing done. In some processing systems the loss of minerals in soaking, washing, and dewatering can be as high as 40 to 70 percent, and the loss of soluble proteins as high as 50 percent (Meuser and Smolnik 1980). The processing technique used for casabe, however, is nutritionally conservative. Waste is limited to the outer peel (<2 percent fresh weight), and the consumption of manicuera makes available the minerals and soluble proteins that would otherwise be lost. This advantage can only be gained if processing is done in small batches and the liquids boiled and consumed shortly afterward, because they deteriorate rapidly in both raw and cooked states. Retention of the peel also increases the nutritional value of cassava products because the peel fraction is higher in both minerals and protein than the pulp.

Cyanide Exposure and the Increased Need for Amino Acids

To estimate the exposure to dietary, cassava-born cyanide in Yapu we determined food intake for 24 adults (12 males and 12 females) using the 3-day weighed intake method during November 1986. Energy and protein values for Tukanoan foods were taken from food composition tables, principally those of Wu Leung and Flores (1961) and Dufour (1988b).

Table 7.3 Sources of Energy and Protein in the Diets of 24 Yapu Adults (means ± SD)

	Energy, % total	Protein, % total
Cultigens: Manioc	79.8 ± 9.00	20.9 ± 13.41
Other	9.0 ± 7.91	14.6 ± 16.28
Wild vegetable products	1.4 ± 4.04	0.8 ± 2.39
Wild animal products	8.5 ± 7.05	61.4 ± 28.73
Store foods	2.1 ± 4.46	2.4 ± 9.63

Table 7.4 Mean Daily Energy, Protein,
and Cyanide Intakes of 24
Yapu Adults

	Mean ± SD
Energy, kcal	2272 ± 746.4
kcal/kg	42.9 ± 12.7
Protein, g	43.3 ± 23.12
g/kg	0.82 ± 0.43
Total Cyanide, mg	20.0 ± 8.29
mg/kg	0.4 ± 0.11
Free Cyanide, mg	9.1 ± 3.24
mg/kg	0.2 ± 0.04

Cyanide values for cassava-based foods were taken from the processing done in the present study and samples collected in Yapu.

Results of the food intake study are shown in Tables 7.3 and 7.4. The overall composition of the diet is similar to that reported previously for this population (Dufour 1983). Total cyanide intakes were on the order of 20 mg/day (0.4 mg/kg/day), and free cyanide intakes were approximately half that value, 9 mg/day (0.18 mg/kg/day).

The metabolic detoxification of dietary cyanide occurs principally via the conversion of cyanide to thiocyanate, which is then excreted in urine. The key enzyme in this reaction contains sulphur, which is derived from sulphur-containing amino acids, methionine and cystine. Reliance on this metabolic pathway increases the need for these two amino acids. For the Yapu diet, cyanide detoxification would require about 2 mg/kg/day of methionine. This estimate may be high, however, as the toxicity of intact cyanogenic glucosides has not been established. If only free cyanide, which definitely requires detoxification, is considered, the methionine requirement would be about 1 mg/kg/day.

What does this imply in terms of the adequacy of the current Yapu diet? The dietary data indicate that adults' crude protein intakes average 0.85 grams per kilogram of body weight per day. This is 96 to 102 percent of the FAO/WHO/UNU Safe Level (1985), depending on how the digestibility of the diet is estimated. Energy intake is 45 kilocalories per kilogram of body weight and appears to be adequate, so we can assume that dietary protein is probably not being used to supply energy. The amino acid pattern of the Yapu diet is compared to the FAO/WHO/UNU suggested pattern

Table 7.5 Yapu Diet Compared to FAO/WHO/
UNU Suggested Pattern (Preschoolers)
for Critical Amino Acids

Amino Acid	FAO	Yapu diet
Lysine	58	70
Methionine + Cystine	25	34
Threonine	34	40
Tryptophan	11	11

requirement for preschool children in Table 7.5. The FAO/WHO/UNU requirement for methionine and cystine is 25 mg/kg/day, and the Yapu diet provides approximately 34 mg/kg/day. Thus, even if the additional requirements for detoxification of 2 mg/kg/day are considered, sulphur-containing amino acids do not appear to be limiting in this diet. This is noteworthy inasmuch as Yapu protein intakes are barely adequate by FAO/WHO/UNU (1985) standards.

Spath's (1981) contention that the reliance on cassava as a dietary staple increases the minimum daily requirement for methionine is valid, but the Yapu data indicate that this increase in need is quite small. I think that given this small increase in need and the limited nature of our understanding of human amino acid requirements, it would be difficult to support Spath's (1971) argument that methionine alone may be acting as a limiting factor in Amazonia.

Conclusions and Implications for Future Research

The results presented here indicate that cassava may not be quite so poor a source of protein and minerals as we have assumed, but as is true of other staple foods, its nutritional value is a function of processing. Although Tukanoans cultivate very bitter varieties of cassava, their processing system is effective in detoxifying the roots. The residual cyanide in food products is low, and the current diet of adults appears to provide adequate quantities of the sulfur-containing amino acids used in the metabolic detoxification of dietary cyanide.

What are the implications of these results for future research? I would like to make two suggestions. First, a number of the health problems associated with cassava use in Africa are the direct result of inadequate processing. Given the preference for high-cyanide cassava varieties in Amazonia, the potential for these same sorts of problems is clearly present if less efficient processing techniques are adopted in the future. Presently, in the more traditional villages like Yapu, cassava processing is highly constrained culturally and there is almost no variation between women or over time in how products are prepared. Cassava processing is, however, an extremely time-consuming activity. As women's expectations change with acculturation, cassava processing techniques may also change. In more acculturated areas like Mitu, there has been a shift to fariña and a virtual abandonment of casabe and associated products. The quality of the fariña for sale suggests that the traditional long fermentation period is being shortened.

Further, since metabolic detoxification of cassava-borne cyanide is dependent on sulfur-containing amino acids, a decrease in the quantity or quality of protein in the current high-cassava diet would increase the risk of cyanide-related health problems. The general assumption is that dietary quality, including animal protein consumption, decreases with acculturation, but there are few empirical data available.

I believe that the strong cultural preference for bitter cassava varieties by at least some native Amazonians deserves more attention. To my knowledge, it is the only example of selection for the more toxic varieties of a given crop. In the Yapu area this selection does not appear to be related to productivity differences between the bitter and sweet cultivars, but it does appear to be related to qualitative differences in the food products made from bitter and sweet cultivars (Dufour 1993).

Notes

1. This research was supported by NSF grant number BNS-8519490, a Fulbright research grant, and an Early Career Development Award from the University of Colorado. I thank Felipa and Cándido Muñoz of Yapu, Vaupés, Colombia, for the processing work at CIAT; T. Salcedo of CIAT for the laboratory analyses; and the Instituto Colombiano de Antropología for its collaboration. I also thank Paul N. Patmore and Richard Wilshusen for their assistance with the fieldwork, and J. Cock, R. Best, and C. Wheatley of CIAT for their support.

2. In Central America and northern parts of South America the plant is referred to as *yuca*, also a Taino word (Carrizales 1984). In Brazil, Paraguay, and Argentina it is referred to as *mandioca* (Albuquerque 1969), and in parts of Colombia, as *mañoco*.

References Cited

Albuquerque, M. de
1969   *A mandioca na Amazonia*. Belém, Brazil: Superintendencia do Desenvolvimento da Amazonia.

Ayernor, G. S.
1985   Effects of the Retting of Cassava on Product Yield and Cyanide Detoxification. *Journal of Food Technology* 20:89–96.

Bourdoux, P., A. Mafuta, A. Hanson, and A. M. Ermans
1980   Cassava Toxicity: The Role of Linamarian. In *Role of Cassava in the Etiology of Endemic Goitre and Cretinism*, edited by A. M. Ermans, N. M. Mbulamoko, F. Delange, and R. Ahluwalia, pp. 15–28. Ottawa: International Development Research Centre Monograph IDRC-136e.

Bruijn, G. H. de
1973   The Cyanogenic Character of Cassava (*Manihot esculenta*). In *Chronic Cassava Toxicity*, edited by B. Nestle and R. MacIntyre, pp. 43–48. Ottawa: International Development Research Centre Monograph IDRC-010e.

Carrizales, V.
1984   Evolución histórica de la tecnología del cazabe. *Interciencia* 9(4): 206–13.

Cock, J. H.
1982   Cassava: A Basic Energy Source in the Tropics. *Science* 218:755–62.
1985   *Cassava: New Potential for a Neglected Crop*. Boulder, Colo.: Westview Press.

Cooke, R. D., and E. N. Maduagwu
1978   The Effects of Simple Processing on the Cyanide Content of Cassava Chips. *Journal of Food Technology* 13:299–306.

Coursey, D. G.
1973   Cassava as Food: Toxicity and Technology. In *Chronic Cassava Toxicity*, edited by B. Nestle and R. MacIntyre, pp. 27–36. Ottawa: International Development Research Centre Monograph IDRC-010e.

Dole, G. E.
1978   The Use of Manioc Among the Kuikuru: Some Interpretations. In *The Nature and Status of Ethnobotany*, edited by R. I. Ford, pp. 217–49. Ann Arbor: Museum of Anthropology, University of Michigan.

Dufour, D. L.
1983   Nutrition in the Northwest Amazon: Household Dietary Intake and Time-Energy Expenditure. In *Adaptive Responses of Native Amazonians*, edited by R. Hames and W. Vickers, pp. 329–55. New York: Academic Press.

1985   Manioc as a Dietary Staple: Implications for the Budgeting of Time and
           Energy in the Northwest Amazon. In *Food Energy in Tropical Ecosystems*,
           edited by D. J. Cattle and K. H. Schwerin, pp. 1–20. New York: Gordon
           and Breach.
1988a   Cyanide Content of Cassava (*Manihot esculenta*, Euphorbiacae) Cul-
           tivars Used by Tukanoan Indians in Northwest Amazonia. *Economic
           Botany* 42(2):255–66.
1988b   The Composition of Some Foods Used in Northwest Amazonia. *Inter-
           ciencia* 13(2):83–86.
1989   Effectiveness of Cassava Detoxification Techniques Used by Indigenous
           Peoples in Northwest Amazonia. *Interciencia* 14:(2)88–91.
1993   The Bitter Is Sweet: A Case Study of Bitter Cassava (*Manihot esculenta*)
           Use in Amazonia. In *Tropical Forests, People and Food: Biocultural Inter-
           actions and Applications to Development*, edited by C. M. Hladik,
           A. Hladik, O. F. Linares, H. Pagezy, A. Semple, and M. Haldey, pp.
           575–88. Paris: UNESCO/Parthenon.

Ermans, A. M., N. M. Mbulamoko, F. Delange, and R. Ahluwalia, eds.
1980   *Role of Cassava in the Etiology of Endemic Goitre and Cretinism*. Ottawa:
           International Development Research Centre Monograph IDRC-136e.

FAO/WHO/UNU
1985   *Energy and Protein Requirements*. Geneva: World Health Organization.

Gomez, G., et al.
1984   Effect of Variety and Plant Age on the Cyanide Content of Whole-root
           Cassava Chips and Its Reduction by Sun-drying. *Animal Feed Science
           and Technology* 11:57–65.

Howeler, R. H.
1985   Mineral Nutrition and Fertilization of Cassava: A Review of Recent
           Research. In *Cassava Research, Production and Utilization*, edited by
           J. H. Cock and J. A. Reyes, pp. 249–320. Cali, Colombia: CIAT.

Hugh-Jones, C.
1979   *From the Milk River*. Cambridge: Cambridge University Press.

Jones, W. O.
1959   *Manioc in Africa*. Stanford, Calif.: Stanford University Press.

Lancaster, P. A., J. S. Ingram, M. Y. Lim, and D. G. Coursey
1982   Traditional Cassava-based Foods: Survey of Processing Techniques.
           Economic Botany 36:12–45.

Meuser, F., and H. D. Smolnik
1980   Processing of Cassava to Gari and Other Foodstuffs. *Starch/Starke*
           32:116–22.

Moran, E. F.
1973   Energy Flow Analysis and the Study of *Manihot esculenta* Crantz. *Acta
           Amazonica* 3(3):29–39.

Nambisan, B., and S. Sundaresan
1985   Effect of Processing on the Cyanoglucoside Content of Cassava. *Journal of Science of Food and Agriculture* 36: 1197–1203.

Nestel, B., and R. MacIntyre, eds.
1973   *Chronic Cassava Toxicity.* Ottawa: International Development Research Centre Monograph IDRC-010e.

Nordenskiold, E.
1924   *The Ethnography of South America Seen from Mojos in Brazil.* Goteborg: Erlanders Boktryckeri Aktiebolag.

Okezie, B. O., and F. V. Kosikowski
1982   Cassava as Food. *Critical Reviews in Food Science and Nutrition* 17(3): 259–75.

Osuntokun, B. O.
1981   Cassava Diet, Chronic Cyanide Intoxification and Neuropathy in Nigerian Africans. *World Review of Nutrition and Dietetics* 36:141–73.

PRORADAM (Proyecto Radargrametrico del Amazonas)
1979   *La Amazonia y sus recursos.* Bogotá: Republica de Colombia.

Renvoize, B. S.
1972   The Area of Origin of *Manihot esculenta* as a Crop Plant: A Review of the Evidence. *Economic Botany* 26:352–60.

Rogers, D. J.
1965   Some Botanical and Ethnological Considerations of *Manihot esculenta.* *Economic Botany* 19(4):369–77.

Roosevelt, A. C.
1980   *Parmana: Prehistoric Maize and Manioc Subsistence Along the Amazon and Orinoco.* New York: Academic Press.

Rosling, H.
1987   *Cassava Toxicity and Food Security.* Uppsala, Sweden: Tryck kontakt.

Sauer, C. O.
1950   Cultivated Plants of Central and South America. In *Handbook of South American Indians,* edited by J. H. Steward, pp. 507–33. Washington, D.C.: United States Government Printing Office.

Schwerin, K. H.
1971   The Bitter and the Sweet: Some Implications of the Traditional Techniques for Preparing Manioc. Paper presented at the annual meeting of the American Anthropological Association.
1985   Food Crops in the Tropics. In *Food Energy in Tropical Ecosystems,* edited by D. J. Cattle and K. H. Schwerin. New York: Gordon and Breach.

Seigler, D. S., and J. F. Pereira
1981   Modernized Preparation of Casave in the Llanos Orientales of Venezuela. *Economic Botany* 35(3):356–62.

Spath, C. D.
1981   Getting to the Meat of the Problem: Some Comments on Protein as a Limiting Factor in Amazonia. *American Anthropologist* 83(2):377–79.

Sponsel, L. E.
1986   Amazon Ecology and Adaptation. *Annual Review of Anthropology* 15:67–97.

Steward, J. H., and L. C. Faron
1959   *Native Peoples of South America.* New York: McGraw-Hill.

Wu Leung, W-T., and M. Flores
1961   *Food Composition Table for Use in Latin America.* Bethesda, Md.: Interdepartmental Committee on Nutrition for National Defense, National Institutes of Health.

8

Epidemiological Factors and Human Adaptation in Amazonia

Carlos E. A. Coimbra, Jr.

Infectious and parasitic diseases rank among the most important challenges posed by the environments to which human populations have to adapt. The epidemiological picture of any population can be conceptualized as the final outcome of the dynamic interaction between a multitude of biological, environmental, and sociocultural variables. Therefore, the traditional "cause-and-effect" approach to disease that still prevails in the biomedical sciences ought to be replaced by a more systemic view in which culture assumes a vital role in mediating the interactions between human beings and potential pathogens.

Within this framework, human ecological studies should look more closely at the interactions between pathogens, human demographic structure, spatial distribution of the population, and its subsistence base, dietary habits, housing patterns, and religion. Adaptation to diseases assumes paramount significance for human survival, as has been extensively demonstrated by medical and biological anthropologists (Alland 1970; Coimbra 1989; Lieban 1973).

The Amazon region has long provided ecologically oriented anthropologists with a fertile field for investigations. Indeed, a lot has been done in this field among Amerindian populations as well as *caboclo* villages and colonization sites. Nevertheless, economic, environmental, and sociocultural change has been the central theme for most recent collective works (see Barbira-Scazzochio 1980; Moran 1983; Prance and Lovejoy 1985; Salati et al. 1983; Schmink and Wood 1984).

Studies carried out among indigenous societies often show a preoccupation with the identification of limiting environmental factors in attempting to explain demography, warfare, and spatial distribution of villages (cf. Hames and Vickers 1983). With few exceptions, epidemiology has been consistently left out of the mainstream of the discussion on human adaptation in Amazonia (see Coimbra 1985, 1987, 1988a; Holmes 1984; Kroeger 1980; Moran 1993; Sioli 1984).

The persistent neglect of epidemiological variables by anthropologists is due to a lack of basic training in the field and/or a lack of interest in carrying out multidisciplinary research with biomedical researchers. A rare exception is, for example, the longitudinal study coordinated by the anthropologist Napoleon Chagnon and the human geneticist and physician James Neel among the Yanomamo (Chagnon 1968; Chagnon and Melancon 1983; Neel et al. 1970).

Implicated in this neglect is the presumption shared by investigators both in anthropology and in biomedical sciences that important disease entities did not exist among isolated (or "virgin-soil," as some would prefer) New World populations. This generalized assumption may have had some influence on the disregard of epidemiology as part of the process of human adaptation to the lowlands, because Amerindians were perceived as not having had to cope with major diseases until the arrival of Europeans.

More recently, though, this picture has begun changing as paleopathological investigations undertaken at different localities in South America document the occurrence of parasites, once believed to be introduced after contact, in pre-Columbian human remains (Allison et al. 1974; Araújo et al. 1985; Confalonieri, Ferreira, and Araújo 1991; Ferreira et al. 1984). Moreover, other human infections such as tuberculosis (Buikstra 1981; Clark et al. 1987), trypanosomiasis (Coimbra 1988a; Rothhammer et al. 1985), and treponematosis (Black et al. 1974) were probably present in pre-Columbian South America in areas where mobility, housing, and alimentary patterns, along with other behavioral components, would allow their endemicity.

This gap becomes even more impressive if one looks at the growing medical and anthropological literature on indigenous South America. The former concentrates its efforts on describing clinical and etiological aspects of various diseases, usually overlooking their sociocultural dimensions, whereas the latter emphasizes the role of social and environmental variables but omits the role of diseases, despite anthropologists' attempts to provide a comprehensive understanding of human adaptation to the region.

The upper Xingu region in central Brazil draws most of the attention from professionals in both fields, although an integration between the two disciplines is far from being achieved. For instance, the longitudinal stud that have been carried out by biomedical researchers from the Escola Paulista de Medicina for more than 15 years have yielded important data on certain diseases that would certainly interest anthropologists, for they might raise questions concerning the adaptation processes of groups in the region (see Baruzzi, Marcopito, and Iunes 1978). Such is the case for, among others, lobomycosis, a unique skin infection that affects only the Kayabí (Baruzzi, Lacaz, and Souza 1979); mansoneliasis, a blood filariid that affects the Aruák-speaking groups in the Xingu park—Waurá, Yawalaptí, and Mehináku (D'Andretta and Silva 1966); and a recently described neurological syndrome that was associated with puberty seclusion rituals (Pinto and Baruzzi 1991; Verani and Morgado 1991).

These examples lead one to raise questions such as: What makes some groups more susceptible than others to certain diseases if, after all, the upper Xingu Amerindian groups live in a reasonably homogeneous ecosystem? To what extent might cultural practices such as seclusion play a role in the outcome of diseases? What is the role of parasites in the process of human adaptation to the different kinds of Amazonian ecosystems? Questions like these could be asked about any indigenous society in the Amazon, and it is unlikely that one would find any convincing answer in the ecologically oriented studies in medical anthropology carried out in the region.

This chapter is less an attempt to answer questions than an effort to raise possible lines of research relevant to a broader understanding of human adaptation in Amazonia. In the discussion that follows, I will draw a general outline of epidemiological fields of inquiry within the context of examples drawn from the ethnographic and biomedical literature.

Coping with Infection and Disease

The biomedical literature on native Amazonians points to the existence of a multitude of parasitic and infectious diseases that, at least under traditional living conditions, tend to occur in endemic levels. As Salzano and Callegari-Jacques (1988) point out, the immunological systems of individuals from these populations are constantly being challenged, as manifested by the high levels of gamma globulin usually found among them.

The presence of antibodies to viral infections among relatively isolated groups has been demonstrated for herpesvirus, Epstein-Barr virus, cytomegalovirus, and varicella, among others (Black 1975; Black et al. 1970, 1974; Salzano and Callegari-Jacques 1988:102–104). The prevalence of antibodies is usually evenly distributed throughout the age groups, suggesting that infection takes place early in childhood. For hepatitis B antibodies, prevalences can vary from 0 to 31 percent in different Yanomamo villages (Soyano et al. 1976), and from 61 to 71 percent among the Kayapó-Xikrín and the Kayapó-Menkrangnotí (Black et al. 1974). Because this virus is present in blood, cultural practices such as scarification can be responsible for the maintenance of high endemicity levels in some populations.

Toxoplasmosis, a protozoan infection that can be of great harm to fetuses, is widely distributed. Among the Xavánte, Neel et al. (1968) found a prevalence rate for *Toxoplasma* antibodies in the order of 100 percent, while a rate of 89 percent was reported for the Kreen-Akarôre (Leser, Camargo, and Baruzzi 1977), 52 percent for Xingu Indians (Baruzzi 1970), and 25 to 59 percent for the Tikúna (Lovelace, Moraes, and Hagerby 1978). It is believed that an important route of transmission of toxoplasmosis is through the consumption of meat, so the epidemiology of this infection among Amerindians could be influenced by the amount of game a group consumes. In their study of the Tikúna, Lovelace, Moraes, and Hagerby (1978) considered that the variation observed between villages could be reflecting different dietary habits: villages with higher fish intake showed lower prevalences of *Toxoplasma* antibodies, while villages with higher game consumption showed higher prevalence rates.

Actually, different dietary habits account for significant differences in the epidemiology of many parasitic infections on the continent. The revulsion for the consumption of raw animal products generally manifested by lowland societies can be highly adaptive, considering that helminth infections can be acquired by eating encisted larvae in animal muscle tissues. For instance, one species of fish tapeworm (*Diphyllobothrium pacificum*) is found in coastal Chile and Peru (Atias and Cattan 1976; Baer et al. 1967), where the consumption of raw or naturally dried fish has taken place since prehistoric times, as is indicated by findings of these eggs in human coprolites (Ferreira et al. 1984). Fish tapeworm infections among lowland Amerindians, who usually cook fish for a considerable amount of time, have not been reported, despite the existence of similar species and/or genera of tapeworms in both freshwater and marine fish in the region (see, for instance, Carvajal and Rego 1985).

Infection by *Paragonimus* species is endemic in many areas of South America, especially Peru and Ecuador, where raw freshwater crabs are consumed as food (Paulson and Paredes 1978; Urrutta 1967; Yokogawa 1969). In Amazonia, where several species of this helminth have been reported (Meira and Correa 1986; Yokogawa 1969), the consumption of raw crabs and other crustaceans is not usual, thus preventing local human populations from acquiring the infection.

The habit of eating the smoked livers of monkeys and wild pigs, observed among different Amazonian groups (Coimbra 1982), may account for the introduction of *Capillaria hepatica* into the community, as has been shown for the Yanomamo (Lawrence et al. 1980) and the Suruí (Coimbra 1982; Coimbra and Mello 1981). The eggs of this parasite are concentrated in the liver, and when first ingested by a predator, they pass in the stools and become infective in the soil. If accidently ingested for the second time, through contaminated food or water, they will develop into full parasites that may account for serious disease.

For intestinal helminthiasis, data from several surveys are available for different groups (see Salzano and Callegari-Jacques 1988). Roundworms, hookworms, and whipworms are by far the most frequent findings, with prevalence rates varying from 70 to 99 percent for *Ascaris*, 40 to 100 percent for hookworm, and 20 to 100 percent for whipworms (see Coimbra and Mello 1981; Holmes 1984; Lawrence et al. 1980; Neel et al. 1968; and Santos, Coimbra, and Ott 1985, among others).

Notwithstanding the high prevalence rates and widespread distribution of these parasites, most authors agree that parasite loads tend to be relatively low (Lawrence et al. 1980; Neel et al. 1968) among Amazonian Indians living under traditional conditions. Unfortunately, few quantitative studies on intestinal parasite loads are available in order to confirm this hypothesis.

Village mobility is considered a major factor in keeping worm loads low enough to minimize the impact of the exploitation exerted by the parasite on the host's blood and nutrients. Other practices might also interfere with the transmission of helminthiasis. Traditional house construction patterns, for example, might influence the transmission of certain parasites such as hookworms, if one compares houses built on stilts (like those of the Waiampí or the Pakaanóva) with the traditional *malocas* with their dirt floors. A comparative study of this kind has not yet been undertaken. Population size, village spatial organization, and water resources also play obvious roles in the epidemiology of these parasites, as they may interfere with the intensity of contact humans might have with infective helminth larvae and eggs. Moreover, the habit of chewing leaves of certain trees, as I have observed among the Suruí, might also affect infection rates; different studies have suggested antihelminthic properties for many Amazonian plant species (Elizabetsky 1986; van den Berg 1993).

So far I have mentioned examples only of behavioral adaptations to parasitic diseases. The role of the host's biological responses, however, conceptualized in terms of antibody production, is also important, for these responses allow human populations to achieve an equilibrium with local parasite strains. This notion fits with the idea generally shared by parasitologists and immunologists that both host and parasites tend to evolve toward a more benign infection pattern because it is not in the "interest" of the parasite to kill its host (Bradley 1977; Busvine 1980; Massad 1987; Parlevliet 1986).

For example, despite the existence of more than 100 different kinds of arbovirus in Amazonia (Pinheiro et al. 1986), as well as different species and/or strains of *Leishmania* (Lainson 1983), one rarely witnesses outbreaks of these infections among indigenes. Virological surveys carried out among these populations found high antibody titers for different groups of arboviruses such as yellow fever, *ilhéus*, and *mayaro* (Black et al. 1970, 1974; Neel et al. 1968). The distribution of antibody titers in the population was not even but showed an increase in prevalence rates according to age. This pattern suggests that as one grows up and increases one's range of activities—fishing, hunting, gathering—the greater becomes one's likelihood of being exposed to mosquitoes, ticks, and other possible vectors of arbovirus and becoming infected.

If somehow this relatively benign host-parasite system is disturbed, serious epidemics might occur. Among recently arrived colonists in Amazonia, epidemics of these and other infections are not uncommon (Coimbra 1988b; Pinheiro et al. 1977). In these cases, the forms of interactions between humans and the environment are likely to be more disruptive, with more extensive deforestation and radical transformation of the landscape, thus exposing susceptible individuals to zoonotic pathogens that would otherwise have been kept in their sylvatic cycle. Outbreaks of leishmaniasis and arboviral infections have been reported from development projects in the region, such as new roads, colonization sites, and urban settlements (Fraiha 1983; Pinheiro et al. 1977).

As illustrated in the preceding examples, the movement of susceptible populations into sylvatic transmission foci might give rise to epidemics. Outbreaks of zoonotic infections probably have taken place among indigenous populations, since the periodic movement of villages is a common behavioral pattern for most groups. Indeed, extensive movements of populations are reported in the ethnographic literature, owing to intertribal warfare (Métraux 1927) and contact with Europeans (Wagley 1977), among other factors. During these movements, it is likely that outbreaks occurred as populations were exposed to new parasite strains to which they had not yet developed immunological defenses. The medical literature reports at least one situation in which the movement of a village into a new area (the Waurá from Xingu) resulted in a serious outbreak of cutaneous leishmaniasis (Carneri, Nutels, and Miranda 1963), probably due to the presence of a different and more virulent local strain of the parasite. Six years later, another medical team visited the same group (Aston and Thorley 1970). They found no cases of active lesions and high antibody titers for *Leishmania*, indicating that the population had been able to achieve a balance with the local parasite strain.

For a last example of major health and disease problems faced by Amazonians, I will comment on diarrheal disease, since it is considered to be a leading cause of mortality, especially in early childhood, among different populations. From an anthropological point of view, this group of infections is also significant because its transmission patterns are closely related to behavioral variables such as diet, weaning, water utilization, waste disposal, and housing construction.

Different organisms can be involved in causing diarrhea. Among isolated Yanomamo villages, eight unique strains of enteropathogenic *Escherichia coli* were identified (Eveland, Oliver, and Neel 1971). Enteropathogenic, invasive, and toxigenic strains of *E. coli*, along with two species of *Shygella*, were isolated among the Suruí and Karitiána Indians (Coimbra et al. 1985). In this case, an incidence rate of diarrheal disease higher than 60 percent was reported for some months of the year among the Karitiána.

Large outbreaks of diarrhea have also been documented. This was the case in the Tiriyó epidemic, caused by rotavirus, which affected 70 percent of the population (Linhares et al. 1971). Recent reports on the findings of a larger serological survey for rotavirus covered 13 different groups and, generally speaking, revealed high prevalence rates of antibodies, thus indicating previous exposure of this group to viruses (Linhares et al. 1986). Prevalence rates for rotavirus antibodies varied from 17.9 percent among the Parakana to 93 percent among the Kubenkrankégn, confirming the widespread distribution of the infection among Indian populations— although, as the authors point out, all sources of human infection and transmission routes are not yet clear (Linhares et al. 1986).

Diarrhea can also be attributed to protozoans such as *Giardia* and amoebas, or to helminths such as *Strongyloides*. In Amazonia, the wide geographic distribution and high prevalence rates reported for these parasites (Coimbra and Mello 1981; Genaro and Ferraroni 1984; Holmes 1984; Lawrence et al. 1980; Santos, Coimbra, and Ott 1985) are indicative of the important role they play in the epidemiology of diarrhea in Amazonia.

Concluding Remarks

In this review, I have attempted to demonstrate the importance of infectious and parasitic diseases in the lives of Amazonian populations. By ignoring the role of pathogens in the process of traditional human adaptation to the region, the present body of knowledge on the subject developed by ecological and medical anthropology is deficient.

I do not want to overemphasize the importance of diseases relative to other environmental variables such as soil fertility or the availability of essential nutrients to humans, since these and other ecological factors have been shown to be important in human adaptations to Amazonia (see Sponsel 1986 for a review of the subject). Nevertheless, the neglect of epidemiological variables often leads to dubious conclusions about the adaptiveness of certain cultural traits and/or behaviors shown by various groups under different circumstances.

Potential parasites are present everywhere and have always interfered with dimensions of human life. In ignoring this fact, one not only overlooks an important aspect of human ecology but also, in many cases, risks misinterpreting observed behavioral patterns.

A short agenda for future work in ecological and medical anthropology in Amazonia should include studies focusing on the adaptiveness of housing patterns, population size and mobility, and dietary habits within an epidemiological framework. Moreover, researchers should look at the significance of traditional medical systems in enhancing a society's adaptiveness to its "microbiological environment." The great majority of Amerindian societies in Amazonia are undergoing rapid changes that affect basic components of their social organization and culture. New pathogens are being introduced all the time, and the high mortality rates that, unfortunately, appear during the first years of contact with most groups are well known (Ribeiro 1956). Few anthropologists have looked at the different sociocultural and environmental variables that are involved with the process of demographic recuperation of these groups following massive depopulation (see Coimbra 1987; Meireles 1988; Ribeiro 1956; Werner 1983).

Finally, the dietary changes that are taking place among Amazonian populations, with an overall increase in the consumption of carbohydrates such as rice and sugar and a decrease in fiber and protein intake, add a totally new dimension to the epidemiological picture of these groups. Besides considering the role of pathogens, we should also look at how the endocrine and other systems are responding to these changes, since malnutrition (Coimbra 1989) and chronic metabolic diseases such as diabetes and hypertension (Flemming-Moran and Coimbra 1990; Vieira Filho 1977, 1981), which are currently being observed among different Amazonian groups, can seriously affect people's capacity to work and compromise their chances of survival.

References Cited

Alland, A., Jr.
1970   *Adaptation in Cultural Evolution: An Approach to Medical Anthropology.* New York: Columbia University Press.

Allison, M. J., A. Pezzia, I. Hasegawa, and E. Gerszten
1974   A Case of Hookworm Infestation in a Precolumbian American. *American Journal of Physical Anthropology* 41:103–106.

Araújo, A. J. G., L. F. Ferreira, U. E. C. Confalonieri, L. Nuñez, and B. M. Ribeiro Filho
1985   The Finding of *Enterobius vermicularis* Eggs in Pre-Columbian Coprolites. *Memórias do Instituto Oswaldo Cruz* 80:141–43.

Aston, D. L., and A. P. Thorley
1970   *Leishmania* in Central Brazil: Results of a Montenegro Skin Test Survey Among Amerindians in the Xingu National Park. *Transactions of the Royal Society of Tropical Medicine and Hygiene* 64:671–78.

Atias, A., and P. E. Cattan
1976   Primer caso humano de infección por *Diphyllobothrium pacificum* en Chile. *Revista Médica de Chile* 104:216–17.

Baer, J. G., C. H. Miranda, R. W. Fernandes, and T. J. Medina
1967   Human Diphyllobothriasis in Peru. *Zeitschrift für Parasitenkunde* 28:277–89.

Barbira-Scazzochio, F., ed.
1980   *Land, People and Planning in Contemporary Amazonia.* Cambridge: Cambridge University Press.

Baruzzi, R. G.
1970   Contribution to the Study of Toxoplasmosis Epidemiology: Serologic Survey Among the Indians of the Upper Xingu River, Central Brazil. *Revista do Instituto de Medicina Tropical de São Paulo* 12:93–104.

Baruzzi, R. G., C. S. Lacaz, and F. A. A. Souza
1979   História natural da doença de Jorge Lobo: Ocorrência entre os índios Caiabí (Brasil Central). *Revista do Instituto de Medicina Tropical de São Paulo* 21:302–38.

Baruzzi, R. G., L. F. Marcopito, and M. Iunes
1978   Programa médico preventivo da Escola Paulista de Medicina no Parque Nacional do Xingu. *Revista de Antropologia* 21:155–70.

Black, F. L.
1975   Infectious Diseases in Primitive Societies. *Science* 187:515–18.

Black, F. L., W. J. Hierholzer, F. P. Pinheiro, A. S. Evans, J. P. Woodall,
E. M. Opton, J. E. Emmons, B. S. West, W. G. Downs, and G. D. Wallace
1974   Evidence for Persistence of Infectious Agents in Isolated Human Popula-
        tions. *American Journal of Epidemiology* 100:230–50.

Black, F. L., J. P. Woodall, A. S. Evans, H. Liebhaber, and G. Henle
1970   Prevalence of Antibody Against Viruses in the Tiriyó, an Isolated Amazo-
        nian Tribe. *American Journal of Epidemiology* 91:430–38.

Bradley, D. J.
1977   Human Pests and Disease Problems: Contrast Between Developing and
        Developed Countries. In *Origins of Pest, Parasite, Disease and Weed Prob-
        lems*, edited by J. M. Cherrett and G. R. Segar. Oxford: Blackwell Scien-
        tific Publications.

Buikstra, J. E., ed.
1981   *Prehistoric Tuberculosis in the Americas*. Evanston, Ill.: Northwestern Uni-
        versity Archaeological Program.

Busvine, J. R.
1980   The Evolution and Mutual Adaptation of Insects, Microorganisms and
        Man. In *Changing Disease Patterns and Human Behaviour*, edited by
        N. F. Stanley and R. A. Joske. London: Academic Press.

Carneri, I., N. Nutels, and J. A. Miranda
1963   Epidemia de leishmaniose entre os índios Waurá do Parque Nacional do
        Xingu (Estado de Mato Grosso, Brasil). *Revista do Instituto de Medicina
        Tropical de São Paulo* 5:271–72.

Carvajal, G. J., and A. R. Rego
1985   Anisaquíase: Uma enfermidade de origem marinha pouco conhecida.
        Ciência e Cultura 37:1847–49.

Chagnon, N.
1968   *Yanomamo: The Fierce People*. New York: Holt, Rinehart and Winston.

Chagnon, N., and T. F. Melancon
1983   Epidemics in a Tribal Population. In *The Impact of Contact: Two
        Yanomamo Case Studies*. Cambridge, Mass.: Cultural Survival, report
        11, pp. 53–78.

Clark, G. A., M. A. Kelley, J. M. Grange, and M. C. Hill
1987   The Evolution of Mycobacterial Disease in Human Populations: A
        Reevaluation. *Current Anthropology* 28:45–62.

Coimbra, C. E. A., Jr.
1982   Notas para uma análise epidemiológica dos achados de ovos de *Capilla-
        ria* sp. em exames de fezes realizados entre os Suruí do Parque Indígena
        Aripuanã, Rondônia. *Boletim* CEPAM (Centro de Estudos e Pesquisas em
        Antropologia Médica) 1:5–6.

1985   A habitação Suruí e suas implicações epidemiológicas. In *Adaptação à enfermidade e sua distribuição entre grupos indígenas da bacia Amazônica,* edited by M. A. Ibañez-Novion and A. M. T. Ott. Brasília: Centro de Estudos e Pesquisas em Antropologia Médica/Belém: Museu Paraense Emílio Goeldi.

1987   O sarampo entre sociedades indígenas brasileiras e algumas considerações sobre a prática da saúde pública entre estas populações. *Cadernos de Saúde Pública* 3:22–37.

1988a   Human Settlements, Demographic Pattern, and Epidemiology in Lowland Amazonia: The Case of Chagas' Disease. *American Anthropologist* 90:82–97.

1988b   Human Factors in the Epidemiology of Malaria in the Brazilian Amazon. *Human Organization* 47:254–60.

1989   From Shifting Cultivation to Coffee Farming: The Impact of Change on the Health and Ecology of the Suruí Indians in the Brazilian Amazon. Ph.D. dissertation, Indiana University.

Coimbra, C. E. A., Jr., and D. A. Mello
1981   Enteroparasitas e *Capillaria* sp. entre o grupo Suruí, Parque Indígen Aripuanã, Rondônia. *Memórias do Instituto Oswaldo Cruz* 76:299–302.

Coimbra, C. E. A., Jr., R. V. Santos, R. Tanus, and T. M. Inham
1985   Estudos epidemiológicos entre grupos indígenas de Rondônia. II. Bactérias enteropatogênicas e gastrenterites entre os Suruí e Karitiána. *Revista da Fundação SESP* 30:111–19.

Confalonieri, U., L. F. Ferreira, and A. Araújo
1991   Intestinal helminths in Lowland South American Indians: Some Evolutionary Interpretations. *Human Biology* 63:863–73.

D'Andretta, C., Jr., and M. P. Silva
1966   Ocorrência de mansonclose entre índios Uaurás (Alto Xingu, Mato Grosso, Brasil). *Revista Paulista de Medicina* 68:182.

Elisabetsky, E.
1986   New Directions in Ethnopharmacology. *Journal of Ethnobiology* 6:121–28.

Eveland, W. C., W. J. Oliver, and J. V. Neel
1971   Characteristics of *Escherichia coli* Serotypes in the Yanomama, a Primitive Indian Tribe of South America. *Infection and Immunity* 4:753–56.

Ferreira, L. F., A. J. G. Araújo, U. E. C. Confalonieri, and L. Nuñez
1984   The Finding of Eggs of *Diphyllobothrium* in Human Coprolites (4100–1950 B.C.) from Northern Chile. *Memórias do Instituto Oswaldo Cruz* 79:175–180.

Flemming-Moran, M., and C. E. A. Coimbra, Jr.
1990   Blood Pressure Studies Among Amazonian Native Populations: A Review from an Epidemiological Perspective. *Social Science and Medicine* 31:593–601.

Fraiha, H.
1983   Leishmanioses tegumentares. In *Saúde na Amazônia*, second edition, edited by A. C. Linhares. São Paulo: ANPES.

Genaro, O., and J. J. Ferraroni
1984   Estudo sobre malária e parasitoses intestinais em indígenas da tribo Nadeb-Maku, Estado do Amazonas, Brasil. *Revista de Saúde Pública* 18:162–69.

Hames, R. B., and W. T. Vickers
1983   Introduction. In *Adaptive Responses of Native Amazonians*, edited by R. B. Hames and W. T. Vickers. New York: Academic Press.

Holmes, R.
1984   Non-dietary Modifiers of Nutritional Status in Tropical Forest Populations of Venezuela. *Interciencia* 9:386–91.

Kroeger, A.
1980   Housing and Health in the Process of Cultural Adaptation: A Case Study Among Jungle and Highland Natives of Ecuador. *Journal of Tropical Medicine and Hygiene* 83:53–69.

Lainson, R.
1983   The American Leishmaniasis: Some Observations on Their Ecology and Epidemiology. *Transactions of the Royal Society of Tropical Medicine and Hygiene* 77:569–96.

Lawrence, D. N., J. V. Neel, S. H. Abadie, L. L. Moore, L. J. Adams, G. R. Healy, and I. G. Kagan
1980   Epidemiologic Studies Among Amerindian Populations of Amazonia. III. Intestinal Parasitoses in Newly Contacted and Acculturating Villages. *American Journal of Tropical Medicine and Hygiene* 29:530–37.

Leser, P. G., M. E. Camargo, and R. G. Baruzzi
1977   Toxoplasmosis Serologic Tests in Brazilian Indians (Kren-Akorore) of Recent Contact with Civilized Man. *Revista do Instituto de Medicina Tropical de São Paulo* 19:232–36.

Lieban, R. W.
1973   Medical Anthropology. In *Handbook of Social and Cultural Anthropology*, edited by J. J. Honigmann. Chicago: Rand McNally.

Linhares, A. C., F. P. Pinheiro, R. B. Freitas, Y. B. Gabbay, J. H. Shirley, and G. M. Berds
1971   An Outbreak of Rotavirus Diarrhea Among a Nonimmune, Isolated South American Indian Community. *American Journal of Epidemiology* 113:703–10.

Linhares, A. C., E. V. Salbe, Y. B. Gabbay, and N. Rees
1986   Prevalence of Rotavirus Antibody Among Isolated South American Indian Communities. *American Journal of Epidemiology* 123:699–709.

Lovelace, J. K., M. A. P. Moraes, and E. Hagerby
1978   Toxoplasmosis Among the Ticuna Indians in the State of Amazonas, Brazil. *Tropical and Geographic Medicine* 30:295–300.

Massad, E.
1987   Transmission Rates and the Evolution of Pathogenicity. *Evolution* 41:1127–30.

Meira, J. A., and M. O. A. Correa
1986   Sobre o *Paragonimus westermmani* no Brasil. Notas sobre um antigo trabalho. *Revista da Sociedade Brasileira de Medicina Tropical* 19:193–94.

Meireles, D .M.
1988   Sugestões para uma análise comparativa da fecundidade em populações indígenas. *Revista Brasileira de Estudos Populacionais* 5:1–20.

Métraux, A.
1927   Les migrations historiques des Tupiguarani. *Journal de la Société des Americanistes*, n.s. 19:1–45.

Moran, E. F.
1981   *Developing the Amazon*. Bloomington: Indiana University Press.
1993   *Through Amazonian Eyes: The Human Ecology of Amazonian Populations*. Iowa City: University of Iowa Press.

Moran, E. F., ed.
1983   *The Dilemma of Amazonian Development*. Boulder, Colo.: Westview Press.

Neel, J. V.
1974   Control de las enfermedades de los Amerindios en transición cultural. *Boletín de la Oficina Sanitaria Panamericana* 77:478–85.

Neel, J. V., W. R. Centerwall, N. A. Chagnon, and H. L. Casey
1970   Notes on the Effect of Measles and Measles Vaccine in a Virgin-Soil Population of South American Indians. *American Journal of Epidemiology* 91:418–29.

Neel, J. V., A. H. Paes de Andrade, G. E. Brown, W. E. Eveland, J. Goobar, W. A. Sodeman, G. H. Stollermann, E. D. Weinstein, and A. H. Wheeler
1968   Further Studies of the Xavante Indians. IX. Immunologic Status with Respect to Various Diseases and Organisms. *American Journal of Tropical Medicine and Hygiene* 17:486–98.

Parlevliet, J. E.
1986   Coevolution of Host Resistance and Pathogen Virulence: Possible Implications for Taxonomy. In *Coevolution and Systematics*, edited by A. R. Stone and D. L. Hawksworth. Oxford: Clarendon Press.

Paulson, G., and L. Paredes
1978   Investigación médico-ecológico y socio-económico en una tribu Cayápa de la provincia de Esmeraldas, realizada por las Universidades de Guayaquil y Esmeraldas en 1973. *Revista Ecuatoriana de Higiene y Medicina Tropical* 31:19–78.

Pinheiro, F. P., G. Bensabath, A. P. A. T. Rosa, R. Lainson, J. J. Shaw, R. Ward, H. Fraiha, M. A. P. Moraes, Z. M. Gueiros, Z. C. Lins, and R. Mendes
1977   Public Health Hazards Among Workers Along the Trans-Amazon Highway. *Journal of Occupational Medicine* 19:490–97.

Pinheiro, F. P., A. P. A. T. Rosa, R. B. Freitas, J. F. S. T. Rosa, and P. F. C. Vasconcelos
1986   Arboviroses: Aspectos clinico epidemiológicos. In *Instituto Evandro Chagas. 50 Anos de Contribuição ás Ciências Biológicas e á Medicina Tropical*, vol. I. Belém: Ministério da Saúde/Fundação Serviços de Saúde Pública.

Pinto, N. R. S., and R. G. Baruzzi
1986   Neuropatia periférica aguda associada a reclusão pubertária masculina em índios do Alto Xingu, Brasil Central. *Revista da Sociedade Brasideira de Medicina Tropical* 19(Supl.):88.
1991   Male pubertal seclusion and risk of death in Indians from Alto Xingu, Central Brazil. *Human Biology* 63:821–34.

Prance, G. T., and T. E. Lovejoy, eds.
1985   *Amazonia.* Oxford: Pergamon Press.

Ribeiro, D.
1956   Convívio e contaminação: Efeitos dissociativos da depopulação provocada por epidemias em grupos indígenas. *Sociologia* 18:3–50.

Rothhammer, F., M. J. Allison, L. Nuñez, V. Staden, and B. Arriaza
1985   Chagas' Disease in Pre-Columbian South America. *American Journal of Physical Anthropology* 68:495–98.

Salati, E., H. D. R. Shubart, W. Junk, and A. E. Oliveira
1983   *Amazônia: Desenvolvimento, Integração e Ecologia.* Rio de Janeiro: Editora Brasiliense/Brasilia: CNPq.

Salzano, F. M., and S. Callegari-Jacques
1988   *South American Indians: A Case Study in Evolution.* Research Monographs on Human Population Biology, no. 6. Oxford: Oxford University Press.

Santos, R. V., C. E. A. Coimbra, Jr., and A. M. T. Ott
1985   Estudos epidemiológicos entre grupos indígenas de Rondônia. III. Parasitoses intestinais nas populações dos vales dos rios Guaporé e Mamoré. *Cadernos de Saúde Pública* 1:467– 77.

Schmink, M., and C. H. Wood, eds.
1984   *Frontier Expansion in Amazonia.* Gainesville: University of Florida Press.

Sioli, H., ed.
1984   *The Amazon: Limnology and Landscape Ecology of a Mighty Tropical River and Its Basin.* Dordrecht: W. Junk Publishers.

Soyano, A., I. Malave, R. Walder, Z. Layrisse, and M. Layrisse
1976   Hepatitis-B Antigen in an Isolated Indian Population (Yanomama Indians), Southern Venezuela. *Revista Brasileira de Pesquisas Médicas e Biológicas* 9:247–53.

Sponsel, L. E.
1986   Amazon Ecology and Adaptation. *Annual Review of Anthropology* 15:67–273.

Urrutta, M. A.
1967   Paragonimiasis en las márgenes del río Napo. *Revista Ecuatoriana de Higiene y Medicina Tropical* 24:315–17.

van den Berg, M. E.
1993   *Plantas medicinais da Amazônia.* Contribuição ao seu Conhecimento Sistemático. Belém: Museu Paraense Emílio Goeldi.

Verani, C., and A. Morgado
1991   Fatores culturais associados à doença da reclusão do Alto Xingu (Brasil Central). *Cadernos de Saúde Pública* 7:515–37.

Vieira-Filho, J. P. B.
1977   O diabetes mellitus e as glicemias de jejum dos índios Caripuna e Palikur. *Revista da Associação Médica Brasileira* 23:175–78.
1981   Problemas de aculturação alimentar dos Xavantes e Boróro. *Revista de Antropologia* 24:37–40.

Wagley, C.
1977   *Welcome of Tears: The Tapirapé Indians of Central Brazil.* Prospect Heights, Ill.: Waveland Press.

Werner, D.
1983   Fertility and Pacification Among the Mekranoti of Central Brazil. *Human Ecology* 11:227–45.

Yokogawa, M.
1969   *Paragonimus* and Paragonimiasis. *Advances in Parasitology* 7:375–87.

CHANGE, CONSERVATION, AND RIGHTS

The first four chapters in part III offer a sample of case studies on ecological aspects of cultural change and economic development in Amazonia. They reveal that most traditional indigenous societies were successful in adapting to the constraints and opportunities of the diverse ecosystems in the Amazon by creating economies and cultures that usually were ecologically and socially sustainable and were based on an intimate empirical knowledge of local ecology. At the same time, these chapters demonstrate how nutrition, health, economy, culture, and society often deteriorate in synergy under Western influences such as resource competition and habitat destruction by recent colonists. The authors raise important questions about the abuse of indigenous rights to resources, traditional territories, and intellectual property. The concluding chapter of the book explores such questions further by examining indigenous societies and anthropology within the broader context of the world system.

In chapter 9, Michael Baksh reports longitudinal observations of deterioration in the quality of life of the Machiguenga in Peru. Traditionally the Machiguenga had a high quality of life, which Baksh assesses in terms of nutrition, health, material goods, social relations, and life satisfaction. After two centuries of contact—including raiding, enslavement, and murder during the rubber boom—the Machiguenga are experiencing a demographic rebound, partly as a result of Western medical assistance. Their quality of life, however, is deteriorating, in part because of increasing pressure on the resource base as a result of their population rebound; in part because of nucleation and sedentarization stimulated by missionization, which has increased community size as much as tenfold; and in part because of resource competition from Andean colonists and the personnel of timber and oil companies. Baksh concludes that research by anthropologists can promote the survival and welfare of indigenous societies by exploring alternative strategies for food and cash production as well as by facilitating the exchange of such information between indigenous groups.

In chapter 10, Allyn Stearman examines the effects on resources of acculturation through missionization and colonization in the case of the Yuquí who inhabit the humid tropical forest near the foothills of the Andes in eastern Bolivia. By moving into one of the most remote areas of Bolivia to escape missionization and settler encroachment, the Yuquí avoided contact with outsiders until 1968, when peaceful relations were established with Westerners. Stearman compares the ecology of the subsistence and economy of traditional and acculturated Yuquí. Nucleation and sedentarization of the Yuquí at the mission has reduced their trekking and dietary breadth and increased their dependence on fishing rather than hunting. Schooling results in children's being left behind with relatives at the village while other family members are on extended foraging trips. This separation also severs an important channel of transmission to younger generations of ethnoecological knowledge and subsistence technology and skills. Coca farmers, commercial fishers, and other transient exploiters of local resources increasingly compete with the Yuquí as well as fragment or modify their habitat. To cope with this situation the Yuquí need information and skills to deal with the political economy of the outside world that is impinging on them. Here is a role for applied research on human ecology that is designed and produced for the indigenous society instead of academia, government bureaucracy, economic developers, or other external agencies.

In chapter 11, Avecita Chicchón describes patterns of land and resource use in forest, savanna, and river ecosystems by three different settlements of Chimane. They inhabit the multiple use zone of the Beni Biosphere Reserve in Bolivia. This reserve was arranged by Conservation International as a debt-for-nature swap. It has a management plan that integrates the interests of both conservationists and indigenes. Chicchón also discusses the policy implications of her research findings for the conservation of biodiversity and sustainable development of the economy of local peoples. She emphasizes that the needs of local people within and adjacent to protected areas must be considered by planners and administrators of protected areas, an arena for co-management by government and community.

In chapter 12, Janet Chernela documents the case of the Awa Binational Biosphere Reserve in Colombia and Ecuador. She examines the roles and interests of each group involved in the formation of the reserve—indigenes, loggers, ranchers, government, and international scientific and conservation agencies. Points of conflict between the different groups had to be negotiated. The governments were concerned about guarding their territorial interests in border zones and preventing activities such as guerrilla movements and narco-trafficking. The Awa were concerned with land demarcation and tenure as well as the right to control and develop their land and resources in sustainable ways. To guard their interests they had to participate in every phase of the decision-making process in the formation of the reserve.

Chernela's study provides an illustration of the political component in human ecology and adaptation. Although in the past indigenes and environmentalists have often found common concerns, in recent years there have been growing criticisms of indigenes by some environmentalists, and in this arena of potential conflicts of interest the ecological anthropologist may usefully serve as a mediator.

Chapter 13, by Leslie Sponsel, concludes part III and the book as a whole by exploring the relationships among the world system, indigenous peoples, and ecological anthropology. The world system is increasingly impacting on indigenous societies and their habitats, largely in deleterious ways. Whereas anthropologists have tended to contribute to the power of colonial and neocolonial entities over indigenes, I argue for greater attention to directly serving and thus contributing to the empowerment of indigenous societies. At a minimum this might be accomplished simply by including indigenes in meaningful ways as colleagues in every phase of research, from initial design to final report. Doing so would also develop a stimulating dialectic between basic and applied research. The chapter is intended to provoke introspective, retrospective, and prospective thought on the role of the ecological anthropologist in the survival and well-being of indigenes in the endangered world of the Amazon.

9

Changes in Machiguenga Quality of Life

Michael Baksh

As cultural, ecological, and economic change intensifies in Amazonia, it is increasingly urgent that cultural-ecological research be concerned with the future well-being of the region's habitants. Such research should be sensitive to the knowledge and expertise of indigenous resource use and the adaptational value of alternative subsistence and economic behaviors (Johnson 1980; Moran 1983; Moran and Herrera 1984; Posey 1983; Sponsel 1986). Cultural-ecological research should also be oriented toward offering recommendations that would lead to improvements in well-being.

The objectives of this chapter are to demonstrate that the Machiguenga Indians of the Peruvian Amazon recently had a very good quality of life and to describe how aspects of their adaptation are changing. An important finding that should come as no surprise to many other observers of Amazonian cultural adaptation is that densely populated Machiguenga communities are not conducive to prolonged high quality of life. Also, Machiguenga well-being is becoming increasingly dependent upon people's ability to develop reliable sources of cash income. The chances of cultural, if not physical, survival by the Machiguenga and other Amazonian societies would be enhanced by additional cultural-ecological research.

Quality of Life

The quality of life concept requires some elaboration here because it means something different to almost everyone. Health practitioners, economists, psychologists, and other researchers all have very different notions of what quality of life means. Curiously, few anthropologists have explicitly adopted and defined quality of life in their research (but see Davis 1986 for development of a "Physical Quality of Life Index"). Yet because of its holistic approach to social science research, anthropology is in the best position to discuss a population's quality of life.

Perhaps the most holistic definition available is that offered by Lore Scheer (1980:145–46):

> Probably most of us could agree on the main goal areas that we consider of value in determining a good quality of life. These would certainly include remaining alive and healthy, having a suitable place to live, working, enjoying leisure time, and receiving an education that prepares us to cope with life's problems. Money alone cannot guarantee health and security; and yet these are the two factors that most decisively determine our quality of life today. [Quality of life also] depends to a considerable extent on how we like our life; on the extent to which our life "satisfies" us and makes us feel that it is worth living.

When we adopt a holistic approach to quality of life, it immediately becomes clear that there are an unlimited number of potential domains or variables to investigate. For the sake of practicality, it is necessary to select a limited set of variables that are capable of describing a population's well-being as fully as possible. And because culture is always changing, it is critical to select domains that, if changed significantly, would bring about the greatest impact on overall well-being.

Minimally, then, quality of life must emphasize first and foremost the fulfillment of basic biological needs. This emphasis is compatible with the cultural-ecological approach, and indeed, quality of life may, in a holistic sense, be thought of as "quality of cultural-ecological adaptation."

In an effort to convey Machiguenga quality of life and the ways in which it is changing, I focus primarily on the domains of food procurement and production, diet, health, availability of material goods, social relations, and life satisfaction. Because Machiguenga cultural-ecological change is proceeding rapidly, due in part to the Machiguenga's own efforts to generate cash, their good level of well-being now appears to be in serious jeopardy. Yet at the same time, their good quality of life is increasingly dependent on their ability to purchase certain essential Western goods.

The Machiguenga

The Machiguenga are an Arawakan-speaking Indian population living in the tropical rain forest of the Peruvian Amazon. They are situated primarily around the Urubamba River but extend eastward into the western headwaters of the Madre de Dios River. They number approximately 10,000, and most continue to rely almost exclusively on the traditional practices of slash-and-burn agriculture, fishing, hunting, and collecting.

Much of this chapter is based on fieldwork conducted in the community of Camaná from September 1979 to November 1980 and from July to August 1981. The village was established in 1976 and so was three to five years old during this period. As described elsewhere (Baksh 1985), the community fissioned in late 1981, and most people moved to a previously unexploited location (although they were joined shortly thereafter by the others).

Fieldwork was also conducted during July 1988, when the "new" site was approaching its seventh year. This visit led to valuable insights regarding recent trends in cash crop involvement and quality of life, some of which are summarized in this chapter.

It is important to note that Camaná is an atypically large community of about 250 people; traditional settlements typically totaled 25 to 35 individuals. The establishment of densely settled communities and the accompanying trend toward permanent village sites are consequences of Western efforts to incorporate tribal groups into the market economy, spread Christianity, and provide education, health care, and goods. The Machiguenga also subscribe to these goals in varying degrees. In any case, Camaná provides a good test case for research on the potential for settlements of high population density to maintain good levels of well-being over time.

As I have argued elsewhere, the Machiguenga—particularly those who live in relatively unacculturated communities—enjoy a very good quality of life (Baksh 1984a; also see Johnson 1978). At a time when a considerable portion of the world's population is hungry, overworked, unhealthy, and/or unhappy, the Machiguenga are decidedly well off. Indeed, to the extent that any society may be said to maintain an excellent quality of life today, one is tempted to describe the Machiguenga's overall well-being as such.

Sources of Cultural-Ecological Change

The major source of Machiguenga cultural-ecological change over the last two centuries is contact with the Western world. At the turn of this century, for instance, the rubber boom fomented such social atrocities upon the Indians as raiding, enslavement, and homicide. Relations with outsiders steadily improved in the first half of the century, owing at least in part to missionary influence and assistance, and improved relations quite possibly reached a climax in the 1970s when contact with outsiders was generally favorable and Western medicine and material items were relatively abundant.

A major tradeoff, however, and one that threatens to disrupt the current good level of well-being in numerous ways, has been the establishment of densely populated and/or permanent settlements. The shift in settlement pattern from seminomadic hamlets to sedentary villages of hundreds of people is a consequence of a desire on the part of Westerners to distribute Christianity, education, health care, and goods, and of a desire by the Machiguenga to obtain some or all of these things.

Aside from changes in settlement patterns, the future poses severe threats to Machiguenga well-being for several other related reasons. Other major sources of change include an increase in population size, increased contact with the outside world, and involvement in cash crop and domesticated animal production for the sake of earning cash.

More specifically, considerable evidence indicates that the Machiguenga are increasing in population size (see Baksh 1984a:328–29). Indeed, it may be predicted that a population explosion is on the horizon because adults are living longer, child mortality is low, and numerous youths are approaching marriageable age. Individuals in the 10- to 14-year-old age bracket represented about one-fifth of the population in 1980, and the majority of females in this cohort have had at least one child by now. This is not an insignificant matter for the Machiguenga's future well-being, because population density in the tribal area is certain to surpass levels achieved under traditional ecological constraints. Minimally, it is expected that wild food resources will be depleted at increasingly faster rates and that food production and consumption will shift in emphasis toward agricultural and domesticated animal foods. Ideally, the population growth rate should be reduced, but it is difficult to imagine how any program of family planning would be adopted by the Machiguenga.

Contact with outsiders and subsequent opportunities for conflict and competition over land and other resources are intensifying as a result of (1) colonists from the crowded Andes settling in the upper Amazon, and (2) exploitation of lumber and other resources by Peruvian and international companies. Oil companies are now well entrenched in Machiguenga territory. And, as a rather perverse example of negative contact with Western civilization, the filming of the movie *Fitzcarraldo* led to the near destruction of a thriving community in the heart of Machiguenga territory.

The Machiguenga need some cash to preserve their achievements in well-being. If nothing else, every Machiguenga family must have access to a machete. Without machetes, and without aluminum cooking pots, Western medicines, and steel axes, the Machiguenga would work considerably harder and suffer more from disease. Machiguenga adults appear to be increasingly preoccupied with acquiring Western goods, perhaps because they fear, correctly, that access to these items can be cut off. The psychological consequences of such technological losses would also be traumatic. In short, their quality of life is inextricably dependent upon the ability to generate cash.

At this point, I will turn to a description of aspects of Camaná's quality of life during the period 1979–81. This will be followed by a similar presentation based on observations made in the summer of 1988.

Food Procurement and Production

Like most other native Amazonians, the Machiguenga are expert farmers, fishers, and foragers. Their reliance upon these subsistence strategies provides them an excellent diet through modest expenditures of labor.

As expert slash-and-burn agriculturalists, the Machiguenga grow the bulk of their food as well as many important nonfood items (e.g., cotton, *barbasco*, medicines). As demonstrated elsewhere (Baksh 1984a:139–249; Johnson 1983; Johnson and Baksh 1987; Johnson and Behrens 1982), the current system of subsistence agriculture is extremely well developed and efficient. One hour of work in Camaná, for example, produces at least 3.5 kg of food. Enough food and other products are produced by the average man working about one hour per day and the average woman working about half an hour per day (Table 9.1). Moreover, the strategy appears to have no prolonged negative impact on the environment.

Because the current system of subsistence agriculture is so well developed and efficient, major changes in the system hold a strong likelihood of being negative. The establishment of permanent settlements alone means that gardens are normally farther from the village every year. Even in Camaná, a settlement surrounded almost entirely by homogeneous soils of good quality (according to community residents), with gardens lying farther from the community every year, travel time to gardens in 1980 was twice that of 1979.

As fishers and forest foragers, the Machiguenga possess an intimate knowledge of the behaviors and availability of animals and plants in their environment. From an etic perspective, they use well-developed and highly appropriate procurement strategies. Given the limited availability of wild foods in their habitat and the normal uncertainties associated with wild food procurement (e.g., not knowing whether food will be

Table 9.1 Mean Hours per Day Allocated to Selected Activities by the
Average Adult Male and Female of Camaná

Activity	Adult Male	Adult Female	Edible Kg Produced/ Procured per Hour[a]
Subsistence Agriculture	1.10	0.60	3.5
Foraging (hunt/collect)	0.54	0.23	0.12 kg meat; 0.23 kg veg.
Fishing	1.64	0.60	0.48
Cash crops (peanuts/beans)	0.25	0.13	0.34
Cattle raising	0.12	0.00	(3–4 live cattle/community)
Chicken raising	<0.10	0.20	(12 live chickens per HH; consumption of few eggs and small amounts of meat)

Note: The average household has 1.22 adult males and 1.41 adult females.

[a]Efficiency is based on yields produced/procured from all adult male and female labor over one year.

obtained or even encountered on a given trip), the Machiguenga do quite well as fishers, hunters, and collectors. The average adult male spent a little over two hours per day procuring wild foods, and the average adult female, about one hour per day (Table 9.1). One hour of fishing yielded 0.48 kg of fish, and one hour of foraging yielded 0.12 kg of meat and 0.23 kg of vegetal products.

Clearly, Machiguenga well-being is influenced to a considerable extent by the availability of wild food resources. As demonstrated elsewhere (Baksh 1984a, 1985), the site of Camaná was initially rich in wild food resources, but after it had been occupied for five years, local game animals in the forest had been significantly reduced and the efficiency of fish procurement was declining rapidly. The severe decline of fish, especially, led residents to work significantly harder and spend more time away from the village in their effort to maintain previous levels of wild food consumption.

It is probable that a decline in the availability of faunal foods will initiate a greater dependence upon agricultural foods, particularly maize. Thus the community of Shimaa, which has less fish and other wild foods than Camaná, spends considerably more time at agricultural production than Camaná because of the need for comparatively large new gardens (Baksh and Johnson 1990; Johnson and Baksh 1987).

In short, the strategies of subsistence agriculture, fishing, hunting, and collecting are well adapted by the Machiguenga for life in their environment. Community members enjoyed a satisfactory diet in 1979–81; the average man worked a total of 3.3 hours per day and the average woman 1.5 hours per day in food production. However, it was apparent that wild food supplies could not be sustained in the vicinity of permanent and/or densely populated Machiguenga settlements. And in the face of declining wild foods, a host of other changes occurred, some of which are discussed below.

Diet

Food supplies were normally more than adequate in Camaná, and measurements of meals made prior to consumption indicated that the diet was quite nutritious. About 84 percent of all calories were derived from subsistence crops, 6 percent from fish, 4 percent from wild forest foods, 2 percent from chicken meat and eggs, and 4 percent from peanuts and beans, which are recently adopted cash crops. For an adult male, a daily diet of 2,840 calories provided about 69 grams of protein and 20 grams of fat. And for an adult female, a diet of 2,029 calories provided about 49 grams of protein and 14 grams of fat. Interestingly, Allen Johnson found that adult males in Shimaa expended 3,202 calories per day, and adult females, 1,924 calories. The most significant reason for the difference between men of the two communities was the larger emphasis upon agricultural production in Shimaa.

As supplies of fish and other wild foods declined through time, people not only worked harder in the attempt to maintain previous levels, but the diet also became less nutritious. Fish availability at meals became erratic toward the end of my fieldwork, and informants often complained that their families were hungry. As described elsewhere, however (Baksh and Johnson 1990), there is little risk of starvation for the Machiguenga.

Although villagers continued to meet their protein needs, the dietary fat (and particularly the essential fatty acid content) of meals consumed in late 1980 was close to, if not below, the minimum requirement recommended by the Food and Agriculture Organization (1980:85) (Baksh 1984b, 1985; Johnson and Baksh 1987). Emically, the relative scarcity of fish and other highly preferred foods was not unimportant to the Machiguenga. Although native Amazonians are unaware of "protein" per se, they are aware of fat in fish and meat, and a scarcity of these foods most basically means a scarcity of foods that taste good and make one feel satiated.

Health

In evaluating a population's well-being it is critical to consider the status of its health, since health is perhaps the most important reflection of the quality of a group's fulfillment of basic biological needs and its adaptive responses to hazards presented by its habitat.

The residents of Camaná were generally quite healthy. Infant mortality was low, and many adults enjoyed long lives. Most individuals were "normal" or close to normal in their weight for height and other anthropometric measurements; few suffered from serious physical disabilities or other health ailments; all had access to a variety of traditional and often important Western health treatments; and most were immunized against the major diseases. Everyone suffered from parasites, wounds, infections, burns, bites, and other problems on occasion, and a few individuals were physically disabled as a result of genetic disorders, accidents, and communicable diseases. On the whole, however, health was generally good.

The introduction of Western health practices corresponded largely to the establishment of bilingual school communities. Indeed, the availability of medicine, along with steel tools and other Western items, has been a major factor in encouraging families to locate near settled school communities. Missionaries affiliated with the Summer Institute of Linguistics (SIL) and, more recently, the Misión Suiza have been the primary advocates and donors of Western health care in the Machiguenga area.

Like many other domains of well-being, this good level of health was precarious and to a large extent dependent upon the outside world. Serious problems that jeopardized the good level of health care were the expense and tenuous availability of medical supplies. Practically all who had received Western medicine were in debt to the village clinic; many people's debts extended over years. Few families were able to make immediate payments, and even then could do so only if a treatment was inexpensive. The main consequence of this dilemma was that without cash it was difficult to buy new supplies. Camaná was normally in debt to another community that had begun charging interest as penalty for late payments. The entire situation was compounded by the fact that medicine prices were rising rapidly. Thus, even when payments were made promptly, they were usually insufficient to purchase replacement supplies because of higher costs.

Another threat to villagers' health in tropical rain forests is that prolonged occupation of a site encourages increased growth of parasite populations (Alland 1970:55; Neel 1974:211). And people are undoubtedly more susceptible to contagious and infectious illnesses and diseases in densely populated village settings (Kaplan, Larrick, and Yost 1984:73). It may be speculated that health concerns alone traditionally discouraged the Machiguenga from establishing densely populated, permanent settlements.

Material Culture and Protection from the Environment

The good quality of life of the Machiguenga is dependent upon the manufacture of several important "traditional" items and the availability of a few critical Western items. The raw materials needed to manufacture such important items as houses, clothes, bows and arrows, net bags, and other food procurement and utilitarian tools are generally readily available to all. And, importantly, the Machiguenga have the time and desire to make such items carefully.

The Machiguenga maintain a great deal of pride in their workmanship. All manufactured items are made of the finest materials available, and care is always taken to guarantee that items will be as practical and long-lasting as possible. Although every item could be made with less effort and in less time and still be of high quality from a practical standpoint, extra care is always taken to improve the appearance of manufactured goods. This diligence is made possible by having the time to do so.

As is the case with wild foods, the resources needed for the manufacture of certain important items become exhausted in the vicinity of a densely populated site after a few years of occupation. Housing materials, for instance, were depleted up to an hour's walk from Camaná by the end of my fieldwork. This was not a major problem at the time, since most structures were expected to last for two to three years without needing significant amounts of new materials, but it was clear that when the time came to make repairs, the labor for all households would be considerable.

The most important Western items are machetes, axes, knives, aluminum cooking pots, fishing tackle, matches, and needles. Although the members of Camaná owned very few items of Western origin—many households were limited to a single machete, an aluminum pot, and a knife, for example—few experienced undue hardship from limited supplies. All would have liked to own more of such items, but accessibility was highly dependent on individual households acquiring cash. The ability to afford such goods appears to be increasingly threatened as the rate of inflation of Peru's economy continues to skyrocket.

Social Relations

A subject deemed to be important in any evaluation of well-being is the qualitative nature of social relations. Some conflict is inevitable in any social group. All conflict in Camaná that I observed or otherwise learned about was recorded and has been documented elsewhere (Baksh 1984a: 397–442). Examples of conflict ranged from minor quarrels between spouses to a single fistfight between two men. In general, however, social relations were quite good. Relations at the level of the household were excellent: sharing and cooperation were abundant and conflict was virtually absent. Relations between closely related households were also excellent, and in general the members of Camaná were compatible with one another. An outstanding social characteristic of the community was its extensive interhousehold exchange of food and labor. A considerable amount of the sharing was not essential for physical well-being but instead reflected and encouraged the maintenance of interhousehold social fellowship.

Conflict arose during the end of my fieldwork, largely as a consequence of the increased scarcity of fish and other faunal foods. Even under the best of social arrangements, Machiguenga adults become increasingly irritable and quarrelsome when they experience declines in the availability of preferred foods, especially those that are high in fat content. Other sources of interhousehold conflict were community-organized labor, particularly for cash crop and cattle projects, community political leadership, and increased costs of health care.

Life Satisfaction

Although life satisfaction is perhaps impossible to measure, subjective evaluations based on ethnographic fieldwork are nevertheless relevant. From both etic and emic perspectives, the residents of Camaná were generally quite happy and satisfied with their lives. All adults had experienced harder and less enjoyable times in the past, but most were currently satisfied with their labor requirements and diet, enjoyed living in a large community, were pleased that their children were obtaining a "Western" education, felt safe from both outsiders and potential health problems, and enjoyed considerable leisure time. Perhaps the most common complaint was the lack of useful Western material items. This was and is, in fact, a valid concern, and the Machiguenga's inability to obtain such goods reliably is perhaps the greatest risk to their current high level of well-being.

Conditions in 1988

The most apparent change in food production I saw in 1988 was a decline in wild food procurement. After having exploited the new site for seven years, people had nearly wiped out local fish and forest game. While few quantitative data could be collected in three weeks of fieldwork, it was nevertheless obvious that people had to travel to distant streams before they stood a reasonable chance of making decent catches. Indeed, people were now traveling upriver past the old site to the most distant streams that were exploited while they lived at the old site. Round-trip travel time to these most distant streams was now two days, versus eight hours from the old site in 1981. Regardless of the yields obtained at these distant streams, the efficiency was extremely low because of the tremendous amount of time spent traveling. The lack of nearby game was also reflected in the fact that men did not carry bows and arrows for short trips out of the village. At the old site, it was common for a man to carry a bow and at least a couple of arrows on garden trips, for example, in case he encountered game along the way. In 1988 it was rare to see anyone with a bow in hand.

Surveys of subsistence gardens indicated no change in crop mixes or areas cultivated. But it must be pointed out that most households had moved their houses from the original sites to their newer producing gardens, largely to minimize travel time.

By 1988 the diet had declined in quality. I ate no forest foods in 1988, for example, and only 17 percent of all meals included some fish (this was largely because I had participated in an overnight fishing trip and contributed my catch to the household feeding me), versus 43 percent of all meals in 1979–81. The diet was already low in fat in 1979–81; in 1988 it must have been well below the daily allowances recommended by nutritional authorities.

Indeed, the nutritional status of the population in 1988 had declined since 1980. As demonstrated in Tables 9.2 and 9.3, weights had declined considerably for most age and sex categories, and as much as 19 percent for 15- to 19-year-old males. Machiguenga heights also appear to have declined from 1980 to 1988 (Table 9.4). In general, individuals most at risk appear to be young children and children in their teens.

I also witnessed considerable illness in 1988. Many people had *gripe*, and an unusually large number of people were suffering from diarrhea to the extent that they could not get out of bed.

Western medicine has been virtually unavailable for years; an inspection of the clinic showed it to be practically empty of medications. This

Table 9.2 Distribution of Weight for Height Data for Adults, School-
Aged Children, and Young Children by Percentage of
Standard

Percentage of Standard	Adults[a]		School-Aged Children[b]		Young Children[c]	
	n	%	n	%	n	%
90+	145	73.2	293	94.8	55	50.5
80–89	41	20.7	15	4.9	36	33.0
70–79	12	6.1	1	0.4	11	10.1
60–69	0	0.0	0	0.0	4	3.7
50–59	0	0.0	0	0.0	1	0.9
Below 50	0	0.0	0	0.0	2	1.8
Total	198	100.0	309	100.0	109	100.0

Note: Percentage of standard is based on Jelliffe (1966:Annex 1).
[a] Males, 20 years and older; females, 19 years and older.
[b] Males, 6–19 years; females, 6–18 years.
[c] All 0–60 months.

lack of access to medicine was reflected in a whooping cough epidemic that killed 10 people in 1986. A new problem is that medicines are hoarded by the *sanitarios* (health promoters) and a few others who can afford to buy them. This came to light when I toured the "clinic." Although I had purchased a few hundred dollars' worth of medicine in Pucallpa and had given it to the community with the understanding that patients would pay the clinic based on the price I had paid, little of this supply remained a few days after I made the donation—the sanitario explained to me that he and a few others had bought most of supplies since their families needed them or would need them someday.

The ability to purchase Western tools has clearly worsened due to the lack of cash. I saw no new machetes, and most of the old ones had been worn down to half or even a third the size of a new one. Some were no longer effective as machetes since they were the length of kitchen knives. Similarly, most cooking pots were old and many were practially useless. Few people owned fishhooks and monofilament line.

The quality of social relations, too, has not gone unscathed as Machiguenga production and economy have worsened. Although I witnessed

Table 9.3 Machiguenga Weights in 1980 and 1988

Age (years)	June 26, 1980 n	June 26, 1980 kg	July 11, 1988 n	July 11, 1988 kg	% of Change 1980 to 1988	p value (t-test)
Males						
0–4	20	10.6	16	9.0	− 15.1	
5–9	18	19.1	20	17.4	− 8.9	.05
10–14	24	29.2	14	25.6	− 12.3	.08
15–19	13	51.7	17	41.8	− 19.1	.01
20+	22	57.6	24	56.4	− 2.1	
Females						
0–4	23	11.0	20	9.6	− 12.7	.10
5–9	23	19.3	12	17.1	− 11.4	.05
10–14	23	31.6	24	26.9	− 14.9	.05
15–19	11	48.1	13	45.7	− 5.0	
20+	40	46.5	41	44.8	− 3.7	

Table 9.4 Machiguenga Heights in 1980 and 1988

Age (years)	June 26, 1980 n	June 26, 1980 cm	July 11, 1988 n	July 11, 1988 cm	% of Change 1980 to 1988	p value (t-test)
Males						
0–4	19	79	15	74	− 6.3	
5–9	18	108	20	108	0.0	
10–14	24	128	14	127	− 0.8	
15–19	13	156	17	146	− 6.4	.02
20+	24	160	43	157	− 1.9	
Females						
0–4	23	81	17	80	− 1.2	
5–9	23	107	12	108	+ 0.9	
10–14	23	130	24	127	− 2.3	
15–19	11	146	13	145	− 0.7	
20+	40	144	41	144	0.0	

no physical conflict and few arguments during my brief visit, it was clear that the village was no longer as tightly knit socially as before. Visiting was still extensive, but sharing had dropped off drastically. This was basically a consequence of there being fewer prized foods available: whereas in the past people carried strings of fish to one another daily, I did not see a single fish taken from one household to another in 1988. Similarly, whereas I commonly received pineapples, bananas, and other garden foods daily from visitors in the past, even these items were not passed along to me.

A second way in which social relations are likely reflected is in house locations. As I noted earlier, most households have relocated their houses to their newer gardens (i.e., away from the nucleus of the community, radiating outward). Although this relocation is largely for practical purposes, it is also apparent that at least some people have moved well beyond the distance necessary to minimize travel time to gardens. Indeed, a few have moved a half hour's walk or more from the village center, leaving large expanses of cultivable, uncleared forest in between.

Before leaving the topic of social relations, it is important to note one event that stunned me and left me saddened to this day. Theft is extremely rare among the Machiguenga. Although most villages can point to a child or two who have reputations for stealing fruits out of gardens or something of this order, major problems are almost unheard of and I was never the target of thievery. Within a few days of my arrival in 1988, however, several machetes were stolen from my room while I was on an overnight fishing trip. (I would not have made an issue of the problem were it not that I had brought a machete for every family and had not yet had the opportunity to see the people to whom I wanted to give these last machetes.) I described the missing machetes to my close friends, who were embarrassed and saddened but not particularly surprised because, as they explained, there were now a lot of *koshinti* (thieves) in Camaná, "like in other villages." They vowed to find the culprit, and did by the next day. As it turned out, the work was not that of an adolescent or youth, as I had expected, but rather that of a 32-year-old man and a 21-year-old man who was serving as my main field assistant! I had known and trusted both for nine years. The machetes were returned and the men apologized profusely. I am convinced that the act was committed not for any personal reasons but out of desperation somehow to improve their free-falling quality of life.

Although I had always played the role of sympathetic listener to many informants, I was kept particularly busy in 1988 listening to my old friends enumerate the problems they faced. They were particularly concerned

about their lack of important Western tools and medicines and their inability to raise cash. They were also astounded at the prices of Western
items. Clearly, people were very depressed. They seemed to feel abandoned, stating repeatedly that "no one was helping them." My impres-
sions of their depression are supported by the fact that beer drinking to
the point of drunkenness had increased significantly over that to which I
was accustomed. Indeed, during tours of the community, it was rare to
visit a household and, if the adults were home, not be offered a bowl of
masato (beer).

Economic Development

Machiguenga communities are attempting to meet their need for cash
primarily through the production of cash crops and domesticated animals.
Camaná's initial efforts focused on the production of beans, peanuts, coffee, rice, chickens, and cattle. By 1981, however, the community had yet
to realize even a modest income for its efforts; the labor expended to
produce these commodities was essentially extra labor added to that
needed for subsistence production, but with very little reward.

The cash crops that have received the most attention from the people
of Camaná are beans and peanuts. Although these crops were first acquired for seed and planted in 1976, it was not until 1980, after five
seasons, that some were finally marketed. Badly timed plantings, poor
drying and storage techniques, communal production and decision making, and lack of transportation to the market were among the reasons for
this delay. Even in 1980 the average household received the equivalent of
only U.S. $6.00, after having contributed 183 hours to the production of
that year's crops alone. From another perspective, it is important to note
that the efficiency of producing cash crops is significantly lower than that
of subsistence crops. Thus, in 1980, peanuts and beans were produced at
a rate of 0.34 kg per hour, which was less than one-tenth the efficiency of
subsistence crops (Table 9.1).

An important change in cash crop production that the Machiguenga
should consider making is a shift from communal garden production to
the cultivation of plots at the household level. One advantage of this shift
would be avoidance of a potential source of interhousehold tension, because each household would be free to choose the extent of its participation and free either to eat or to sell the yields. Second, household
production is more efficient: individuals and small groups work at higher
productive rates than large, cooperative groups. Finally, potential losses
would be minimized: gardens would not only be established at different

locations but also planted at different times. These two characteristics would provide maximum assurance of success for the community as a whole, although some individual households could conceivably suffer important losses. A number of households were experimenting with personal plots of peanuts and beans in 1981, while also participating in the village's cooperative project to raise these crops.

Another endeavor to raise cash is the tending of cattle. Camaná normally had three or four cows but, as of late 1981, had failed to market a single animal. Several reasons contributed to an inability to increase the herd, and in any case, several problems related to marketing the animals remained to be resolved. Over a period of one year, the average household contributed 52 hours of labor toward the maintenance of the cattle project. This expenditure of labor will increase drastically if the community is successful at increasing the herd size, unless several specific problems of pasturage are minimized. Poor fencing and the lack of appropriate pasturage were major problems.

Chickens offer perhaps the highest growth potential for cash sales. They can be raised relatively easily (one to two dozen animals currently require about 100 hours of labor per year), are easy to market, and command decent prices. Like other attempts to earn cash, however, chicken production is of little success. This is largely due to a high mortality rate: many newborn chicks die because of poor nutrition, and over one-third of all mature birds are eaten by wildcats. Minimally, improved feeding techniques and secure housing need to be adopted.

In 1988, Camaná's ability to produce cash was no greater than it had been a decade before. Indeed, people had almost abandoned efforts to raise peanuts and beans on a scale that would be economical for marketing. They made a few more attempts to grow these crops while at the new site, but production and marketing problems continued. Similarly, rice and coffee have not done well.

I have only been able to hint at ways in which economic development might be improved (see Baksh 1984a:250–86 for more details). The point is that research by anthropologists on alternative strategies of food and cash production is critical and can contribute to appropriate economic development. A major contribution that anthropologists should make toward the well-being of Amazonian societies is to document and subsequently facilitate the exchange of subsistence and economic-development knowledge and expertise among such populations (Sponsel 1986:82).

It is clear that Camaná progressed little in its efforts to generate income during the 1980s. The inability to produce a cash crop efficiently, together with the fact that the 250 members of the community made such an impact on the local environment of their "new" site over almost seven years, led to a decline in their quality of life in several important ways. It is clear that if the Machiguenga are to have any chance of sustaining the high quality of life that they have recently enjoyed, it will be necesary for them to limit the size of settlements and to generate cash to purchase critical Western goods.

Conclusions

Involvement in the market economy did not increase for the community of Camaná during the 1980s. Indeed, the community has not yet adopted a commodity that can be produced efficiently and marketed easily. As a consequence, its ability to obtain critical Western tools such as machetes and cooking pots and Western medicines such as penicillin and immunizations against various infectious diseases is precarious at best. And when cash is generated, the rapid rate of inflation of Peru's economy weakens what otherwise might be attractive purchasing power. If the Machiguenga could generate cash in proportion to the increased costs of outside goods, the inflation problem would be minimized—but this appears unlikely in the foreseeable future. Importantly, should the availability of steel tools be cut off (due to expense or lack of access), the efficiency of agricultural food production would decrease significantly, greater dependence would rest upon wild food procurement, overall subsistence work time and effort would increase drastically, and diet and health would be less secure.

Amazonian cultural ecologists and other anthropologists are in an important position to contribute to appropriate economic development. A major contribution would be to facilitate the exchange of subsistence and economic knowledge and expertise between societies. For example, because the Machiguenga are experts at producing subsistence crops, their knowledge and skills would no doubt benefit nonindigenous groups settling in the Amazon. Similarly, because the Machiguenga lack experience in raising and marketing crops and animals for cash, which they sorely need, they would no doubt benefit from learning the skills of others.

References Cited

Alland, Alexander
1970   *Adaptation in Cultural Evolution: An Approach to Medical Anthropology.*
        New York: Columbia University Press.

Baksh, Michael
1984a   Cultural Ecology and Change of the Machiguenga Indians of the Peruvian Amazon. Ph.D dissertation, University of California, Los Angeles.
1984b   The Significance of Dietary Fat for Machiguenga Subsistence Practices and Health. Paper presented at the 83rd annual meeting of the American Anthropological Association, Denver, Colorado.
1985   Faunal Food as a "Limiting Factor" on Amazonian Cultural Behavior: A Machiguenga Example. *Research in Economic Anthropology* 7:145–75.

Baksh, Michael, and Allen Johnson
1990   Insurance Policies Among the Machiguenga: An Anthropological Analysis of Risk Management in a Non-Market Economy. In *Risk and Uncertainty in Tribal and Peasant Societies,* edited by Elizabeth Cashdan, pp. 193–227. Boulder, Colo.: Westview Press.

Behrens, Clifford A.
1986   Shipibo Food Categorization and Preference: Relationships Between Indigenous and Western Dietary Concepts. *American Anthropologist* 88(3):647–58.

Davis, Bruce E.
1986   Quality of Life in Small Island Nations in the Indian Ocean. *Human Ecology* 14(4):453–71.

Food and Agriculture Organization (FAO)
1980   *Dietary Fats and Oils in Human Nutrition.* Food and Nutrition Series, no. 20. Rome: FAO.

Jelliffe, D. B.
1966   *The Assessment of the Nutritional Status of the Community.* Geneva: World Health Organization.

Johnson, Allen
1978   In Search of the Affluent Society. *Human Nature* 1(9):50–59.
1980   On the Appropriate Development of the Lands of Amazonia. Paper read at the 26th annual meeting of the Pacific Coast Council on Latin American Studies, Laguna Beach, California.
1983   Machiguenga Gardens. In *Adaptive Responses of Native Amazonians,* edited by R. Hames and W. Vickers, pp. 29–63. New York: Academic Press.

Johnson, Allen, and Michael Baksh
1987   Ecological and Structural Influences on the Proportions of Wild Foods in the Diets of Two Machiguenga Communities. In *Food and Evolution: Toward a Theory of Human Food Habits,* edited by Marvin Harris and Eric B. Ross, pp. 387–405. Philadelphia: Temple University Press.

Johnson, Allen, and Clifford Behrens
1982   Nutritional Criteria in Machiguenga Food Production Decisions: A Linear-Programming Analysis. *Human Ecology* 10(2):167–89.

Kaplan, Jonathan E., James W. Larrick, and James A. Yost
1984   Workup on the Waorani. *Natural History* 9:68–75.

Moran, Emilio F.
1983   Growth Without Development: Past and Present Development Efforts
          in Amazonia. In *The Dilemma of Amazonian Development*, edited by
          Emilio F. Moran, pp. 3–23. Boulder, Colo.: Westview Press.

Moran, Emilio F., and Rafael Herrera
1984   Human Ecology in the Amazon Basin. *Interciencia* 9(6):342–43.

Neel, James
1974   Control of Disease Among Amerindians in Cultural Transition. *Bulletin*
          of the Pan American Health Organization 8:205–11.

Posey, Darrell
1983   Indigenous Ecological Knowledge and Development of the Amazon. In
          The Dilemma of Amazonian Development, edited by Emilio F. Moran, pp.
          225–57. Boulder, Colo.: Westview Press.

Scheer, Lore
1980   Experience with Quality of Life Comparisons. In *The Quality of Life:*
          Comparative Studies, edited by Alexander Szalai and Frank M. Andrews,
          pp. 145–55. Beverly Hills: Sage Publications.

Sponsel, Leslie E.
1986   Amazon Ecology and Adaptation. *Annual Review of Anthropology*
          15:67–97.

10

Neotropical Foraging Adaptations and the Effects of Acculturation on Sustainable Resource Use

The Yuquí of Lowland Bolivia

Allyn MacLean Stearman

For many generations, the Yuquí Indians successfully exploited the tropical rain forest of lowland Bolivia as true foragers. Their understanding of the dynamics of the tropical forest ecosystem, their mobility patterns, and their effective social strategies contributed to this adaptive success. Eventually, incipient encroachment by Bolivian settlers into Yuquí territory led to contact with missionaries and sedentarization of the first band of Yuquí in 1968. Although many of their previous subsistence patterns underwent significant changes as the result of missionization, for almost two decades the Yuquí continued to provision themselves primarily from forest products. By the late 1980s, however, new waves of colonists began moving into the area, leading to competition for resources, which resulted in a serious depletion of fish and game. These and other effects of colonist incursion, such as environmental alteration and habitat fragmentation, have contributed to the Yuquí's increasing dependence on cultivated crops and food subsidies provided by the mission.

Yuquí Ethnohistory and Habitat

Linguistic and historical evidence indicates that the Yuquí are probably remnants of a larger Tupí-Guaraní–speaking population that migrated into what is now lowland Bolivia a few centuries prior to the European invasion. Wars with the Spaniards led to the reduction of Guaraní populations in lowland Bolivia and their ultimate incorporation into the emergent mestizo, or "mixed," society as part of the evangelization efforts of Catholic missionaries. A few groups apparently escaped the process of missionization and acculturation until well into the twentieth century by retreating into inaccessible areas of the tropical forest. The Yuquí are most likely descendants of these fugitives and were among the last of the forest nomads in Bolivia to undergo sedentarization and acculturation.

Today the Yuquí number less than 150, having suffered population loss from disease and infrequent but deadly encounters with Bolivian hunters and loggers in the years prior to contact. There is little evidence indicating what their original numbers might have been, and Yuquí themselves remember few events of their past. Nonetheless, it is quite certain that their unusual lack of cultural elaboration, to be described briefly below, can be attributed to deculturation as the result of their long-term isolation and gradual but steady population loss (Stearman 1984).

By their own reports and those of the missionaries who accompanied them during the initial years of contact in the 1950s and 1960s, the Yuquí avoided detection and survived as true foragers by moving almost constantly, rarely camping in any one location for more than three to four days. They built no structures, using only a few palm fronds to cover their hammocks during cold or rainy weather; and they could not produce their own fire, which had to be carefully preserved. The Yuquí had no religious specialists, wore no clothing, did not make use of body ornamentation, had only a rudimentary cosmology, did not construct canoes and could not swim, and had a limited tool inventory. Their material culture consisted primarily of a black palm bow over 2 m in length, two types of arrows, an agouti incisor nocking tool, a string hammock made from *Cecropia* bark, a baby sling of the same fiber, and a few rudimentary palm baskets (see Stearman 1989b for a more extensive description of these articles). Most remarkably, they practiced no horticulture whatsoever and had no significant external source of food. Trading relationships did not exist, since all non-Yuquí were considered enemies and Yuquí bands, probably few in number, seldom came in contact with one other.[1]

In 1968, the first of what were believed to be three remaining bands of Yuquí was successfully contacted by a group of North American Protestant missionaries and settled on a mission station on the Chimoré River (64°56′50″ W and 16°47′00″ S). At the time of contact, this band numbered 43 people. Including the two additional bands whose populations at contact in the late 1980s numbered 23 and 24 individuals, respectively, the Yuquí occupied a range that encompassed approximately 4,500 km² (fig. 10.1).

The Chimoré mission station, Biá Recuaté ("place of the people"), is located near the base of the Andes at an elevation of about 250 m and is covered by moist tropical forest. The area is marked by continuous activity of white-water rivers that periodically overflow their banks or change

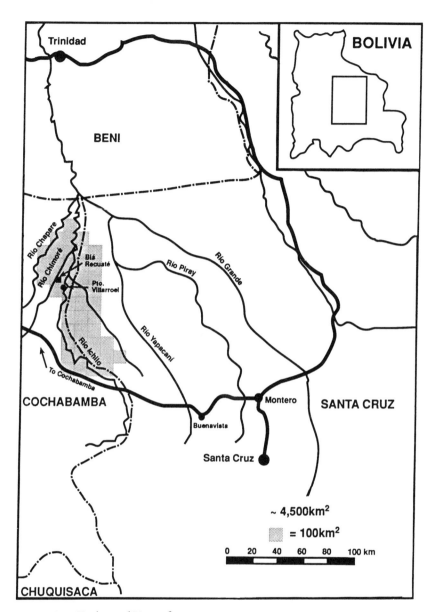

Figure 10.1. Traditional Yuquí foraging territory.

course, creating large flooded areas of palm forest, primarily *Iriartea* and *Socratea*, and patches of arrow cane (*Gynerium saggitatum*), in addition to other microhabitats formed or influenced by these disturbances. The region is known for its very short dry season, usually the months of July and August, which also experience periodic cold fronts, or *surazos*, frequently accompanied by strong winds. Temperatures may vary from 39°C in February to 4°C in July, and rainfall averages 4,000 mm annually.

The Yuquí's ability to lead a successful foraging existence in this region prior to and following contact (although in a modified form) depended on a series of interlinked environmental and cultural factors. These factors included an understanding of the dynamics of the Neotropical ecosystem in which they foraged and the development of cultural responses to that ecosystem.

Traditional Foraging Patterns Among the Yuquí

Ecological Diversity, Patch Dynamics, and Mobility

The nature of the Yuquí's successful relationship with their environment is best understood in terms of the dynamics of the forest they inhabited. Of particular interest and importance is the habitat diversity, or "texture," found in the Neotropical forest that provides the mosaic of resources exploited by the Yuquí.

The spatial and temporal texture of Neotropical forests is created by "patch dynamics," the continuous opening of gaps of various sizes and shapes in the forest canopy caused by natural processes such as river activity and tree falls (Begon, Harper, and Townsend 1990). This disturbance regime contributes to the constant turnover of species in any given area, and thus it is an important factor in maintaining biological diversity not just in superficial terms of absolute species number but, more importantly, in terms of species composition (Denslow 1987; Denslow et al. 1990; Foster 1980; Gentry and Terborgh 1990; Hartshorn 1978; Putz and Brokaw 1989; Salo et al. 1986).

Gap formation gives rise to site-specific assemblages of flora and fauna different from those normally found under the closed canopy. Herbaceous and/or fruit-bearing, light-tolerant pioneer species, which often are important game animal attractants (Foster 1980; Fragoso 1991; Levey 1988a, 1988b), proliferate under these circumstances (Odum 1971). Canopy trees at the edges of gaps also tend to produce larger fruit crops than they do in closed forest, show less seasonality in fruit production, have longer fruiting episodes, and often produce asynchronously with conspecifics (Levey n.d.). Far from being a place of "homogenous complexity"—a biome rich in species but with a predictable "evenness" over the landscape—the Neotropical forest is better described as exhibiting constant variation in time and space.

The patchwork mosaic of the Neotropical forest also has been shown to provide select foraging sites with resource flushes, particularly fruit and the animals that feed on it. For example, the dense, monospecific stands of fruit-bearing trees, or "oligarchic forests," that form in Amazonia as a consequence of severe flooding, shallow soils, or frequent disturbance are important sources of nutrition for humans as well as wildlife (Peters et al. 1989). In other instances, large quantities of a given resource—fish, honey, or white-lipped peccaries—are also harvested from a single patch, providing the group with substantial nourishment over extended periods of time.

Finally, the constant disturbance caused by river activity and windstorms in the Yuquí region results in the formation of resource patches that are not so widely distributed over the landscape as to make foraging unfeasible. Each of these factors contributes to the biological diversity necessary for Yuquí foraging success. This habitat variation and the ability to use it to advantage through high mobility forms the core of Yuquí traditional subsistence strategies.

It is clear that in the years prior to contact, the mobility patterns of the Yuquí were determined primarily by two factors: (1) the Yuquí's knowledge of fruiting phenologies and locations of important plant resources; and (2) their knowledge of fish and game behavior, and particularly of animals' feeding habits. Because the two factors are intimately related, it is difficult to separate them analytically; and from the Yuquí perspective, hunting and gathering are often synchronous activities. Yuquí patterns of social interaction such as those manifested in task performance result in foraging strategies that contribute to the effective exploitation of the forest mosaic.

Social Adaptations and Foraging Effectiveness

Although women tend to do more gathering and men more hunting, these are not mutually exclusive activities and can be combined in a number of ways. Gathering often occurs during a hunt, carried out opportunistically by a group of men as they move through the forest in search of game, or opportunistically by both men and women when women are actively participating in the tracking, calling, and retrieving of game (and even in the killing if the animal is wounded or can be taken by hand). Gathering is also done by women who accompany hunters to exploit currently available plant resources in the area where the hunt is to occur and to check on the status of resources intended for future use; by groups of men and women whose primary interest is in gathering a previously noted resource but who may hunt or fish along the way as a secondary activity; and by groups of women who make special trips for the purpose of exploiting a known resource but who may encounter game animals, particularly fossorial or slow-moving species, that can be killed by hand. In the past, the band's daily movements were in large part determined by which of these strategies was most promising. Women frequently accompany men on the hunt and actively participate in hunting activities, although they do not use the bow to hunt game. Several of the older men confirmed that in the years prior to contact, some women learned to use a small bow well enough to kill fish.

This overlap of gender roles and simultaneous foraging activities led to an extremely effective mode of exploitation of forest resources. Although I have documented amounts of fish, game, honey, and plant products brought back by Yuquí parties following daily or extended foraging episodes (Stearman 1989a, 1989b, 1990), it is evident that a great many items never reach camp and thus escape inclusion in any inventory.

The Yuquí have an almost uncanny ability to cognitively mark resources for later use. Much of this marking is achieved through group rather than individual memory. Very little conversation strays far from people's primary interest in food getting. During rest periods or at night, hunting stories are retold and a verbal record of each day's expedition is shared with the group. Since redistribution of food was so critical to Yuquí survival prior to contact, and hoarding of food was virtually impossible given that each band lived in a single camp, there was no advantage to keeping food source information from one's peers. This constant sharing of information further contributed to effective resource use in that items noted but left unexploited by one foraging party could be utilized by another.

Diet Breadth and the Forest Mosaic

The Yuquí's diet includes all edible plants known to them and most animals. Their only functional dietary taboos include insects (including palm grubs but not bee larvae), bats, and snakes. Given the opportunity, they consume carrion eaters and all mammalian carnivores. Other dietary taboos, particularly those involving large game animals, are often ignored by those Yuquí temporarily affected by them. Game meat and fish are the preferred foods, although fishing was restricted primarily to nonriverine sources prior to contact. Until that time, the Yuquí avoided large rivers, where they were likely to encounter mestizos and run the risk of being shot. Even had they not feared for their safety, the Yuquí lacked the technology to harvest river fish efficiently. Nonetheless, oxbow lakes or depressions in the forest floor (the latter often the result of multiple tree falls in which complete uprooting creates root pits that may be of considerable size) were and continue to be extremely important, rich sources of fish, as well as sites where turtles and caiman may be found. These lakes and ephemeral ponds are periodically replenished by stream overflow and are exploited with the bow and arrow, by hand, with fish baskets, or with *barbasco* (Yuquí: *chimbó*) vine poison. Although these sites are heavily utilized during the dry season when fish become concentrated and sluggish in the increasingly shallow and rapidly heating water, they are surveyed for potential catches throughout the year.

Although numerous foraging activities are carried out while hunting, the dietary preference for meat means that when it is plentiful, virtually nothing else is eaten. Thus, while Yuquí men and women carry out alternative strategies for resource use, the primary focus is always on securing large amounts of meat that will carry the group along for several days at a time. Knowing the fruiting phenologies of plant taxa enables the Yuquí to successfully harvest arboreal mammalian species such as primates, terrestrial mammalian species such as tapir, peccary, deer, and paca, and the larger avian species such as curassow, guan, and tinamou. Once a fruit source is located, it frequently serves a dual purpose: it can be exploited for the game animals it attracts and for the fruit itself, since many of the fruits eaten by animals may also be edible by humans (Redford, Klein, and Murcia 1992).

Episodes of resource scarcity, primarily during the dry season, were mitigated by high mobility, a fine-tuned knowledge of local habitats, and the availability of "keystone resources" that could see the Yuquí through periods of dietary stress. Although the concept of keystone resources is defined by ecologists in a number of ways, one application of the term involves critical resources that carry a population through periodic lean times (Terborgh 1986:371–72). Fish are an important keystone resource for the Yuquí during the dry season, when other food sources are unavailable. Honey is another keystone resource; honey consumption increases during periods of scarcity not only because additional carbohydrates are needed to replace seasonally scarce sources of calories but also because bees store honey during the dry season in preparation for scarcities of their own during the rains, when fruit is plentiful but nectar and pollen are in short supply (Kempff Mercado 1980:2). Hence, supplies of honey tend to be greater precisely at the time of the year when human foragers must find replacements for calories normally provided by other resources.

Like many foraging peoples, the Yuquí eat the entire contents of a hive, including pollen (its digestibility by humans is still being debated), royal jelly, propolis (a substance reported to contain antibiotic properties [Dadant and Sons 1975]), and fat-rich larvae. And on those days when nothing else was available, the Yuquí ate starchy palm hearts, cooked or raw. To the Yuquí, who nonetheless like this food and its mild taste, palm heart was "starvation food," meaning that it was not as satisfying as meat, fish, honey, or oil-rich palm fruits, but they could stay alive on it for short periods of time until they located a more nutritious food source.

The Effects of Social and Ecological Change on Traditional Yuquí Subsistence Patterns

Contact and Sedentarism

Contact with outsiders and sedentarism had almost immediate impacts on Yuquí strategies for exploiting resources, with overt as well as more subtle effects on their habitat. Sedentarism, however, was a slow process that took an additional five years once peaceful contact had been achieved in 1968. During the interim, the Yuquí continued to make extended treks of several months' duration, returning each time to a site near the missionary station on the Chimoré River. According to mission personnel, these treks slowly shortened until the Yuquí took up permanent residence at the mission camp. From that time hence, foraging trips tended to be of a single day's duration, with individuals or small groups leaving camp early each day to return in the evening. Until recently, as will be discussed below, extended overnight trips were relatively rare.

Once relations of trust had been established between the Yuquí and the missionaries, Yuquí men were taught to use firearms and given opportunities to purchase them in exchange for fish, game, or labor supplied to mission personnel. In general, younger men acquired firearms more readily than senior males, who were somewhat fearful of these weapons and consequently had greater difficulty in learning to use them safely and effectively. Many of the older men were also reluctant to work for others—which, by traditional custom, meant loss of esteem—to earn the cash necessary to purchase a firearm. Consequently, within a short period of time, younger hunters were beginning to eclipse the senior Yuquí men in hunting success, relegating them to positions of lesser status within the group (Stearman 1989a).

Another technological innovation, the use of canoes, also began to create inequalities among hunters. Only a few Yuquí hunters, again tending to be the younger men, learned to make dugout canoes and handle them on the treacherous Chimoré River. This not only extended their hunting range up and down the river but also gave them access to the area on the opposite bank. As might be expected under conditions of sedentarism, the immediate environs around camp quickly felt the impact of frequent hunts. Since access to the other side of the river was restricted by the availability of canoes, this area did not experience the same hunting pressure as did the camp side and therefore continued to provide good hunting (Stearman 1990).

Metal tools such as axes and machetes increased the Yuquí's ability to secure fruit and honey, but with several negative consequences exacerbated by their sedentary existence. Like every other activity associated with subsistence, fruit and honey gathering initially was concentrated in those areas near camp but gradually expanded outward as resources were overexploited. Instead of climbing trees to extract fruit and honey, the Yuquí now felled these trees with axes. In cases where the trees were large, the expenditure of energy was much greater than had they been climbed, although the threat of death or injury from falling was eliminated.[2] At the same time, honey trees were also felled, affecting available hiving locations for bees, at least in areas contiguous to camp. In the past, the massive and sharply pointed bow stave was used as a pry bar to extract honey from bee holes, more often than not leaving a space suitable for rapid recolonization by new swarms.

Although many preferred species, such as primates, were nearly eliminated from the 5-kilometer radius around camp most frequently hunted by the Yuquí, others were not. This was due in large part to the availability of an alternative and dependable source of meat in the form of river fish. Stress on the most heavily hunted areas around camp was mitigated by the abundance of fish in the Chimoré River and the Yuquí's access to new technologies for exploiting this resource. In addition to canoes, the Yuquí had also learned to use hook and line and gill nets, supplied to them through the mission store. Fish were taken from the river year-round, but with periodic windfalls coming between flood stages that left fish trapped in ponds on the beaches. Because several men or boys fished the river each day and shared their catch with the entire band, the pressure to hunt on a daily basis was lowered significantly.

The frequent appearances of large, mobile herds of white-lipped peccaries were also important in maintaining Yuquí dietary levels under conditions of sedentarism. With firearms, the Yuquí were able to kill up to 16 or 20 at a time, representing a significant amount of meat that could be smoked and eaten over several days. Since these herds moved through the area quite regularly and the Yuquí were now able to travel up and down the river in canoes to track the animals' crossings, sedentarism did not seem to negatively affect the Yuquí's ability to exploit them. Having more efficient technologies may actually have improved their success rate, but apparently without severely depleting these herds, which can reach sizes of 150 to 200 individuals. After almost 19 years of hunting in the same area, in 1983 the Yuquí were not only still harvesting adequate numbers of collared and white-lipped peccaries to meet their dietary needs but also continuing to find capybara, deer, and tapir regularly.

Continual access to river fish and periodic windfalls of large herding mammals evidently created a delicate equilibrium allowing the Yuquí to remain sedentary foragers. In the long view, however, sedentarism forced the Yuquí to focus their subsistence base on a few keystone resources that had become important year-round. The 5-kilometer high-use zone extending outward from the mission continued to provide game, although on a much reduced basis, as did the extended-use zone comprising an additional 5-kilometer radius. Both areas enjoyed the artificial effect of having the surrounding forest, so long as it was intact, serve as a source for restocking prey species. Thus the apparent sustainability of Yuquí subsistence under conditions of sedentarism was precarious, and any perturbation was likely to have deleterious effects on Yuquí well-being.

Although indications in 1983 were that resources, especially game animals, were still keeping pace with exploitation by the Yuquí, even with an increase in population, it would be naive to assume that this equilibrium could be maintained indefinitely. For example, Yuquí population is now increasing much faster than the probable growth rate under precontact conditions. With the advent of mission intervention inhibiting female infanticide,[3] with daily medical attention that has lowered mortality, and with the successful contact and incorporation of two more bands in 1986 and 1989, Yuquí numbers have grown from 43 at initial contact in 1968 to 127 in 1990. Ideally, the problem of population growth could be mitigated by setting up satellite villages in more remote areas of the forest where either colonist or Yuquí hunting as yet has had little effect on existing faunal resources (see also Sponsel 1981). However, three factors have interceded to make the success of this plan unlikely.

First, the Yuquí mission, Biá Recuaté, is now considered part of the Bolivian nation and as such is required by law to provide primary education to Yuquí children. This places Yuquí parents in the untenable position of having to leave children behind with relatives (something that is not part of Yuquí tradition and creates tension in the community) in order to go off on an extended foraging trip. Second, the Yuquí are now dependent on the availability of medical attention, commercial goods they now consider necessities, and the social environment fostered by the mission, which offers daily activities as well as security from the outside world. Consequently, the Yuquí have no desire to return to their previous isolated existence as forest dwellers.

Third, and most importantly, the area where the Yuquí live is rapidly being settled by mestizos who are seriously and perhaps irreversibly affecting the resource base on which the Yuquí depend. If resource competition from colonists and habitat fragmentation due to land clearing by settlers continues at its present pace, the establishment of satellite communities would offer only a temporary solution to the growing problem of meat scarcity. Primarily as a result of settler encroachment, perturbations that could destabilize the resource equilibrium achieved under conditions of sedentarism are now in evidence.

The Effects of Settler Incursion on Yuquí Resource Use

Research results obtained in 1988 indicate that the Yuquí are currently experiencing resource stress and that much of this stress can be attributed to the movement of colonists into their foraging territory. A drop in daily per capita meat consumption from 440 g to 200 g between 1983 and 1988 is perhaps the most direct indicator of the results of this intrusion. A more detailed account of this problem has been published elsewhere (Stearman 1990); however, a brief review of the more pertinent aspects of this encroachment is relevant here.

Colonists in the Yuquí area are engaged primarily in the production of coca, which is harvested approximately three times a year. The crop requires little attention, freeing colonists to return to their places of origin to engage in other economic activities between harvests. Colonists plant very few food crops because they do not remain in the area long enough to tend them and there is no real economic need to engage in subsistence farming. Consequently, coca growers, much more than traditional settlers, depend on fish and game for meat. Although they often use hunting and fishing technologies that are not much more sophisticated than those presently employed by the Yuquí, colonists are more agressive in their exploitation in order to acquire a surplus, often to sell to other colonists.

In addition, many colonists are ex-miners who are adept at using dynamite to kill fish, a highly destructive fishing technology that affects the entire reproductive cycle of resident species. Those colonists who hunt often use dogs that are skilled at tracking and bringing game to ground. As yet, the Yuquí have not come to appreciate the use of hunting dogs and find the few that have been introduced into camp both a nuisance and a source of disputes over meat presumably stolen from the open houses by these pets. Because of dietary preferences, colonists tend to pursue certain types of game animals, particularly the large mammals whose meat resembles that of domestic animals (see Beckerman 1978; Redford and Robinson 1987). Thus, to borrow a forestry term, colonists tend to "high grade" the forest in selecting the larger, more desirable game animals.

With the disturbance to the landscape caused by settled agriculturalists, many of the migratory animals, especially white-lipped peccaries, apparently have moved out of the area entirely or have disappeared (see Campos 1977). As of 1990, the Yuquí had not seen a white-lipped peccary in five years. Indications are that tapir, deer, and capybara are also in decline. The latter are not considered edible by colonists but are a crop nuisance and so are killed whenever encountered.

The advent of colonization in the region opened new transportation routes and brought more traffic through the area. It was not long until local fishers saw an increase in the demand for fish as well as the feasibility of long-distance transport of their product. In 1987, fishers began coming up the Chimoré River from nearby port towns in boats outfitted with ice chests and large gill nets capable of spanning the entire river. Within a matter of months the river had been fished out. Differences in Yuquí fishing success between 1983 and 1988 were remarkable, even accounting for seasonal variation. The take for the 56-day sample in 1983 was 1,055 kg, while that for the same period in 1988 was only 59 kg.

The loss of large game mammals and fish has resulted in what appears to be overexploitation of smaller, less desirable species that are now being hunted at apparently unsustainable rates. In 1983, five species (red brocket deer, tapir, capybara, collared peccary, and white-lipped peccary) accounted for 63 percent, by weight, of all game taken; in 1988 no tapir, capybara, or white-lipped peccary was captured, although the total weight of meat taken remained about the same. The difference in 1988 was made up by harvesting larger numbers of smaller animals. Thus, in 1983, small animals (<5 kg) comprised 62 percent of the take by weight, while in 1988 they made up 88 percent.

This trend is also reflected in the increased numbers of both individuals and taxa harvested: in 1983, 156 individual animals representing 27 taxa were captured, as compared to 348 individuals representing 44 taxa in 1988. The Yuquí are also having to undertake longer and farther trips to find game to meet their needs. During the 1983 research period, only two overnight hunts occurred; in 1988 this number increased to 19 for the same length of time. Further exacerbating the problem was the continued scarcity of fish. As of mid-1990, the Chimoré River still had not returned to its former abundance, even though commercial fishing and the use of dynamite had been greatly curtailed.

Market Integration and Resource Use

As the result of increasing contact with colonists and other Bolivians, the Yuquí are gradually being drawn into the national market economy. Previously, the mission store provided for their needs in a highly paternalistic and artificial economic system whereby the Yuquí earned wages from the mission by doing chores (mowing the airstip, maintaining mission buildings, etc.), and the wages could then be converted into trade goods. While the mission was scrupulous in charging fair prices for the goods it provided (normally cost plus transportation fees), through this system the Yuquí gained little understanding of the mechanics of a market economy.

Now they are venturing out to colonists' homesteads and small villages, which each year move closer to Biá Recuaté. The colonists, often in need of fresh meat, fish, and fruit, encourage the Yuquí to give up their small supplies of forest and river products in exchange for store-baked bread, candy, and cookies, items rarely available at the mission store. As has been the case with many indigenous peoples who have little else to trade, the commercialization of forest products that may be part of the subsistence base becomes an all too common pattern (Stearman and Redford 1992). The colonists are also unconcerned about cheating the Yuquí, who, as newcomers to the system, are easily taken advantage of in a world that operates under the maxim "buyer beware."

As resources are further depleted by competition from settlers and the Yuquí's own subsistence demands, which are exacerbated by sedentarism, a growing population, and a desire to provide forest products to colonists in exchange for consumer goods, the Yuquí will be forced to clear more and more of their forest for crops to meet both subsistence and market needs. In doing so, they are sealing the fate of many of the local wildlife and plant populations on which they have traditionally depended. For the present, however, the mission continues to supply the Yuquí with staples such as rice, corn, soy and wheat flour, and pasta, much of it donated, an undependable and habituating dietary subsidy that tends to mask the faltering natural system.

Conclusion

The sustainability of traditional Yuquí subsistence depended on a fine-tuned knowledge of the environment and on freedom of movement over a large territory to exploit resources within it. With sedentarism, sustainability was maintained with the addition of river fish to the diet as well as the continuing presence of large herding animals that moved through the area on a relatively dependable basis. But this system remained in equilibrium only as long as the natural resources of the local catchment area continued to be supplemented by external inputs. Restocking of the Chimoré River from upstream and down, along with continual replacement of game species from unhunted areas of the forest, prevented a resource deficit. The distances and areas involved in sustaining this restocking are unknown. What is certain is that once the critical keystone resources of fish and large game were depleted as a result of competition from settlers now occupying portions of these restocking areas, the apparent stability of Yuquí subsistence was threatened. They are now compensating for declining meat yields by harvesting larger numbers of smaller species and going farther to get them. From all indications, foraging is no longer functioning at a level that will indefinitely sustain either the Yuquí or the faunal resources they draw upon.

For the present, the Yuquí still enjoy the freedom of the hunt, a way of life far removed from what they view as the monotonous toil of working a field. Although the Yuquí are gradually learning to become agriculturalists, status, prestige, and respect, for both men and women, are determined by one's ability to use the forest knowledgeably and productively. The complex mosaic of the forest, however, is being rapidly and perhaps irrevocably altered by colonists clearing homesteads, and now by the Yuquí themselves. If the Yuquí eventually become recipients of a legally titled territory, it is unlikely that this area will be large enough to support the diversity and density of game animals necessary for long-term sustainable hunting if foraging increasingly becomes a means of meeting demands for trade goods. Under these conditions, the Yuquí face the almost inevitable prospect of joining the ranks of other indigenous peasants of Amazonia who trade farm surplus for commodities in a system known for its gross exploitation of the native producer.

Even so, there exists the strong possibility that the Yuquí as a people may not survive the process of acculturation. As a small, technologically simple, and politically unsophisticated indigenous population that was thrust suddenly into membership in a nation-state, the Yuquí are ill-prepared to deal with the changes that are now affecting their lives. They are responding in understandable ways to the seductiveness of becoming participants in Bolivian society without fully comprehending the consequences of this participation in terms of their cultural persistence as a people. Unfortunately, the Yuquí still lack the leadership skills and knowledge of the outside world to make informed decisions concerning their own future: to carefully select those aspects of the Western world that they feel will best suit their own interests and not be swayed by people claiming to know what those interests should be. If they do not have the time and opportunity to acquire such skills, these changes will irrevocably alter the Yuquí's fragile cohesiveness and lead to their destruction as a people.

Acknowledgments

Research support for the results described here was provided by the National Science Foundation (BNS-8706958 and BNS-9010248), the Charles A. Lindbergh Fund, the L. S. B. Leakey Foundation, the Explorer's Club, the Amazon Research and Training Program of the University of Florida, and the Division of Sponsored Research, University of Central Florida. A version of this paper was presented at the American Anthropological Association invited session, "Tropical Forest Ecology, The Changing Human Niche, and Deforestation," in New Orleans, November 29–30, 1990. I would like to acknowledge those colleagues whose helpful comments and criticisms contributed to the development of many of the ideas presented here: Bob Bailey, Chris Canaday, Pete Feinsinger, Tom Headland, Kent Redford, and Les Sponsel.

Notes

1. The fissioning of bands into smaller units was evidently a frequent event occasioned by arguments, commonly over sexual transgressions. Normally, these fragmented bands would reunite after a few days or weeks as tempers cooled. On at least three occasions, however, the group presently at the Chimoré mission fissioned permanently, and relations were so hostile between the members that once separated, they did not see each other again until many years later, when missionary contact reunited them. By then, the original protagonists had died and many of the younger band members were little concerned about the divisive event.

2. In December 1990 a Yuquí hunter died as the result of a fall from a tree that he had climbed to retrieve a game animal. This recent event and others in the past in which Yuquí have lost their lives or have been severely injured make the fear of falling from a tree a very real one.

3. Although greatly discouraged by the missionaries, infanticide, particularly of infant females, does occur from time to time. From the Yuquí perspective, a first-born female is undesirable for very pragmatic reasons. A Yuquí woman knows that she will most likely outlive her husband. Without an adult son to hunt for her, she will have a difficult time surviving in her later years. While daughters are esteemed as well, their husbands cannot be counted on to provision the mother-

in-law in addition to other family members. Thus the necessity of having an older male child overrides other concerns of Yuquí women.

References Cited

Beckerman, Stephen
1978   Comment on Ross. *Current Anthropology* 19:17–18.

Begon, Michael, John L. Harper, and Colin R. Townsend
1990   *Ecology. Individuals, Populations, and Communities.* Boston: Blackwell Scientific Publications.

Campos, R.
1977   Producción y pesca y caza en una comunidad Shipibo en el río Pisqui. *Amazonia Peruana* 2(2):34–56.

Dadant and Sons, eds.
1975   *The Hive and the Honey Bee.* Hamilton, Ill.: Dadant and Sons.

Denslow, Julie S.
1987   Tropical Rainforest Gaps and Tree Species Diversity. *Annual Review of Ecology and Systematics* 18:431–52.

Denslow, Julie S., J. C. Schultz, P. M. Vitousek, and B. R. Strain
1990   Growth Responses of Tropical Shrubs to Treefall Gap Environments. *Ecology* 71:165–79.

Foster, Robin B.
1980   Heterogeneity and Disturbance in Tropical Vegetation. In *Conservation Biology: An Evolutionary-Ecological Perspective*, edited by Michael E. Soule and Bruce A. Wilcox, pp. 75–92. Sunderland, Mass.: Sinauer.

Fragoso, José
1991   Effect of Hunting on Tapirs in Belize. In *Neotropical Wildlife Use and Conservation*, edited by J. G. Robinson and Kent H. Redford, pp. 154–62. Chicago: University of Chicago Press.

Gentry, Alwyn H., and John Terborgh
1990   Composition and Dynamics of the Cocha Cashu "Mature" Floodplain Forest. In *Four Neotropical Rainforests*, edited by Alwyn H. Gentry, pp. 542–64. New Haven: Yale University Press.

Hartshorn, Gary S.
1978   Treefalls and Tropical Forest Dynamics. In *Trees as Living Systems*, edited by P. B. Tomlinson and M. H. Zimmerman. New York: Cambridge University Press.

Kempff Mercado, Noel
1980   *Flora apicola subtropical de Bolivia.* Santa Cruz, Bolivia: Universidad Mayor Gabriel Rene Moreno.

Levey, Douglas J.
1988a   Spatial and Temporal Variation in Costa Rican Fruit-Eating Bird Abun-
         dance. *Ecological Monographs* 58(4):251–69.
1988b   Tropical Wet Forest Treefall Gaps and Distributions of Understory Birds
         and Plants. *Ecology* 69(4):1076–89.
n.d.   Habitat-Dependent Fruiting Behavior of an Understorey Tree, *Miconia
         centrodesma*, and Tropical Treefall Gaps as Keystone Habitats for Frugi-
         vores in Costa Rica. Unpublished manuscript used by permission of the
         author.

Odum, Eugene P.
1971   *Fundamentals of Ecology.* Second edition. Philadelphia: Saunders.

Peters, Charles M., Michael J. Balick, Francis Kahn, and Anthony B. Anderson
1989   Oligarchic Forests of Economic Plants in Amazonia: Utilization and
         Conservation of an Important Tropical Resource. *Conservation Biology*
         3(4):341–49.

Putz, Francis E., and N. V. L. Brokaw
1989   Sprouting of Broken Trees on Barro Colorado Island. *Ecology* 70:
         508–12.

Redford, Kent H., Burt Klein, and Carolina Murcia
1992   The Incorporation of Game Animals into Small Scale Agroforestry Sys-
         tems in the Neotropics. In *Traditional Resources Use in Neotropical
         Forests*, edited by K. H. Redord and C. Padoch, pp. 333–58. New York:
         Columbia University Press.

Redford, Kent H., and John Robinson
1987   The Game of Choice: Patterns of Indian and Colonist Hunting in the
         Neotropics. *American Anthropologist* 89(3):650–67.

Salo, J., R. Kalliola, I. Hakkinen, Y. Makinen, P. Nimela, M. Puhakka,
and P. D. Coley.
1986   River Dynamics and the Diversity of Amazon Lowland Forest. *Nature*
         322:254–58.

Sponsel, Leslie E.
1981   The Hunter and the Hunted in the Amazon: An Integrated Biological
         and Cultural Approach to the Behavioral Ecology of Human Predation.
         Ph.D. dissertation, Cornell University.

Stearman, Allyn M.
1984   The Yuquí Connection: Another Look at Sirionó Deculturation. *Ameri-
         can Anthropologist* 86(3):630–50.
1989a   Yuquí Foragers in the Bolivian Amazon: Subsistence Strategies, Prestige,
         and Leadership in an Acculturating Society. *Journal of Anthropological
         Research* 45(2):219–44.
1989b   *Yuquí: Forest Nomads in a Changing World.* New York: Holt, Rinehart
         and Winston.

1990　The Effects of Settler Incursion on Fish and Game Resources of the Yuquí, a Native Amazonian Society of Eastern Bolivia. *Human Organization* 49(4):373–85.

Stearman, Allyn M., and Kent H. Redford
1992　Commercial Hunting by Subsistence Hunters: Sirionó Indians and Paraguayan Caiman in Lowland Bolivia. *Human Organization* 51(3):235–44.

Terborgh, John
1986　Community Aspects of Frugivory in Tropical Forests. In *Frugivores and Seed Dispersal*, edited by A. Estrada and T. H. Fleming. Dordrecht: W. Junk Publishers.

11

Faunal Resource Use by the Chimane of Eastern Bolivia

Policy Notes on a Biosphere Reserve

Avecita Chicchón

Thanks to a number of scientific reports on declining biological diversity in the tropics due to human activities, many governments, nongovernmental organizations, and the general public have become more aware of the environmental consequences of tropical habitat destruction.

Many tropical countries have begun to establish and/or consolidate protected areas within their national boundaries. Whereas early attempts to protect natural areas implied the relocation of local peoples to areas away from their traditional lands, causing enormous social problems (see Turnbull 1972), there are now serious efforts to incorporate the needs and views of local peoples into the management of protected areas (Chernela 1990; Miranda et al. 1989).

One important issue to take into account when designing a management plan for a protected area is how the people living in the area use natural resources. Fauna is a key resource because it supplies people with essential nutrients for their subsistence. The abundance or scarcity of fauna influences the quality of life of populations who live at a subsistence level.

The purpose of this chapter is to describe and analyze the ways in which the Chimane, who live in the Beni Biosphere Reserve of lowland Bolivia, use faunal resources. The focus of the analysis is on three Chimane settlements within the reserve. The first is Puerto Méndez, a settlement located along the Maniqui River and the southern boundary of the reserve, eight kilometers from the town of San Borja (pop. 13,000). Puerto Méndez has been continuously occupied by several generations of Chimane, and it suffers more environmental and social constraints than the other two settlements, owing to habitat destruction and demographic pressure by nonindigenous peasants.

The second settlement is Chacal, also located along the Maniqui River, one day's journey downstream by canoe from San Borja. Chacal was established in 1983; it lies close to savanna and forest resources within the reserve. Third, there is Chaco Brasil. This settlement is located along the banks of a slow-flowing river that is an old course of the Maniqui, here referred to as the Old Maniqui River (Río Maniqui Viejo). Chaco Brasil was established in 1964 and is relatively distant from nonindigenous settlements, but close to forest resources within the reserve.

Chimane responses to resource availability are flexible and diverse. Indigenous use of faunal resources is largely patterned by social and ecological factors, namely, resource availability and access to markets. When the Chimane lived at low population densities, it was possible for them to move seasonally to different areas within their ethnic territory to exploit fauna (see Riester 1978). Now that their resource base has been reduced because of the presence of nonindigenous landholdings, some Chimane have changed the way they use resources. While some prefer to move to areas where demographic pressure is not yet a problem (Chacal), others have chosen to stay in one place in order to have better access to market circuits (Puerto Méndez). In this sense, sedentarization also influences their use of resources.

Since the early 1980s, many nonindigenous people who used to work on ranches in the area have broken their bonds with their patrons to take advantage of new economic opportunities, especially in agriculture. These new peasants have established settlements in gallery forest areas where they are able to cultivate land. In many cases this has meant less land for the Chimane who lived in the same region and who used resources extensively. The Chimane who live closer to the town of San Borja have been more affected than others because nonindigenous people also find it economically advantageous to live close to town.

The Chimane and the Beni Biosphere Reserve

The Chimane are an indigenous group in the Bolivian Amazon who subsist by practicing shifting agriculture, hunting, fishing, and gathering. Numbering approximately 5,000 individuals (Comisión Socio-económica 1989), the Chimane occupy a vast forested area between the lowland eastern slopes of the Andes and the Beni savanna in the Ballivián province of the Beni department (fig. 11.1).

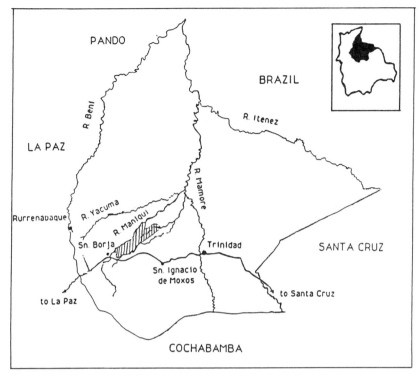

Figure 11.1. The department of Beni in Bolivia. The Beni Biosphere Reserve is shown as a shaded area.

Although the Jesuits established missions in this area as early as the 1690s, the Chimane were never successfully settled in missions. Since the 1950s, new mission posts have been established by Catholic Redemptorists in the upper Maniqui River area and by Evangelical New Tribes missionaries near San Borja. Previously, only some Chimane had been directly influenced by missions, but now a growing number of Chimane are influenced through bilingual schools established in their villages.

The Beni Biological Station was created in 1982 through the efforts of Spanish and Bolivian natural scientists. In 1986, the station was declared a biosphere reserve by UNESCO's Man and the Biosphere Program (fig. 11.2). The biosphere reserve concept attempts to bridge the gap between conservationists' and local people's interests (Batisse 1982). A biosphere reserve is a type of protected area made up of a representative sample of major ecosystems. Zoning of a biosphere reserve includes an undisturbed

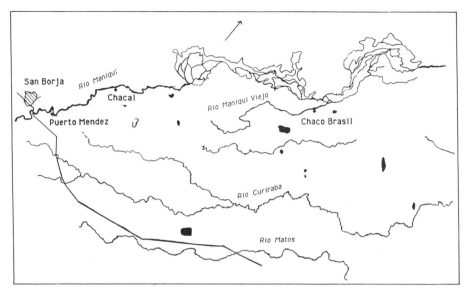

Figure 11.2. The Beni Biosphere Reserve.

core area; a buffer zone around the core area where controlled, minimal use of resources and scientific research are permitted; a multiple use zone where a diversity of resource use activities take place; and a stable cultural zone where local people are expected to carry out traditional subsistence practices. The Beni Biological Station is one of three biosphere reserves in Bolivia, but the only one that has a management plan incorporating the interests of biological conservation and local peoples.

In 1987, Conservation International, a Washington, D.C., nonprofit organization, engineered the first ever debt-for-nature swap that paid a small fraction of Bolivia's external debt in return for the government's guaranteeing improved protection of the Beni Biosphere Reserve and the adjacent Chimanes Forest. These protected areas became well known internationally, but not locally. For the most part, local people were not aware that they lived in a protected area, and those who were did not know what to expect from living in an area that had special status. Much groundwork needed to be done by reserve administration officials to incorporate local people's needs and considerations.

In 1990, after indigenous peoples from the Chimanes Forest had marched from the Beni to La Paz to call government attention to their demand for land, the government promulgated the 22611 Supreme Decree on September 24, 1990. This decree legally established an indigenous territory in the Chimanes Forest. It also established that 35,000 hectares of the Beni Biosphere Reserve along the Maniqui River had the dual role of indigenous territory and protected area. This new zone was consistent with the one that the administration of the reserve had previously designed as a multiple use zone.

The reserve encompasses 135,000 hectares of forest and savanna rich in plant and animal species. Recent studies have registered more than 80 mammal species and more than 386 types of birds (Miranda et al. 1989: 247). This area supports 13 of Bolivia's endangered species, such as some species of primates, spotted cats, and river otters.

Some 800 Chimane reside in the reserve, which lies in the northeasternmost region of their ethnic territory. Most Chimane live in groups of several extended household clusters along the alluvial terraces of the Maniqui and Curiraba rivers and in old courses of the Maniqui such as the Maniqui Viejo (Old Maniqui) and Maniquicito. Other people living in the reserve include cattle ranch personnel in the savanna areas and nonindigenous peasants who subsist mainly by cultivating land for cash crops such as rice and maize and by practicing some hunting.

Environment

The area of the reserve is classified as a subtropical life zone in Holdridge's system (1967). There are low temperatures from April through November caused by cold winds that come from Antarctica and are known locally as *surazos*; temperatures may drop to 7°C. Average yearly temperatures range from 23°C to 28°C. Annual rainfall was above 1,500 mm in 1989. The rainiest month was March, with a registered value of 331.6 mm (Estación Metereológica de San Borja 1989).

The reserve includes a mosaic of gallery forests and savanna areas. This mixture represents a transition into the natural Moxos savannas. Nearly 70 percent of the area of the reserve undergoes flooding during the wet season (Miranda et al. 1989); consequently, seasonal streams and oxbow lakes have tremendous importance to Chimane who use resources in the reserve.

Methods

The data for this chapter were collected during 15 months of fieldwork (Chicchón 1992). After carrying out a survey in the reserve from September through December 1988, I selected three contrasting settlements, Puerto Méndez, Chaco Brasil, and Chacal, for further study and comparison, in order to obtain an in-depth understanding of Chimane resource use in the reserve.

Hunting and fishing yields were recorded during five time periods of 30 consecutive days each (150 days in 1989). Yields in Puerto Méndez were recorded from January through February (wet season) and from July through August (dry season). In Chaco Brasil, yields were recorded from March through April (wet season) and June through July (dry season), and in Chacal, during the dry season of September through October. The study population included seven conjugal households in Puerto Méndez (43 individuals), five in Chaco Brasil (34 individuals), and seven in Chacal (40 individuals). Hunters were usually male heads of household. There was a total of sixteen hunters: five frequent hunters in Puerto Méndez, five in Chaco Brasil, and six in Chacal. More people fished. Men, women, and children contributed to different degrees to the acquisition of fish. Fishing was an almost daily activity for men, who used hook and line; fishing with poison was a seasonal group activity for men and women.

Hunting

For the Chimane hunters surveyed, the most common hunting weapon was the bow and arrow. Many, however, also owned firearms that they used especially to hunt large animals. Firearms were often shared within an extended household cluster. Chimane sometimes borrowed firearms from nonindigenous neighbors, who expected to receive some game in return for the favor. The most important limitation on the use of firearms was the availability of ammunition, a prized asset that could only be obtained through market exchanges.

Table 11.1 shows a significant difference between weapons used in hunting in each settlement (chi square = 15.95990; sig. = 0.0140). Bows and arrows were used in 50 percent and 47 percent of the hunts that took place in Chaco Brasil and Chacal, respectively, while they were used in only 19 percent of the hunts in Puerto Méndez. Firearms were used in half the total hunts recorded for Puerto Méndez, 53.3 percent in Chacal, and only 16.7 percent in Chaco Brasil. This result clearly shows that Chimane who live in settlements that are closer to market circuits are able to obtain ammunition more frequently than those who live in Chaco Brasil. The Chimane of Chaco Brasil depend largely on itinerant traders to bring market goods; ammunition is not a product that is often provided by these traders.

The total amount of game obtained in all three settlements during the research period was 879.08 kg, consisting of 113 individuals of 14 mam-

Table 11.1 Weapons Used in Hunting (percent)

Weapon	Puerto Méndez (n = 26)	Chaco Brasil (n = 36)	Chacal (n = 15)
Bow and arrow	19.2	50.0	46.7
Firearm	50.0	16.7	53.3
Machete	26.9	25.0	0.0
Other[a]	3.9	8.3	0.0
Total	100.0	100.0	100.0

Note: chi-square = 15.95990, D.F. = 6, sig. = 0.0140
[a]Shovel, bare hands, with help of dogs.

mal species (82.2 percent), one tortoise (6.2 percent), and several different bird species (11.7 percent). As a group, ungulates represented the greatest proportion of kills by weight, with collared peccaries (*Tayassu tajacu*) and white-lipped peccaries (*T. pecari*) representing 523 kg (59.5 percent) of the total catch. Second in importance were rodents: agoutis (*Dasyprocta* sp.), pacas (*Agouti paca*), capybaras (*Hydrochaeris hydrochaeris*), and squirrels (*Sciurus* spp.), which together made up 155.28 kg (17.7 percent) of the total catch. Edentates were third in importance at 97.87 kg (11.13 percent). This group was represented by anteaters (*Tamandua tamandua*) and armadillos (*Dasypus novemcinctus*). Carnivores, represented by coatis (*Nasua nasua*), made up 40.65 kg (4.6 percent), and four species of primates (*Saimiri boliviensis*, *Cebus apella*, *Alouatta* sp., *Aotus* sp.) composed 35.79 kg (4.1 percent) of the take. Birds and tortoises combined made up only 26.81 kg (3.05 percent) of the total catch (fig. 11.3).

There were important differences among the types of game taken in each settlement (Table 11.2). In Puerto Méndez, almost 35 percent of the catch was made up of rodents, while ungulates and edentates represented 15.6 percent each. Primates were the least common mammals taken in Puerto Méndez. In Chaco Brasil, the different categories of game were more evenly distributed. There, the combined category of birds and reptiles composed 26 percent of the catch. Among the mammals, primates were the most common (24 percent), whereas edentates and rodents represented 16 percent and 14 percent of the catch, respectively. The most common game animals caught in Chacal were ungulates, represented by white-lipped peccaries (56.1 percent of the catch). Second in

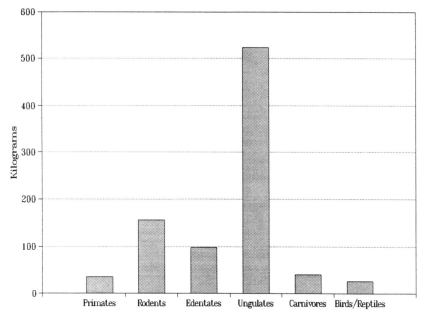

Figure 11.3. Weight of total game captured, by type of game.

importance were primates (16.5 percent), and third, edentates (16.5 percent). There were no small or medium-sized rodents or carnivores hunted
for food in Chacal (fig. 11.4).

A closer look at the hunting sites offers an explanation for the differences in types of game caught in each settlement (fig. 11.5). Puerto Méndez is located in an area that had traditionally been occupied by Chimane.
In 1989, it was surrounded not only by agricultural plots and fallows that
belonged to Chimane but also by plots and fallows of nonindigenous
peasants. Two peasant villages near Puerto Méndez were located next to
the road that linked San Borja with other towns in the Beni. As a consequence, more than 40 percent of the game taken in Puerto Méndez was
hunted in either swiddens or fallows, and the types of game caught (rodents and edentates) were those that thrive in secondary growth.

The Chimane who live in Puerto Méndez spent an average of 4.9 hours
in each hunt (n = 29) and traveled an average distance of only 2.45 km
to hunt. If these Chimane wanted to hunt larger animals they would have
had to travel farther and spend more time hunting. Instead, they opted to
stay in the vicinity of their village to hunt smaller animals. Thirty percent
of the hunts in Puerto Méndez took place on the edges of an oxbow lake.

Table 11.2 Number and Type of Game Species Taken by Settlement
During Research Period

	Puerto Méndez	Chaco Brasil	Chacal	Total
Primates				
Saimiri boliviensis	0	7	0	7
Cebus apella	1	3	0	4
Alouatta sp.	1	2	1	4
Aotus sp.	0	0	4	4
Total	2 (6.3%)	12 (24%)	5 (16.5%)	19 (16.7%)
Rodents				
Agouti paca	2	5	0	7
Dasyprocta sp.	7	0	0	7
Hydrochaeris hydrochaeris	1	1	2	4
Sciurus sp.	1	1	0	2
Total	11 (34.4%)	7 (14%)	2 (6.6%)	20 (17.7%)
Edendata				
Tamandua tamandua	1	6	0	7
Dasypus novemcinctus	4	2	5	11
Priodontes maximus	0	1	0	1
Total	5 (15.6%)	9 (16%)	5 (16.5%)	19 (16.8%)
Artiodactyla				
Tayassu tajacu	5	2	0	7
T. pecari	0	3	17	20
Total	5 (15.6%)	5 (10%)	17 (56.1%)	27 (23.9%)
Carnivora				
Nasua nasua	3 (9.4%)	5 (10%)	0	8 (7.1%)
Reptile				
Geochelone carbonaria	0	6 (12%)	1 (3.3%)	7 (6.2%)
Birds	6 (18.8%)	7 (14%)	0	13 (11.7%)

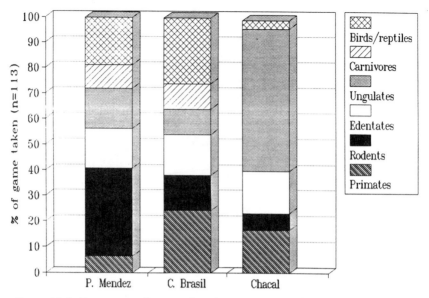

Figure 11.4. Percentage of game taken, by game type and settlement.

Game taken there included capybaras and birds that were probably encountered in the area while people were fishing.

Chimane from Chaco Brasil spent an average time of 6.33 hours per
hunt (n = 38) and traveled an average of 2.78 km per hunt. A little over
30 percent of the catch in Chaco Brasil was taken in the forest, while 25
percent was hunted in fallows. Savanna sites had little importance in
Chaco Brasil, but sites on the edges of water sources (the river, lakes)
were important because in such areas fishing and hunting activities could
be combined.

Chacal was located close to both savanna and forest resources. During
the time when hunting yields were recorded, white-lipped peccaries were
hunted near salt licks and mud baths in savanna patches within the reserve. It was clear that the Chimane had a great cultural preference for
peccary, and they often organized group trips to obtain this resource.
Over 70 percent of the catch was obtained in savanna areas where armadillos were also abundant. Five overnight hunts were recorded in Chacal,
whereas only one took place in Chaco Brasil and none in Puerto Méndez.

The extra effort taken to travel farther (an average of 11 km per hunt,
n = 14) and to spend more time hunting (an average of 14 hours) in
Chacal was justified by the type of game obtained—peccaries. This
finding is consistent with those for other lowland South American groups,

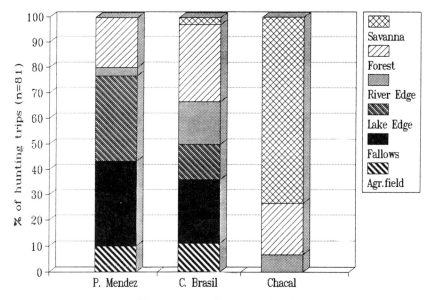

Figure 11.5. Percentage of hunting trips, by site and settlement.

for whom peccaries ranked first in weight and number of individuals taken (Sponsel 1986; Vickers 1984).

Fishing

A little over 13 percent of the hunts recorded during the research period were also fishing trips. Probably the true focus of many of those "hunts" was to fish, but if game such as birds or capybaras was encountered on the river edges, the opportunity to hunt it was not missed.

The most common fishing instruments included hook and line, bow and arrow, and fish poison. Nets were occasionally used in Puerto Méndez, and fishing with machetes was common in all three communities. There were seasonal differences in the use of fishing instruments. Fish poison was used particularly during the dry season when water levels were low.

In terms of successful outcome, fishing offered the Chimane a more secure source of food than did hunting. Fishing could be carried out daily in nearby water sources, and most of the time, at least small fish were certain to be caught.

In terms of quantity of food acquired, fishing contributed 509.93 kg (36.7 percent) of the total amount of meat (1,391.36 kg) obtained in all three settlements during the research period. Fishing contributed 60.5

Table 11.3   Percentage of Fishing Trips in Which Various Fish Species
Were Caught

Fish Species	Puerto Méndez	Chaco Brasil	Chacal	Average %
1. *Prochilodus nigricans*	41.2	18.2	32.0	30.5
2. *Pimelodus cf. maculatus*	2.4	58.4	24.0	28.3
3. *Serrasalmus* sp.	3.5	46.8	40.0	26.2
4. *Pimelodina flavipinnis*	3.5	36.4	40.0	21.9
5. *Triportheus* sp.	2.4	39.0	16.0	19.3
6. *Serrasalmus cf. nattereri*	7.1	35.1	0.0	17.6
7. *Pterygoplychthys multiradatus*	30.6	0.0	4.0	14.4
8. *Hoplias malabaricus*	22.4	1.3	16.0	12.8
9. *Salminus maxillosus*	21.2	2.6	0.0	10.7
10. *Curimata* sp.	16.5	6.5	0.0	10.2
11. *Hoplosternum littorale*	22.4	0.0	0.0	10.2
12. *Sorubimichtys planiceps*	7.1	9.1	20.0	9.6
13. *Pseudoplatystoma fasciatum*	9.4	11.7	4.0	9.6
14. *Pterygoplychthys* sp.	20.0	0.0	0.0	9.1
15. *Schizodon fasciatum*	1.2	14.3	4.0	7.0
16. *Hoplosternum thoracatum*	15.3	0.0	0.0	7.0
17. *Roeboides* sp.	2.4	3.9	24.0	5.9
18. *Hoplerytrinus unitaeniatus*	11.8	1.3	0.0	5.9
19. *Raphiodon vulpinus*	9.4	1.3	4.0	5.3
20. *Ageneious* sp.	0.0	10.4	8.0	5.3
21. *Megalodoras irwini*	9.4	0.0	0.0	4.3
22. *Hypophthalmus* sp.	7.1	1.3	0.0	3.7

percent (284.16 kg) of the total amount of meat obtained in Puerto Méndez; 30.6 percent (162.98 kg) in Chaco Brasil, and 13.5 percent (62.79
kg) in Chacal. Across settlements, there appears to be a trend toward
emphasizing fishing activities more where large game is unavailable;
Puerto Méndez and Chacal represent either extreme of the spectrum of
large game availability. In addition, fishing is often more important than
hunting because in comparison to mammals, fish have a higher percentage of edible tissue and are more energetically efficient in converting
food to edible tissue (Leslie Sponsel, personal communication).

Table 11.3 *Continued*

Fish Species	Puerto Méndez	Chaco Brasil	Chacal	Average %
23. Ishij[a]	7.1	0.0	4.0	3.7
24. *Phractocephalus hemiliopetrus*	0.0	5.2	8.0	3.2
25. Cotyij[a]	1.2	2.6	8.0	2.7
26. *Rhytiodus* sp.	4.7	0.0	4.0	2.7
27. *Gymnotus* sp.	5.9	0.0	0.0	2.7
28. *Pterodoras granulosus*	5.9	0.0	0.0	2.7
29. *Astronotus ocellatus*	2.4	1.3	8.0	2.7
30. *Cichla ocellaris*	1.2	0.0	12.0	2.1
31. Pasha'[a]	3.5	0.0	4.0	2.1
32. Taquedye[a]	0.0	2.6	0.0	2.1
33. Tetra	2.4	0.0	0.0	1.1
34. *Leiarus* sp.	2.4	0.0	0.0	1.1
35. *Acestrorhunchus* sp.	2.4	0.0	0.0	1.1
36. *Potamotrygon* sp.	0.0	2.6	0.0	1.1
37. *Plagioscion squamosissimus*	0.0	1.3	0.0	0.5
38. *Loricariichtys cf. maculatus*	1.2	0.0	0.0	0.5
39. *Hemisorubim platyrhynchos*	1.2	0.0	0.0	0.5
40. *Leporinus trifasciatus*	1.2	0.0	0.0	0.5
41. *Leiarius marmoratus*	0.0	1.3	0.0	0.5
42. *Colossoma macropomum*	0.0	0.0	4.0	0.5
Total no. of fishing trips	85	77	25	187

[a]Name in the Chimane language.

Overall, the most common fish caught were sábalo (*Prochilodus nigricans*), bagre (*Pimelodus* sp.), piranha (*Serrasalmus* sp.), blanquillo (*Pimelodina flavipinnis*), and sardina (*Triportheus* sp.) (Table 11.3, fig. 11.6). There were also important catches of small Callichtyidae and Loricariidae fish in small oxbow lakes near Puerto Méndez during the dry season. Among the larger fish, the most common caught were dorado (*Salminus maxillosus*), paleta (*Sorubimchtys planiceps*), and surubí (*Pseudoplatystoma fasciatum*).

A number of small sardinas (subfamily Tetragonopterinae, family

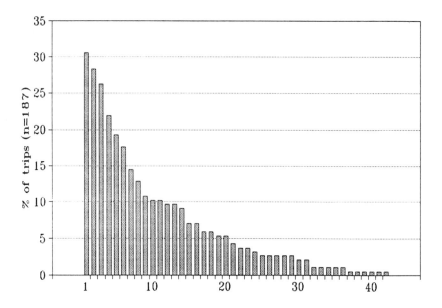

Figure 11.6. Percentage of fishing trips on which various species were harvested. Species identification numbers correspond to those in Table 11.3.

Characidae) were caught on the river edges with machetes. These fish were used as bait to obtain larger fish and were underreported because they were rarely consumed.

Fishing yield differences among the settlements may be explained in terms of the number of people fishing and the location and seasonality of the fishing sites. Although hunting is primarily a male activity, and usually male heads of households or adolescent males hunt, fishing is carried out by men and women, young and old. Fishing with *barbasco* (fish poison) usually results not only in food procurement but also in a social event that allows for strengthening ties of reciprocity through the distribution of fish.

As I mentioned earlier, Puerto Méndez and Chacal are both located on the Maniqui River, and Chaco Brasil is located on an old course of the Maniqui. The characteristics of the two rivers are quite different. The water level of the Maniqui Viejo is getting lower every year and the current is not as strong or as fast as that in the Maniqui; therefore, the fish caught in each environment are of different types. Many of the fish caught in Chaco Brasil year-round are piranha or piranhalike fish (*Serrasalmus* spp.) that remain in low-water rivers or flooded areas where there is underwater vegetation (Goulding 1980). These fish were not a common catch in the Maniqui, although they were sometimes caught in oxbow lakes in the vicinity of Puerto Méndez and when the water was low at Chacal.

Whereas most fishing in Chacal, and nearly all that in Chaco Brasil, took place in rivers, half of the fishing trips in Puerto Méndez took place in nearby oxbow lakes (fig. 11.7). These were important fishing sites, especially during the wet season when the Maniqui was in full flood and dangerous to navigate.

Seasonal streams were preferred sites for catching fish with barbasco because they could be dammed with little difficulty. Chimane from the reserve commonly use three types of fish poison: *chito'*, *conofoto'*, and *vashi'*. There are two kinds of plants that produce chito': *Tiphrocia vogeli* and *T. toxica*, both cultivated shrubs. The leaves of the shrub are hand squeezed and diluted in the water to poison the fish. Conofoto' is the resin of a tree (*Hura crepitans*). The tree is tapped and the resin is mixed with mud and then diluted in water to poison fish. The third type of fish poison, vashi', comes from a woody vine (unidentified) that is gathered in the forest and cut into pieces of about 50 cm each, which are tied in bunches 10 to 15 cm long, placed in the water, and beaten to release the poison. The Chimane report that conofoto' is the most effective fish poison of the three, followed by vashi' and chito'.

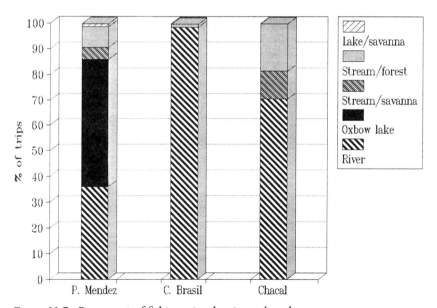

Figure 11.7. Percentage of fishing trips, by site and settlement.

Summary and Notes on Policy

This chapter has examined the ways in which Chimane use faunal resources in three settlements located in the Beni Biosphere Reserve. Their resource use is not homogeneous; each settlement represents a particular scenario. In general terms, the Chimane system of resource use responds to ecological and socioeconomic factors such as resource availability near the settlements and participation in the market economy.

Game was more important than fish as a source of meat in Chacal (86.5 percent of total amount of meat) and Chaco Brasil (64 percent), while game contributed only 30.7 percent of the total amount of meat obtained in Puerto Méndez.

The Chimane of Chacal had the advantage of receiving no competition from other people for available resources. They were favorably located near forest and savanna areas that were accessible by canoe and foot. Peccaries were the focus of hunting efforts in this settlement. Fishing was a secondary option because hunting provided sufficient meat.

In Chaco Brasil, the Chimane did not control the availability of market goods. Therefore, their technology was clearly more traditional than in the other two settlements. Only when ammunition was available did they organize long trips to obtain large mammals; otherwise they were satisfied with the variety of game available near their settlement, which was located close to primary forest.

Puerto Méndez represents an extreme case in which local animal resources are less varied and abundant than in the other two settlements. Puerto Méndez is located near the town of San Borja and is surrounded by agricultural plots and fallows belonging to Chimane and nonindigenous peasants. If the Chimane who live in Puerto Méndez want to obtain larger game, they have to carry out long hunts away from their base settlement. Instead, they have chosen to stay in their settlement, hunt smaller animals available nearby in secondary forest, and practice more fishing in the oxbow lakes and streams in the vicinity of their settlement. This "sedentary option" is strongly linked to the desirability of having access to market circuits of the regional economy. Many Chimane from this settlement have begun to practice occasional wage labor for their nonindigenous neighbors to obtain cash that can in turn be used to buy market goods. Because Puerto Méndez is located near San Borja, the Chimane who live there are also occasional recipients of public services. They have a bilingual school, and some Chimane participate in occasional seminars offered to train health promoters.

At the time of my research, the Chimane from Puerto Méndez and Chacal had better access to products that were obtained through market exchanges. These Chimane were able to obtain ammunition for their firearms regularly. Additionally, Chimane from Puerto Méndez were more effective in obtaining fish because they used modern technology such as nets. Furthermore, they could market their agricultural products for cash because they were favorably located near market circuits. There appears to be a trend toward intensifying agricultural activities when hunting becomes less successful. The production of cash crops permits the Chimane to participate in the market economy and at the same time to maintain a reliable source of food.

This discussion reveals that there is more to take into account in a management plan than the location of specific Chimane settlements. The Chimane use faunal resources mainly for subsistence, but the availability of the resources is limited by the presence of nonindigenous people who are competing for the same land. The situation of Puerto Méndez is a case in point.

Resource use policy in a biosphere reserve needs to incorporate the different ways in which local peoples make use of particular resources. A management plan that intends to regulate the use of faunal resources in a protected area must respect and be responsive to indigenous resource use systems. It is important to take into account the environmental and social factors that affect resource use in order to avoid many potential social and nutritional problems.

The administration of the Beni Biosphere Reserve faces the dual challenge of protecting biodiversity while respecting indigenous resource use within the reserve. Although many important steps have already been taken toward incorporating the indigenous view into the management of the reserve, there is still much to be done. Just as there is no single Chimane resource use system, there is no one answer to the regulation of resource use. Because top-down remedies have proven to be ineffective, sensible answers must be sought in conjunction with the local people to be affected by potential regulations. Because it is impossible to arrive at an answer with each particular household, it is critical that the administration of the reserve facilitate institution building among local peoples. Where local organizations already exist, they should be strengthened in order to encourage more participation in diagnosing, analyzing, and solving actual and potential problems regarding the use of faunal resources.

The Chimane are and inevitably will be affected by the expansion of the market economy. In the past, the demand for pelts, hides, and live animals led local people in the Beni to use resources unsustainably. Currently, Chimane use of fauna is primarily for subsistence. However, the need for cash could lead them to exploit fauna above sustainable harvest rates. It is therefore important that the administrators of protected areas, together with local people, find ways to generate income through the establishment of programs that could benefit local people both financially and nutritionally.

The importance of fauna for the Chimane and other indigenous groups goes beyond economic gain. The uses of animals and the understanding of animal behavior are embedded in traditional knowledge. This knowledge, however, is not enough to guarantee the long-term availability of resources. There are external factors, such as the impact of the market economy, that could trigger a number of processes that would eventually result in the depletion of faunal resources. Competition for land and natural resources with nonindigenous peoples is a proven threat to the cultural survival of indigenous groups. It is therefore important to find answers within the market economy to guarantee the viability of indigenous groups and the conservation of natural resources. Once their resource base is respected, local people would, in turn, more readily contribute to the successful conservation of natural resources.

Acknowledgments

I would like to thank Lisa Naughton, Kent Redford, and Allyn Stearman for very helpful comments on an earlier version of this chapter. Richard Piland contributed with critical insights and comments. Leslie Sponsel provided important comments and editorial suggestions. Funds for this research were provided by the Inter-American Foundation.

References Cited

Batisse, M.
1982   The Biosphere Reserve: A Tool for Environmental Conservation and
        Management. *Environmental Conservation* 9(2):101–14.

Chernela, Janet
1990   The Role of Indigenous Organizations in International Policy Development: The Case of an Awa Biosphere Reserve in Colombia and Ecuador.
        In *Ethnobiology: Implications and Applications*, edited by D. Posey et al.,
        pp. 57–72. Proceedings of the First International Congress of Ethnobiology. Belém: Museu Paraense Emílio Goeldi.

Chicchón, Avecita
1992   Chimane Resource Use and Market Involvement in the Beni Biosphere Reserve, Bolivia. Ph. D. dissertation, Department of Anthropology, University of Florida.

Comisión Socio-económica
1989   *Bosque Chimanes: Estudio socio-económico*. Report prepared for the president of Bolivia.

Estación Metereológica de San Borja
1989   *Registros Climáticos*.

Goulding, Michael
1980   *The Fishes and the Forest*. Berkeley: University of California Press.

Holdridge, Leslie
1967   *Life Zone Ecology*. San José, Costa Rica: Tropical Science Center.

Miranda, Carmen, Carlos Navia, Marco Ribera, Elvira Salinas, and Jaime Sarmiento
1989   Plan de manejo de la Estación Biológica del Beni. Manuscript.

Riester, Jurgen
1978   *Canción y producción en la vida de un pueblo indígena (los Chimane: Tribu de la selva oriental)*. La Paz, Bolivia: Los Amigos del Libro.

Sponsel, Leslie
1986   Amazon Ecology and Adaptation. *Annual Review of Anthropology* 15:67–97.

Turnbull, Colin
1972   *The Mountain People*. New York: Simon and Schuster.

Vickers, William
1984   The Faunal Components of Lowland South American Hunting Kills. *Interciencia* 9(6):366–76.

12

Sustainability in Resource Rights and Conservation

The Case of an Awa Biosphere Reserve in Colombia and Ecuador

Janet M. Chernela

A number of new development schemes reflect growing concerns for both environmental conservation and self-determination of indigenous peoples. The new trends emerge amid criticism that neglect for these issues by international development agencies has resulted in increased environmental degradation and decreased community autonomy. In response to such criticism, a new species of development program combines guidelines for environmental preservation and protection, appropriate land-use management, and respect for ethnic lifeways. Foremost among these new models is that of the biosphere reserve. Yet the new form raises questions regarding the sustainability of indigenous self-governance within a larger institutional context. The matching of diverse priorities is not easy. If it is to be accomplished to any extent, it will be, as the case of the Awa binational biosphere reserve well illustrates, the result of negotiation among interested parties.

Although indigenous organizations and anthropologists have recognized the importance of indigenous peoples in policies that affect them (Anderson 1982; Davis 1982; Salazar 1977; Schwartzman 1984; Weiss 1988), few authors have investigated the motivations and strategies of Indians as actors in the negotiating processes that determine policy formation and implementation. Taking as its subject the case of a proposed Colombian-Ecuadorian biosphere reserve in which an Awa ethnic reserve is a central component, this chapter examines the participation of indigenous organizations in the interplay between government and other decision-making institutions. The chapter contrasts two stages in the formation of the reserve: first, the early demarcation and institutionalization

of an Awa ethnic and forest reserve in Ecuador, and second, the later for-
malization of binational participation in a meeting of government officials
and Indian representatives from both Ecuador and Colombia. Although
Ecuadorian Indian associations maintained a high level of participation in
the early phases of planning the reserve, they and their Colombian counterparts refused comparable participation in the governing apparatus of
the reserve, established at a policy-making meeting held by representatives of both nations in Colombia in 1987.

This chapter attempts to explain the apparently inconsistent role of
the indigenous organizations by examining and analyzing the fit between
their own interests and those of other actors in the decision-making processes toward planning the reserve. By focusing on the interests of the
native peoples incorporated within a reserve, the chapter draws attention
to the potential limitations of a biosphere reserve in meeting some of the
priorities of native peoples.

Development and Decision Making

For heuristic purposes, we may speak of development programming as
falling into three categories: (1) "center-generated" development programming; (2) grass-roots, or "periphery-generated," innovation; and
(3) negotiated, or combined, "center-periphery" programming.

In conventional, center-generated development, policy planning is typically initiated by an agency at a national or international level. Decisions
regarding any single project are subject to a government's or an agency's
broader policy goals. These may or may not match the specific needs of
the area and peoples targeted to benefit by them.

In grass-roots, or periphery-generated, innovation, a local association
or organization proposes a resource management scheme intended to
benefit its own constituency and secures the financial or technical support
required to implement it. Historically, local groups have relied on the
assistance of intermediaries, such as church groups, who provide them
with necessary linkages to sources of available resources. Increasingly,
however, locally based groups engage in coalition building, which offers
them self-representation and allows them to create their own linkages to
resources.

It is the third category of program development that is the subject of
this chapter. Center-periphery programming entails the collaboration of
entities from both the "center" and the so-called periphery. Of the three,
it is this category that is the most challenging and complex of all programming methodologies because it involves the negotiations of different

actors with divergent agendas. It also underscores the important role of negotiation and political interplay in the outcome of all development or resource management projects. This combined strategy diverges from conventional development models in that it recognizes the active role of so-called beneficiary groups, who are conventionally viewed as passive recipients of "assistance." Moreover, it differs from a conventional development perspective in regarding all actors, including government agencies, as interest groups. This category is of greatest importance because it describes the fastest growing area of development, due to the increasing political strength of grass-roots organizations and new opportunities available to them to participate in center-born development proposals.

The Biosphere Reserve

The biosphere reserve is a defined, protected area type that forms part of UNESCO's larger program, "Man and the Biosphere" (MAB). Since the first biosphere reserve was designated in 1976, there have been at least six biosphere reserves proposed in the Neotropics alone. Approval for all reserves depends upon decisions by the Man and the Biosphere International Coordinating Council. The biosphere type of protected area is characterized by multiple-use zoning and is intended to include areas comprising a range of land-use techniques and environmental conditions. The goals of the projects, likewise, are multifaceted, including the restoration of environmentally devastated areas ("reclamation or restoration zones"); the preservation of pristine or endemically rich regions ("natural or core zones") and areas of traditional use patterns ("stable cultural zones"); the establishment of areas of resource management experimentation ("multiple use areas"); and the establishment of protective buffer zones ("manipulative or buffer zones").

An Awa Binational Biosphere Reserve

As it is now designed, the proposed binational Awa Biosphere Reserve would include approximately 300,000 hectares in Ecuador and another 800,000 hectares in Colombia and would affect between 7,000 and 10,000 Awa.[1] A core zone of pristine forest will be selected for absolute protection. An area or areas determined to be traditional Awa territories will form the "ethnic reserve" component of the biosphere reserve. Surrounding these protected lands would be sectors inhabited by non-Awa homesteaders and marked for restoration and experimentation in appropriate land-use management. Between the various use zones, buffer areas are planned to serve as boundary markers and to inhibit encroachment into protected sectors.

The initiation and implementation of such a project involves the participation of numerous actors and interest groups. These include government officials and agencies at national and local levels; scientific investigators; environmentalists and environmental agencies; and local indigenous populations and their national organizations. I shall examine the roles and interests of each of these groups as they contribute to the formation of the binational reserve.

Ecuadorian Government and the Awa

Despite a number of anthropological studies (Ehrenreich 1984, 1985; Kempf and Ehrenreich 1980; Ortiz 1937; Osborn 1968), the Awa population of Ecuador eluded the attention of the national government until the early 1980s. In 1982, when Ecuadorian newspapers reported the presence of Colombian gold miners in the northwestern region of Tobar Donoso, the Ministry of Foreign Relations dispatched a commission to investigate matters. That commission, known as the Tobar Donoso Commission, confirmed reports of Colombians in the area, as well as the additional undocumented presence of numerous indigenous inhabitants. The commission recommended surveillance of the region, precise demarcation of the little-known border, and issuance of citizenship documentation to all indigenous residents.

The government had several reasons to take interest in the poorly known region. Colombian frontier areas were becoming increasingly ungovernable, and there was a strong likelihood that the Colombian-Ecuadorian border could become a refuge for guerrilla movements, narco-trafficking, small-scale mining, and other undesirable activities unless a government presence was in place. Moreover, the productive areas of northern Ecuador had no viable gateway to Pacific ports. A roadway that proceeded along the Colombian-Ecuadorian border would provide producers access to the sea, thus decreasing the cost of northern exports. Besides bringing development to the region, it would provide the necessary governmental presence near the border.[2] Relations with Colombia had been cooperative for at least 60 years, dating back to 1926, and binational responsibility might be desirable.

To begin efforts to regularize a formal Ecuadorian presence in this frontier zone, the Ministry of Foreign Relations proceeded to build a coalition of national-level governmental agencies that would contribute their resources to the specific purpose of demarcating an Indian reserve and documenting the populations living along the ill-defined border. In 1983 the government transformed the informal investigative group into the Inter-Institutional Tobar Donoso Commission, composed of six government ministries (Foreign Relations, Agriculture, Education, Health, Public Works, and Agrarian Reform).

The explicit purpose of the commission was the development of the region, including the growth of agricultural production, as well as the creation of mechanisms to "preserve . . . 'Awa' . . . native culture, presently in danger of extinction" (Ministry of Foreign Relations 1983). With encouragement from international funding sources, this coalition of government agencies was expanded to include one nongovernmental organization, the National Federation of Indian Nations, or CONAIE (Macdonald and Chernela n.d.).

The presence of a national Indian federation early in the history of the Tobar Donoso Commission was one of the first instances in which an indigenous federation was assured representation in government planning that would affect its own constituency. Moreover, as treasurer and sole dispersal agent for funds related to a number of significant projects, CONAIE played a strongly decisive role in any planning that affected Awa communities.

Between 1984 and 1986 the joint Tobar Donoso Commission, with assistance from international nongovernmental agencies such as Cultural Survival,[3] accomplished several major objectives, including demarcation of approximately 80,000 hectares of Carchi province as Awa territory and issuance of citizenship cards to over 1,100 adult Awa, as well as compensation to and removal of settlers from the demarcated area (Macdonald 1986:33).

In order to adequately demarcate the border and provide full documentation to the inhabitants of the region, the cooperation of numerous public agencies was required. Under the coordination of the Ministry of Foreign Relations, therefore, the Tobar Donoso Commission expanded considerably, eventually incorporating more than 15 governmental agencies representing virtually every national ministry.

Demarcation of Indian Lands in Ecuador

Efforts to demarcate Awa territory were punctuated by disputes and disagreements due to claims and counterclaims for the same lands. Ranchers entering from the eastern highlands and lumbering companies from the western lowlands had both appropriated lands claimed by Awa communities. Solutions eventually were achieved through negotiations and compensation in which indigenous organizations and public agencies worked jointly.

Indian and government representatives report that the collaborative demarcation process resulted in cooperative ties between the Indians and government agencies of the commission. One of the principal liasons between the government and the indigenous organizations writes that "relations between government officials involved with the project, CONAIE National Federation of Indian Nations members, and Awa leaders are very good, and have ensured the participation of the Awa on all levels of project planning" (Levy 1988:3).

Once demarcation was accomplished, the legal designation of the lands raised significant questions. The Ecuadorian forestry law of 1981 guaranteed that forested lands in the categories "protective," "regenerative," or "in permanent use" would be protected by the national government.[4] Prior to that legislation, lands that were not visibly in use could be expropriated, and tropical forest Indians wishing to gain title to their lands were often forced to clear forests rather than risk losing forested lands to competitors.

The new legislation prompted the framers of the Awa reserve to incorporate the guarantees of the forestry legislation into their land title. A "forest reserve" would provide the Awa with more titled land than would an Indian reserve. However, forested lands were state owned. The national Indian organization, CONAIE, aware of land disputes underway in the eastern tropical forests, opposed application of the forest reserve form of land title to Indian lands. After months of negotiations, the communities and the commission agreed to combine two pieces of legislation, one regarding forest reserves and the other Indian communities, in order to create a unique Indian/forest reserve. The final demarcation produced a land claim of approximately 120,000 hectares for a population of about 1,800. The question of land ownership, however, remained unresolved.

Ecuadorian Indigenous Organizations

Awa settlement pattern is traditionally dispersed, with nuclear family households united loosely through kinship ties into some eight larger social groupings (James R. Levy, personal communication, 1987). As is the case in other lowland indigenous societies, Awa traditional leadership is neither wide-reaching nor coercive. Ehrenreich described the Awa of 1978 this way:

> There are no pan-tribal, or even pan-household organizations, no social clubs, men's houses, age sets or grades, sodalities or ritual associations in existence among the Awa in their "traditional" pattern of culture. . . . The Awa share a common language (Awapit) and a sociocultural pattern distinct from other groups and they are endogamous within the group. However, there has traditionally been little to no "tribal" consciousness or identity strongly professed or held by the Awa . . . nor has there been a formal political structure per se. . . . Political decisions are an individual or household prerogative. . . . In the absence of a formalized political structure, all important political, economic and social decisions are made at the individual or household . . . level. (Ehrenreich 1989:50)

With increasing white contact, however, the Awa recognized the advantage of a political structure capable of uniting the Awa nation and allowing for representation of all its constituent units. The Awa perceived the need for links to existing national-level indigenous organizations and for spokespersons to negotiate with the state in support of their interests.

Following a model established by the Shuar of southern Ecuador (see Salazar 1981), the Awa in 1983 created a federation comprising 15 regional centers. Each regional center includes all inhabitants of the area and is governed by a locally elected council. Representatives from the centers attend federation assemblies and maintain representation in CONAIE, thus linking each Awa regional center to a national Indian network.

In addition to demarcation, collaboration between the Awa, governmental agencies, and CONAIE resulted in numerous projects, including the construction of meeting facilities and medical stations, agricultural programs, and a bilingual educational program.

The Awa Federation and CONAIE also joined the Ministry of Foreign Relations in presenting a number of proposals to international funding agencies to implement resource management programs in the area. Among the approved proposals were plans for a consortium of government and nongovernment agencies to create a program to teach techniques for sustainable resource management.

Environmental Preservation and Awa Territories in Colombia

In contrast to the strong participation by national-level agencies in Ecuadorian Awa land demarcation, Colombia's policy of decentralization left land titling to local-level officials. Several attempts had been made by the Colombian Institute of Land Reform (INCORA) to establish Awa territories, but rights to the lands were contested by commercial interests and regional politicians who represented them. Demarcation procedures were indefinitely interrupted. At the time of the 1987 binational meeting to commence plans for a biosphere reserve, the 6,000–8,000 Colombian Awa had neither an organization for self-representation nor secure land tenure.

Attention was drawn to the area by the presence of a research station at La Planada with programs in both natural resources and social assistance. In 1982, the year in which Ecuadorian public administrators took interest in the area, Colombian ecologists began initiatives to create a biosphere reserve that would include native Awa territory, non-Indian areas of resource management experimentation, and a region of biological preservation in what they regarded as an important and endangered habitat.

The region occupied by and surrounding the Awa is of significance to naturalists for numerous reasons. Lying within the southern extension of a bioregion whose core is the Choco area of southern Pacific Colombia, the area inhabited by the Awa may be one of the most biologically diverse in the world. The area presents a wide variety of habitats, including humid tropical forests, low montane forests, upper and lower *páramo* zones, and high montane forests. Among these habitats are two of the world's most endangered ecosystems: tropical wet forests (including one of the few remaining true cloud forests), and the ecologically distinct páramos.[5]

The area includes over 300,000 hectares of pristine tropical montane wet forest and is estimated to have one of the highest concentrations of endemic species known today (Orejuela 1987:121). The various ecosystems that comprise the area contain large numbers of both migratory animals and endemic species of plants and animals, including endangered tropical ungulates, carnivores, primates, and avian species.[6] This rare wealth of biota includes the only species of bear found in South America, the spectacled bear (*Tramaretos ornatus*), declared endangered by the international conservation community.

Moved by the perceived urgency of preserving and studying the biological diversity of the area, a Colombian nongovernmental agency, the Foundation for Advanced Education (FES),[7] in collaboration with World Wildlife Fund–U.S., created La Planada Research Station, the first natural reserve and biological study station in the area. Situated near a region of severe land degradation caused by inappropriate methods of land use and competition for fragile, depleted soils, the research station began an educational program in sustainable resource management among the populations living adjacent to the station. Later, FES, along with the regional Development Agency of Nariño and the regional Office of Indian Affairs, initiated a broad community action program involving health, nutrition, and environmental education. FES regards the well-being of the natural environment as inextricably linked to the economic and social well-being of the populations living in association with it. Yet issues of land tenure were not within FES's priorities or powers. Land demarcation, then, continued to lag due to opposition from local agrarian interest groups and their political allies.

The eventual reexamination of Awa land rights in Colombia resulted from demands made by the national Indian organizations of both Colombia and Ecuador. When the important binational meeting to plan the reserve took place in August 1987, it was attended by representatives of both Ecuadorian and Colombian Indian organizations. In Colombia, groups concerned with land rights were the National Indian Organization of Colombia (ONIC), founded in 1984, and its strongest member group, the Regional Indian Council of Cauca (CRIC), founded in 1972.

Two Types of Participation

In Ecuador, the national Indian organization, CONAIE, played an active role in policy making in the earliest stages of the project. As a result of CONAIE's influence and participation, several programs were developed that involved the collaboration of Indians and state agencies. Despite this previous record of active participation, in the later phases of project development the Indian organizations refused full incorporation into the decision-making apparatus that governed project planning.

In contrast to the collaborative participation characteristic of the early stages of the project in Ecuador, the later strategy in the formation of the biosphere reserve can best be described as "selective participation." Nowhere is this strategy better illustrated than in the participation of the indigenous associations at the binational meeting at La Planada, Colombia, in August 1987, for the planning of the Awa binational biosphere reserve. There, participating indigenous organizations from both Ecuador and Colombia refused the opportunity to participate in the leadership of the meeting.

The indigenous organizations at La Planada, surprisingly, declined participation in the coalition formed to draft the plan for the reserve, although they were to be accorded representation within the joint policy-making body. Moreover, they declined to name a representative to the board of directors chosen to lead the meeting. The tactic they chose, instead, was the peripheral participation of a minority caucus. What was the rationale behind this strategy? Why did the indigenous organizations agree to attend the binational meeting, yet decline to participate in important decision-making coalitions?

The purpose of the binational meeting was to bring together Colombian and Ecuadorian public officials and Indian representatives to prepare a joint statement regarding procedures for furthering a carefully delineated binational project.[8] The written statement, or *Acta*, resulting from that meeting was to contain the rationale and objectives of the project and present a schedule for accomplishing first-stage goals. It was hoped that a consensus would be arrived at, committing both countries to a common agenda.

The Ecuadorian delegation, composed of government officials, hoped for collaboration from Colombia to achieve its own goals of border protection. The Colombian delegation consisted of political officials as well as environmentalists. Whereas the Colombian delegation might have responded reluctantly to a project initiated by Ecuador, its environmentalists, who had first proposed the biosphere reserve in Colombia, took the strongest stand in favor of the binational project. More importantly, Colombia's border concerns were posing increasing difficulties for the government, and public officials favored a "controlled presence." The proposal had received international approval and support, and both delegations were eager to see the plan developed.

From the point of view of Colombian and Ecuadorian delegations, the meeting at La Planada was successful in achieving its stated goals. When a general consensus was reached among Colombian and Ecuadorian officials to pursue the binational reserve, the final document proposed a reserve substantially larger than the area initially envisioned by either Colombian environmentalists or the Ecuadorian commission.

The Indian delegations, on the other hand, were less than satisfied with the meeting's accomplishments. Rather than joining the delegations of their own nation-states, the represented Indian organizations (the Awa, CONAIE, ONIC, and CRIC) chose instead to maintain a separate and united indigenous constituency. They presented their goals as a list of demands to appear in a separate section of the meeting document.

Over one-half of the recommendations presented by the Indian groups directly concerned land tenure. Those remaining addressed issues of political autonomy. The priorities placed on land and self-determination were, first, the particular concerns of the indigenous groups that were not shared by other actors and, second, the concerns most vulnerable to compromise by powerful, competing interest groups.

In Ecuador, the Awa ethnic and forest reserve was created from a synthesis of two laws, one specifying forest reserves and the other specifying Indian rights. The result was that ownership of the Awa reserve was not in the name of the Awa but rather in the name of the Ecuadorian state. One recommendation, suggesting that Ecuadorian Awa lands become "legalized as the common property of the Awa Federation," illustrates the rationale of the independent strategy of the indigenous organizations in pursuing their own priorities.

From the point of view of the Ecuadorian public officials who worked to create the reserve, the legal terms are satisfactory. But these same terms are not satisfactory to the Awa, who hope in the future to change them. With the help of national Indian organizations of both countries, the Awa will be supported in their campaign to alter the legal status of their reserve. While political elites may concede to these changes, they cannot, or would not, initiate them.

With regard to legislation guaranteeing indigenous communal ownership of lands in perpetuity, the Colombian system of *resguardos* offers more secure tenure to indigenous peoples than does Ecuadorian law.[9] In this instance, the indigenous associations of both countries may want to play on the competition between nations for most favorable image. They might challenge one government's policy by comparing it to that of the other, in order to get the strongest possible policy.

The strongly stated commitment to land rights and self-determination in the separate statement does not imply disapproval of the biosphere proposal. Another recommendation proposes "similar binational projects for other indigenous groups . . . where . . . [they] are divided by frontiers. Indians must participate in decision-making at every stage of every project." This statement demonstrates the importance of this project to indigenous groups divided by frontiers and underscores the role of the project as a potential model, if Indians are assured leadership, for international accords where indigenous peoples are concerned. The recommendation reveals the indigenous alliance's approval of the project and demonstrates that their selective participation is a strategy intended to safeguard their interests and autonomy, rather than an outright denunciation.

The recommendations of the indigenous alliance clearly and specifically enumerate general Indian rights in both countries that the national governments of Ecuador and Colombia will be expected to support. These recommendations were considered important enough by the directorate to be included as a chapter rather than as an appendix, but were not integrated into the document. While the existence of the demands does not mean that they will necessarily be put into effect, they cannot be dismissed, since they form part of the act. The presence of international agencies may serve to ensure that these proposals are kept.

Discussion

Although the stated goals of a biosphere reserve would appear to be favorable to the indigenous inhabitants of an area, certain potential threats remain, which the Awa recognize. Such considerations determine the strategies and roles played by them and other indigenous organizations.

For example, given the political contexts of the project, politicians who are accountable to competing interest groups might attempt to block implementation of certain measures, such as the demarcation of Awa lands. There is also room for potential conflict between the environmentalist supporters of restricted areas (the biologically preserved "core") and the use patterns and subsistence needs of the Awa. Yet another danger might stem from the inclination of partisan politicians to settle for symbolic rather than real progress, so long as the meetings churned out a continual flow of broadly stated objectives. The result could be a delay in demarcating the Colombian portion of the reserve, and control of the Ecuadorian commission by political and economic interests that prefer keeping the Tobar Donoso region open for ranching or large-scale lumbering.

Because of these possibilities, along with the political realities affecting internal relationships among institutions within countries and external relations between the two countries, and because of the multiple interests influencing policy within each country, the role of the indigenous organizations is crucial.

The indigenous participants recognized the special interests of their own constituency. Their strategy was based upon an assessment of the political environment in which they recognized that land ownership, their highest priority, was not a priority shared by other groupings of actors. Although conservationists sought indigenous support as a means of protecting remaining wildlands, native organizations tended to view environmental activists, commercial developers, and public officials as one undifferentiated grouping when their own land rights were concerned. Although government officials and environmentalists do not share identical agendas, both groups would favor state ownership of reserve lands. This was the case in Ecuador, where the lands were demarcated but remained under government ownership; in Colombia, demarcation procedures had been interrupted. The Indians wanted full, uncontested rights to their own lands. The position they took was non-negotiation. Faced with the possibility that their demands could not be accomodated within the coalition, they declined the opportunity to enter it. By remaining apart and presenting their demands as a separate body, they were able to preserve their demands intact.

The Role of International Agencies

The inclusion of the Indian nongovernmental organization in the coalition of government agencies early in the process in Ecuador was due in part to conditions attached to international funding sources. In the formation of the binational reserve, international agencies played a key role in encouraging the participation and strengthening the bargaining positions of both indigenous and environmentalist groups.

In the long run, a biosphere reserve including both Ecuadorian and Colombian Awa could be perceived by governments as problematic if the reserve were seen as a territorial exchange, or if allegiances between Colombian and Ecuadorian Awa were seen as eroding national identities or loyalties. Under such conditions, the role of an international oversight body may be critical in avoiding potential conflicts. On the other hand, if tensions did develop, the participation of international agencies could be perceived as counter to the interests of national governments. Such countervailing forces are among the creative tensions that contribute toward policy development.

Conclusion

As program designers become increasingly aware of the shortcomings of conventional development paradigms, several schemes for new development models emerge. These alternative development strategies address themselves to concerns that include both native communities and deteriorating environments.

Although the biosphere reserve is exceptional in providing for environmental protection, restoration of deteriorated lands, and respect for native peoples, in its present form it does not guarantee effective control by native peoples over their traditional resources and lands. From the point of view of Indian groups, then, the project is a satisfactory one *if* sustainable development is accompanied by "sustainable control" of their own resources. This explains the apparently inconsistent strategies in the participation of native organizations in the plans for a biosphere reserve.

In the early stages of the Tobar Donoso project in Ecuador, indigenous associations sought full participation in decision making and implementation of the project plans. When they later perceived that their political autonomy or fundamental interests were threatened, as in issues relating to land rights at the binational meeting with Ecuadorian and Colombian public officials, they altered their strategy to emphasize selective participation and hard-line bargaining tactics. They refused an invitation to participate in the board of directors of the meeting and insisted on the inclusion of a list of demands in a separate section of the binational Acta, carefully articulating the positions of the indigenous organizations. Their demands focus on guaranteed land rights and autonomy in social and political life. By refusing participation in the formal binational structure, and by remaining simultaneously inside, as decision makers, and outside, as lobbyists of the official political process, their independent strategic posture allowed them to instigate policy proposals that government agencies might informally favor but could not formally support, and to spur governments to act decisively when they might not otherwise do so.[10]

In name and stated policy, the binational project proposes an "Awa reserve." Even so, the Awa are aware that their participation is necessary at every level of decision making in order to ensure that their interests and priorities are met. These may not always coincide with the goals of one or both governments, of private sector interests, or of environmental and scientific entities also involved in the project. Were a biosphere reserve to be established, certain areas would be set aside for preservation, devastated areas would be targeted for restoration, and indigenous land-use methods might provide a model for sustainable land use. Such goals are potentially compatible with the Awa's own objectives. Yet unless their participation and their rights to their own lands are ensured, even a reserve established in their name may endanger their existence.

Acknowledgments

Versions of this chapter were presented in the symposium "Parks and People" at the New England Latin American Studies Association, Tufts University, October 17, 1988, and at the First International Congress of Ethnobiology, Belém, Brazil, 1988; an earlier version of the paper appears in the Proceedings volume of that Congress (Chernela 1990). The author wishes to thank David Maybury-Lewis, Theodore Macdonald, Jason Clay, Patricio Zuquilandia, Carlos Villareal, James Levy, William Smith, Eduardo Gamarra, Donald Klingner, Luis Montaluisa,

Horacio Pai, Alfredo Jiménez, Jorge Orejuela, Cristien Samper, Martin Von Hildebrand, Dennis Glick, and the persons who made it possible for me to attend the binational meeting in La Planada, Colombia.

Notes

1. According to Levy (1988), there are approximately 1,800 Awa in Ecuador and another 6,000 to 8,000 in Colombia. Osborn (1968:594) estimates the Colombian Awa population at 3,500. Since the studies were carried out two decades apart, the discrepancies in figures may represent demographic growth. Yet the figures presented by both authors are estimates based neither on sampling methods nor on careful censusing. Further research is required before reliable estimates of the Colombian Awa population may be made.

2. This road network would link Chical with Alto Tambo and Tobar Donoso. Ehrenreich (1989:53) reports that plans for the road have been halted.

3. Cultural Survival, an American-based indigenous-advocacy organization, assisted the Tobar Donoso Commission in demarcating the Awa reserve and issuing citizenship documentation to Awa. Cultural Survival's collaboration with the Tobar Donoso Commission is outlined in Leon (1984:87–88) and Macdonald (1986:33–36).

4. This law is known as the Ley Forestal y de Conservación de Areas Naturales y Vida Silvestre.

5. Páramos are unusual in surviving great surface temperature fluctuations (up to 30 degrees in a single day), extreme exposure to ultraviolet light, and extreme seasonality in rainfall.

6. Where detailed investigations have been carried out, as at La Planada, the most extensively studied site in the middle levels of the western Andes of Colombia, surprisingly rich species diversity has been observed. For example, 500 bird species have been identified within an area of about 200,000 hectares; a full 30 of these species are endemic to the region. Similarly, in the same area, more than 400 species of epiphytes have been identified, including numerous orchids and various forms of bromeliads (Orejuela 1987).

7. Fundación para la Educación Superior.

8. A more detailed account of this meeting may be found in Chernela (1990).

9. Colombia has more land, proportionally, in the ownership of indigenous societies than any other country in Latin America. Moreover, resguardos, as these territories are called, may not be sold or otherwise transferred out of the dominion of the owning Indian group.

10. Efforts to title Awa territories were begun shortly after the binational meeting. The program is supported by World Wildlife Fund–U.S., coordinated by FES, and involves the participation of Colombia's Office of Indian Affairs, the National Indian Organization, ONIC, and the Colombian Institute for Land Reform (INCORA).

References Cited

Anderson, Ellen
1982   The Saskatchewan Indians and Canada's New Constitution. *Journal of International Affairs: The Human Rights of Indigenous Peoples* 36(1): 125–48.

Chernela, Janet M.
1990   The Role of Indigenous Organizations in International Policy Development: The Case of an Awa Biosphere Reserve in Colombia and Ecuador. In *Ethnobiology: Implications and Applications*, edited by Darrell A. Posey et al. Proceedings of the First International Congress of Ethnobiology. Belém, Brazil: Museu Paraense Emílio Goeldi.

Davis, Shelton
1982   Working Toward Native Resource Control. In *Native Resource Control and the Multinational Corporate Challenge: Aboriginal Rights in International Perspective*, edited by Sally Swenson, pp. 5–6. Boston: Anthropology Resource Center.

Ehrenreich, Jeffrey
1984   Contact and Conflict: An Ethnographic Inquiry into the Impact of Racism, Ethnocide, and Social Change on the Egalitarian Coaiquer Indians of Ecuador. Ph.D. dissertation, New School for Social Research.
1985   Isolation, Retreat, and Secrecy: Dissembling Behavior Among the Coaiquer Indians of Ecuador. In *Political Anthropology in Ecuador: Perspectives from Indigenous Cultures*, edited by J. Ehrenreich. State University of New York at Albany, Society for Latin American Anthropology and Center for the Caribbean and Latin America.
1989   Lifting the Burden of Secrecy: The Emergence of the Awa Biosphere Reserve. *Latin American Anthropology Review* 1(2):49–54.
1990   Shame, Witchcraft, and Social Control: The Case of an Awa-Coaiquer Interloper. *Cultural Anthropology* 5(3):338–45.

Kempf, Judith, and Jeffrey Ehrenreich
1980   Field Report: The Coaiquer. *Newsletter of the Latin American Anthropology Group*, pp. 7–10, Washington, D.C.

Leon, Lydia
1984   Cultural Survival Projects—1984. *Cultural Survival Quarterly* 8(4): 86–91.

Levy, James R.
1988   Planning Resource Management in Indigenous Territories of Pacific Tropical America: Experiences of the Binational Awa Project in Ecuador and Colombia. Manuscript.

Macdonald, Theodore
1986   Anticipating *Colonos* and Cattle in Ecuador and Colombia. *Cultural Survival Quarterly* 10(2):33–36.

Macdonald, Theodore, and Janet Chernela
n.d.   Politics, Development, and Indians: A Comparison of Two Resource
          Management Projects in the Ecuadorian Rain Forest. Manuscript to
          appear in *The Social Impacts of Deforestation in Latin America*, edited by
          Suzannah Hecht and James Nations. Forthcoming.

Ministry of Foreign Relations (Ecuador).
1983   Proyecto de desarrollo en la zona Tobar Donoso. Manuscript.

Orejuela Gartner, Jorge E.
1987   La reserva natural "La Planada" y la biogeografía andina. *Humboldtia*
          1(1):117–48.

Ortiz, S. E.
1937   Notas sobre los Koaikeres. *Indearium* 1:24–33.

Osborn, Ann
1968   Compadrazgo and Patronage: A Colombian Case. *Man* n.s. 3:593–608.

Salazar, Ernesto
1977   *An Indian Federation in Lowland Ecuador.* Copenhagen: International
          Work Group for Indigenous Affairs, document 28. Copenhagen.
1981   La federación Shuar y la frontera de la colonización. In *Amazonia
          ecuatoriana: La otra cara del progreso*, edited by Norman E. Whitten, Jr.,
          pp. 59–81. Ediciones Mundo Shuar, Ecuador.

Schwartzman, Stephen
1984   Indigenists, Environmentalists, and the Multilateral Development
          Banks. *Cultural Survival Quarterly* (8)4:74–75.

Weiss, Gerald
1988   The Tragedy of Ethnicide: A Reply to Hippler. In *Tribal Peoples and
          Development Issues*, edited by John Bodley, pp. 124–133. Mayfield,
          Calif.: Mayfield Publishing Co.

13

Relationships Among the World System, Indigenous Peoples, and Ecological Anthropology in the Endangered Amazon

Leslie E. Sponsel

Five hundred years ago Amazonia was not an endangered biome, even though indigenous peoples had already lived there for millennia. Although the destruction of the Amazon started with Western colonization centuries ago, only in recent decades has this destruction reached a level that increasingly endangers the entire region. Economic development has been achieved through deforestation and other forms of environmental degradation. It has also been achieved through the imposition of sudden and profound ecological, economic, and cultural changes on indigenous societies. In the process, many have become extinct, and many others are endangered. Some people euphemistically call these changes the advance of civilization and progress. Others honestly label it ecocide, ethnocide, and genocide.

Three things are now alarmingly clear. The futures of indigenes and ecosystems of the Amazon are intimately interrelated and increasingly influenced by Western society. The future of the Amazon is uncertain at best, especially if trends continue. And the future of the Amazon is likely to be determined within the next few decades, if it is not already too late to avoid disaster.

As it has in the past, so in the future human adaptation in Amazonia will depend on the flexibility and resilience of indigenous populations, their cultures, and the ecosystems they inhabit. But the future of Amazonia also depends on the adaptability of Western society—its willingness to learn from indigenous knowledge and wisdom as well as from its own past mistakes in order to develop sustainable relationships with both ecosystems and indigenous societies. In turn, this adaptability depends on

Western society's appreciating the instrinsic as well as the extrinsic value of indigenes and ecosystems, and on respecting and defending the basic human rights of indigenes.

Considering some of the historic occasions of the early 1990s—the Columbian quincentenary, the Earth Summit, the United Nations' International Year of Indigenous Peoples—and the 1990s as the turning point for a new century and millennium, in 1995 it is not only appropriate but even vital to critically rethink Western society's relationship to the indigenous peoples and tropical forests of the world. This historical juncture also provides an opportunity and serves as a catalyst for us to rethink the role of anthropologists, both individually and collectively. It is becoming increasingly clear that purely academic interests in the Amazon can no longer be maintained, considering the gravity and urgency of the growing crisis of ecocide, ethnocide, and genocide. There is also increasing concern among indigenous peoples about the role of anthropologists, as is reflected in the foreword to this book. For these and other reasons, the situation in the Amazon demands a paradigm shift in anthropological research on human ecology and other topics. Accordingly, the primary concern of this book has been to make some contribution toward that goal. Let us now examine these and related matters in greater detail to conclude this book.

Deforestation

Tropical deforestation threatens to diminish the quality of organic and human life on planet Earth as a whole because of the vital environmental services, economic resources (including medicines), and aesthetic value of forest ecosystems. Deforestation and extinction are nothing new, but their recent magnitudes are certainly reason for alarm and action (Grove 1992). Current rates of deforestation throughout the tropics exceed 30 hectares per minute (Repetto 1990). During 1981–85, deforestation rates were higher in Latin America than elsewhere in absolute area (43,000 km^2/ year) and percentage of total forest area (0.64 percent/year) (Anderson 1990:4). The associated spasm of extinction resulting from habitat destruction in the tropics is rare if not unique in geological history (Jablonski 1991; Raup 1988). Wilson (1992) estimates that three species are becoming extinct each hour in the tropical rain forest. There is certainly no precedent in the prehistory and history of indigenous societies for the deforestation that has been occurring at an exponential rate in Amazonia since the 1980s.

Causes

Deforestation involves complicated phenomena and multiple causes. The specific combination of proximate causes varies in time and space from country to country, and even regionally within a country. But the ultimate causes are usually the same—the greed of outsiders and, to a much lesser extent if at all, the needs of locals. Sometimes the latter do not have any alternative for economic survival but to pursue activities that contribute to deforestation.

Under normal circumstances, deforestation is not caused by shifting (swidden or slash-and-burn) horticulture. Traditional indigenous populations are low in density and fairly mobile, and they practice a rotational subsistence economy with polycropping, adequate fallow periods, and ample areas of forest held in reserve for future gardens (Carneiro 1988). In general, swidden farming is efficient, productive, and sustainable. It contributes to deforestation only when it is not practiced in traditional ways, when population pressure develops, and/or when cash crops are introduced for export in a market economy. Admittedly, one or more of these new conditions are rapidly developing in many areas of Amazonia.

Most population growth in Amazonian countries is taking place not so much in the forest as in boom towns and especially in cities, but these in turn put pressure on the land and resources in the adjacent forests (Godfrey 1990; Lugo 1991). The government of Brazil tried to relieve the population problem in the poverty- and drought-stricken, arid northeast sector of the country by designing a scheme to relocate people along the Transamazon Highway, but the initiative was far from successful (Moran 1988; Smith 1978). Such *shifted* (in contrast to shifting) farmers usually do not know how to farm or in other ways adapt in the tropical forest, and they are another factor contributing to deforestation in the Amazon. By far the most important cause of deforestation in Brazil, however, has been the conversion of forest to pasture that appears to be for cattle ranching but is really for profit from land speculation. About 85 percent of the deforestation in the Brazilian Amazon is caused by only some 500 ranches (Hecht 1989; Hecht and Cockburn 1989).

Forest conversion for establishing massive monocrop plantations for agricultural produce, timber, or paper pulp is another cause of deforestation (McNeill 1986; Margolis 1977)—but except for the infamous Jari project, this kind of activity has been fairly limited in the Amazon so far. Hydroelectric dams like the Balbina (Fearnside 1989a; Gribel 1990) and mining projects like Carajas are other important causes of deforestation in Brazil. The timber in the lakes formed behind the dams is not cut but simply left to die and decompose, thus polluting the waters. The enormous Carajas iron mine smelts ore with the use of charcoal produced from the surrounding forest (Fearnside 1989b). Otherwise, commercial logging has not been a major cause of deforestation in Amazonia, although it could well become so in the future as Japan and other tropical timber importers turn to this region after depleting the forests of Southeast Asia and Melanesia. Even selective logging, where less than 10 percent of the trees are cut, can still damage more than half the trees in the forest (Myers 1992).

In Brazil, these and other schemes for economic development have been integral parts of the military's initiative to conquer its frontier, integrate the area economically and politically, and assimilate or exterminate the indigenes, all in the name of national security and economic progress. Much of this destruction is financed by international lending organizations, notably the World Bank. Such banks are supported partly by taxpayers in the United States and other developed countries (Bushbacher 1986; Guimaraes 1991; Hecht and Cockburn 1989; Katzman 1975; Moran 1983; Poelhekke 1986; Schmink and Wood 1992; Treece 1989).

Consequences

The consequences of deforestation are manifold—evolutionary, genetic, environmental, social, economic, medical, political, and aesthetic. They range from impacts on local people and wildlife to global warming and rising sea levels. In all aspects and at all scales they can be far reaching and even catastrophic (Bunyard 1987; Cook, Janetos, and Hinds 1990; Molion 1989; Myers 1992; Sioli 1987).

Species are unique, closed genetic units; species extinction is forever. In a few years, human activity can destroy millions of years of organic evolution. Moreover, the extinction of any species has a multiplier effect, influencing numerous other species because of the great diversity and complexity of the tropical forest ecosystem, which is characterized by multiple linkages and interdependencies between species. The erosion of biodiversity through habitat destruction and species extinction eliminates forever possibilities for future evolution, germ plasm for agriculture, food and pharmaceutical products, and industrial materials (Barrau 1982; Pimentel et al. 1992; Plotkin 1991; Smith and Schultes 1990; Smith et al. 1992; Wilson 1989).

In Amazonia, about half the rainfall circulates in the water cycle of the local ecosystem. Massive deforestation will disrupt this cycle and probably lead to increased aridity regionally and far beyond, with detrimental effects on agricultural activity and productivity (Salati 1987).

A neglected consequence of deforestation is disease. Transients and colonists introduce new diseases from the outside to local residents, some triggering devastating epidemics. Endemic diseases such as malaria are aggravated by changes in the forest ecology and are also contracted by colonists and transients (ICHI 1986; and see chapter 8, this book).

Solutions

Also multiple and complex are any solutions for deforestation. Westerners have treated the forests as obstacles to development rather than as foundations for sustainable land and resource use. Governments, for example, often define colonists' claims and land improvements in terms of their converting forested land into farms and pastures, even providing financial incentives for their efforts in doing so. The future of the forests lies not in conservation alone, in the sense of mere preservation, but also in sustainable land and resource management of existing forests as well as regeneration of deforested areas where feasible (Anderson 1990b; Barrett 1980; Clay 1988; Eden 1990; Fearnside 1990a; Foresta 1991; Gómez-Pompa, Whitmore, and Hadley 1991; Head and Heinzman 1990; Hecht and Cockburn 1989; Lugo, Clark, and Child 1987; Myers 1992; Ryan 1992).

If Westerners afford the forest itself any value, often it is only for logging. So-called minor, secondary, or nontimber forest products have been grossly undervalued and neglected. An economic assessment of one hectare of forest indicates its value for different uses: $1,000 if clear cut for timber, $2,960 if converted to pasture, $3,184 if converted into a *Gmelina arborea* plantation for pulpwood and timber, and $6,820 if used for the extraction of fruit and latex and occasional selective logging. The exploitation of nontimber forest products can be a nonconsumptive and sustainable use of forest, and at the same time most profitable in comparison to other uses (Peters, Gentry, and Mendelsohn 1989; see also Godoy and Lubowski 1992). The hunting of wildlife for subsistence and/or commercial purposes by indigenes (traditional and acculturated), colonists, and others also needs to be carefully considered (Redford and Padoch 1992; Robinson and Redford 1991; and see chapters 5 and 9–12, this book).

Other factors that need to be calculated include the environmental services provided by the forest, such as soil and moisture retention. One promising development is ecological economics, which seeks to expand the scope of neoclassical economics by integrating natural laws and natural resource constraints into analyses of costs, benefits, and values, and by considering the long term as well as the short term (Farnworth et al. 1983; Fearnside 1989c; Katzman and Cale 1990; Repetto 1987, 1992). (For a discussion of extractive industries and reserves, see Browder 1992; Bunker 1984; and Fearnside 1989d. Ehrlich and Ehrlich 1992 review the value of biodiversity.)

An important part of the solution to deforestation must be fundamental changes in the attitudes, values, and practices of the nonindigenous world, particularly the frontier mentality, materialism, and consumerism of Western society (Bodley 1990:6–7; Hvalkof 1989). Western exploitation of the Amazon has been predicated on ignorance, driven by greed, and operated for external interests rather than the benefit of locals. Environmental and social impact assessments need to be made as an integral and meaningful part of the planning, implementation, and monitoring phases of all economic development projects, instead of appealing to such assessments for public relations and damage control, usually after policy decisions have already been made and implementation begun (Fearnside 1986).

Frontier and Development

The Amazon is one of the last frontiers on planet Earth. Frontiers are peripheral to the centers of economic and political power in the world system. A frontier is generally viewed as a wilderness, unpopulated or underpopulated, unused or underused, and therefore rich in resources that are unlimited and free for anyone to exploit to make a quick profit (Dickenson 1989). Frontiers are usually rife with direct and indirect forms of violence, initially caused spontaneously by colonists, and largely beyond the control of the nation-state (Amnesty International 1992; Bodley 1990; Miller 1993). The national government gradually acquires control over the frontier through its military, administrators, missionaries, colonists, and other representatives. This government targets the frontier for integration for purposes of national security, economic development, modernization, and civilization, usually initially through missionization (Bodley 1990; Hecht and Cockburn 1989; Schmink and Wood 1992).

Most outsiders consider the indigenes on the frontier to be, variously, subhuman or barely human, wild, savage, prehistoric survivals, anachronistic, backward, primitive, simple, unsophisticated, inefficient, unproductive, lazy, wasteful, destructive, ignorant, and irrational. The conquest of the frontier rests on such racist and ethnocentric beliefs and values, as well as on their associated behavior, including missionization, warfare, administration, reservations, and other forms of direct and indirect violence. In the process of conquering and developing the frontier, social and economic justice, equity, and rights for the people of the forest are disregarded, as are the rights of future generations of humanity (Amnesty International 1992; Berwick 1992; Hecht and Cockburn 1989:193–209).

More often than not, the net effect on the indigenous societies is dispossession, displacement, depopulation, detribalization, dehumanization, demoralization, and dependence, or, at worst, ecocide, ethnocide, and genocide (Bodley 1988, 1990; Burger 1987; Hemming 1987; Miller 1993; Wolf 1982). In Brazil from 1900 to 1957, for example, the number of indigenous cultures declined through extinction from 230 to 87 (Ribeiro 1972). This horribly destructive process continues during the closing years of the twentieth century. In this respect, during 500 years Western civilization has made, morally, little progress. The Yanomami are among its latest victims, as we shall see later (and see chapters 9–10 in this book).

Ultimately we face a matter of values: the gross failure of the West to recognize the intrinsic as well as extrinsic value of indigenes and their environment, combined with the myopic pursuits of a materialistic consumer society that considers only the benefits of resource exploitation and economic development and does not adequately assess their ecological, social, and psychological costs in both the short term and the long term (Bodley 1985; Crosby 1972; Myers 1993; Repetto 1992; Sponsel 1986; Wolf 1982). Western economic development and the consumer society are analogous to cancer—uncontrolled growth that eventually destroys the host. Unlike cancer, Western society is supposed to be rational, knowledgeable, humane, and civil. Yet it has been repeatedly demonstrated that Western society does not know how to develop Amazonia without destroying the environment and the indigenous inhabitants (Hecht and Cockburn 1989; Sponsel 1992a; Stone 1993). The loss of cultural and biological diversity, not to mention human lives, impoverishes the biosphere, humankind, and even future evolution and adaptation, given the immensity, diversity, richness, and fragility of Amazonia.

Economic development and modernization are partly rationalized as contributing to improvements in quality of life and other aspects of progress. Anthropologist George Appell (1975:31) provides a reality check:

> Every act of development involves, of necessity, an act of destruction. This destruction—social, ecological, or both—is seldom accounted for in development projects, despite the fact that it may entail costs that far outweigh the benefits arising from the development. And I use the term development here to cover all those activities usually incorporated under such terms as economic, educational, and agricultural planning and development.

Appell (1975:33) goes on to provide a more accurate definition of development (also see Appell 1988 and chapter 10 in this book):

> A development act is any act by an individual who is not a member of a local society that devalues or displaces the perception by the members of that society of their relationship with their natural and social world. By this definition we can include in the act of development planning the local school teacher, the local doctor, as well as the economic, agricultural, and educational experts who work in the major centers of the developing country and who are ultimately responsible for the lower-level acts.

The Indigenous World

Jason Clay (1989:1), who worked for many years with Cultural Survival, has observed:

> Virtually all the world's tropical forests are populated, usually by indigenous peoples. In order for local, state or international interests to exploit forest resources, the rights of indigenous groups must be denied and the groups themselves displaced. It is no accident, therefore, that indigenous peoples are disappearing at an even faster rate than the tropical forests upon which they depend. Their own survival is intricately linked with that of their forests. They also represent our best first line of defense against the destruction of the forests.

Yanomami

Until recently the Yanomami were often described as the largest unacculturated indigenous society remaining in the Amazon. There are about 20,000 people in the Yanomami nation. Their territory straddles the border between the states of Brazil and Venezuela. Although archaeological research in their territory has been negligible, genetic and linguistic evidence indicates that the Yanomami have been a distinctive population for at least 2,000 years.

Although the Yanomami have experienced centuries of intermittent and diverse contact with representatives of Western society (Ferguson 1992), only in recent decades has this contact intensified to the point that Yanomami society is now threatened with extinction through the invasion of their territory first by road construction in the 1970s and then by gold miners in the 1980s. The road reduced some Yanomami to hunger, disease, beggary, alcoholism, and prostitution. Subsequently, an apparently spontaneous invasion of miners, which peaked in 1987, aggravated the situation, depleted game resources, and added mercury and other pollutants to the environment (Berwick 1992; Sponsel 1994).

In Venezuela, very near the border with Brazil, during late July of 1993, at least 16 Yanomami, including women, elderly people, children, and infants, were brutally massacred by Brazilian gold miners. Several were decapitated. Bodies were mutilated in other ways (Albert 1993). Again in Venezuela, this time in late November of 1993, at least 19 Yanomami were found dead, presumably of mercury poisoning, although details remain obscure at this writing. Thus the Columbian holocaust continues in the Amazon to this day, with the Yanomami being among the latest victims.

Yanomami have been subjects of research by some three dozen anthropologists from several countries for over a century. Yet proposals by Survival International for a Yanomami park in Brazil to protect their basic human rights and allow them gradually to adapt to Western society lacked such fundamental information as the amount of land necessary to sustain their traditional subsistence economy in the long term (i.e., carrying capacity requirements) (Fearnside 1990b; Ramos and Taylor 1979).

Decades of pressure from advocacy groups have finally, in recent years, forced the former presidents of Brazil and Venezuela to take some positive measures to protect the Yanomami. However, persistent political and economic crises in both countries, and other factors such as international economic interests, do not leave much room for optimism. The Yanomami continue to suffer and even die from the invasion of gold miners. An even greater number die from diseases, most of them preventable. To compound the tragedy of the situation, the impact of both diseases and illegal miners could be greatly reduced if the governments of Brazil and Venezuela would only assume their responsibilities toward indigenous residents and according to international agreements they have signed regarding health care and human rights (see Albert 1992; Arvelo-Jiménez and Cousins 1992; Chagnon 1992:207–246; Pallemaerts 1986; Sponsel 1979, 1981, 1993; Survival International 1991; Turner 1991). (The Yanomami are not the only indigenous society plagued by gold miners. There are more than half a million gold miners in Amazonia. The mercury they use in processing the gold is a major pollutant [Malm et al. 1990; Martinelli et al. 1988].)

Successes

Although many indigenous societies, like the Yanomami, are threatened with imminent extinction, others have avoided genocide and ethnocide, experienced a population rebound after initial depopulation by Western contact diseases, selectively accepted Western culture, and maintained their territorial integrity and ethnic identity (e.g., Hern 1992). Among such successful indigenous societies are the Shuar of Ecuador, Shipibo of Peru, Kayapó of Brazil, and Ye'kuana of Venezuela.

It is a myth that all indigenous peoples are inevitably destined to suffer extinction—biological or cultural (Bodley 1990). This is not to imply that culture is static. A major message of this book is about the dynamics of cultural and environmental systems in space and time. Change is inevitable, and it is what adaptation is all about (Steward 1955). Cultural extinction, however, is not inevitable, except in the minds of the so-called realists (Bodley 1990:Ch. 10). But the rubric "realist" is a misnomer. The "realists" are unrealistic because they fail to confront their own involvement—at least indirect, if not direct—in change as an economic and political process, often a destructive one, induced by Western society in Amazonia and elswhere. They also fail to recognize that conscious choices are actually made by economic and political actors to induce genocide, ethnocide, and ecocide, and they fail to effectively oppose such choices and their dire consequences.

Knowledge and Education

The Shuar nation of Ecuador has in large measure maintained its identity, self-determination, and territory. The Shuar have managed to control the schooling of their children by offering Western education through radio broadcasts to villages, instead of following the usual method of sending children away for most of the year to distant boarding schools, most of them run by missionaries. Radio broadcasts to villages allow children to grow up with family and community, thereby benefiting from both worlds—bicultural and bilingual education in the Western and the indigenous systems. Western education is necessary if people are to adapt to the outside world, although there is plenty of room in which to render it of more practical relevance to indigenes. Indigenous education is necessary to adapt to the indigenous world, including the forests and rivers.

Culture is socially learned and shared behavior, and therefore education is a cross-cultural universal, even though indigenous systems of education may be very different from Western ones. When children remain in their village they continue to learn from the older members of their families and community in the indigenous system of education. This education includes the knowledge, technology, and skills needed for survival, subsistence, and adaptation in the forest and associated ecosystems. Children who are sent away from the village to boarding schools miss this indigenous education and grow up less competent in basic survival and subsistence skills than do children who remain in the village and benefit from its traditional educational system (see chapter 11 in this book).

Boarding school education is a situation that needs not only to be systematically documented but also urgently rectified as one of the main causes of ethnocide. The inherent racism and ethnocentrism of Western education in Amazonia must be challenged, while, simultaneously, indigenous culture, language, and education must be fully recognized and appreciated if these peoples and their ecosystems are to survive.

The importance of indigenous knowledge, technology, and skills is demonstrated by the fact that any colonists who have successfully settled in the forests and floodplains of Amazonia, regardless of their "racial" and cultural heritage, have survived by adopting indigenous ways. Indeed, this practice is the key to the success of the rubber tappers and other so-called *caboclos*, *ribereños*, mestizos, and criollos who live in the Amazon. These people number in the hundreds of thousands and make up a syncretic culture that emerged historically mainly in the riverine contact zone between the indigeneous and Western worlds (Hecht and Cockburn 1989; Hiraoka 1985, 1989; Padoch 1988).

The significant contributions of indigenous societies to humanity are not sufficiently recognized and appreciated (Crosby 1972, 1986; Weatherford 1988). As just one example, consider manioc, or cassava, which was probably originally domesticated in the northwest Amazon. In recent centuries and decades it has been introduced throughout the tropical world from Africa to Asia to Oceania. It is the fourth most important source of energy in the tropics, providing food for humans and livestock (see Hawkes 1989; Mowat 1989; chapter 7, this book).

Political Movements and Environmentalists

By far one of the more promising developments since the 1970s has been the political mobilization of indigenous communities through various regional organizations in Amazonia as well as larger associations such as the World Council of Indigenous Peoples (Bodley 1990:ch. 9, app. D and E). In recent years this movement has even begun to be felt in the growing influence of indigenes in the United Nations. Another hopeful development is the joining of forces by rubber tappers and indigenes to call for the establishment of extractive reserves in the Brazilian Amazon (Allegretti 1990; Lutzenberger 1987; Schwartz 1989; Schwartzman 1989).

The Coordinating Body of the Indigenous Peoples' Organizations (COICA) issued a statement to environmentalists that is also relevant to ecological anthropologists. While applauding the efforts of environmentalists to conserve the Amazon forest, they express concern that indigenes not be neglected. They assert that indigenes are the original inhabitants, ecologists, and conservationists of Amazonia, and that these facts as well as their land rights and other human rights should be recognized. They call for active and effective collaboration between environmentalists and indigenes (COICA 1990).

Fortunately, there is growing recognition of the need for such collaboration by many environmentalists (Kempf 1993; McNeely and Pitt 1984; McNeely et al. 1990a, 1990b). This convergence of indigenous and environmentalist concerns appears to have been realized in Colombia, where President Barco's government in 1988 decided that the best way to conserve the forests of Amazonia was to entrust them to the indigenous peoples who depended on them for survival by officially recognizing their rights to ancestral lands (Bunyard 1989, 1993). The convergence of indigenous and environmentalist interests and political forces is a very promising development, but it is too recent to permit us to detect its ramifications (Clay 1991; COICA 1990; González 1992).

At the same time, it is troubling that some environmentalists have been rather careless in their criticisms of indigenes (e.g., Redford 1990, 1991, 1992; cf. Sponsel 1992a). Indigenes deserve special consideration, for not only are they the descendants of the original peoples of Amazonia, but in many ways they are also the ultimate artists, theologians, philosophers, scientists, librarians, engineers, and guardians of the forest. Furthermore, if anyone knows how to use natural resources sustainably, without irreversibly degrading or even completely destroying the forest ecosystem, it is most indigenous societies. Indeed, it can be argued that they have actually enhanced biodiversity through swidden cultivation, agroforestry, and other traditional practices. This is not to deny that indigenous societies have a significant impact on their forest habitat, but to recognize that their environmental impact, even cumulatively, is usually within the realm of natural disturbances such as gaps created by tree falls. This situation is in sharp contrast to the environmental impact of Western civilization in the Amazon (Sponsel 1992a). It is worth repeating that 500 years ago Amazonia was not an endangered biome, but it has increasingly become so with Western penetration, mostly within recent decades.

Anthropology

More than a century of anthropological research, publishing, and teaching have had surprisingly little effect in changing the colonial relationship between so-called civilization and so-called primitive peoples in frontier zones like the Amazon. The section on anthropology from the neglected but nonetheless historically important "Declaration of Barbados"—a document issued after a symposium on interethnic conflict in South America in which most participants were anthropologists from South America—provides some insight into this matter:

> Anthropology took form within and became an instrument of colonial domination, openly or surreptitiously; it has often rationalized and justified in scientific language the domination of some people by others. The discipline has continued to supply information and methods of action useful for maintaining, reaffirming, and disguising social relations of a colonial nature. Latin America has been and is no exception, and with growing frequency, we note nefarious Indian action programmes and the dissemination of stereotypes and myths distorting and masking the Indian situation—all pretending to have their basis in alleged scientific anthropological research.
>
> A false awareness of this situation has led many anthropologists to adopt equivocal positions. These might be classed as the following types:
>
> 1. A scientism that negates any relationship between academic research and the future of people who form the object of the research, thus eschewing the political responsibility that the relationship contains;
> 2. A hypocrisy manifested in a rhetorical protestation based on first principles, which skillfully avoids any commitment to a concrete situation;
> 3. An opportunism that, although it may recognize the present painful situation of the Indian, at the same time rejects any possibility of transformative action by proposing the need "to do something" within the established order; this position only reaffirms and continues the system.
>
> The anthropology now required in Latin America is not that which relates to Indians as objects of study but rather that which perceives the colonial situation and commits itself to the struggle for liberation. In this context, we see anthropology providing, on the one hand, the colonized peoples with data and interpretations about both themselves and their colonizers that might be useful for their own fight for freedom and, on the other hand, a redefinition of the distorted image of Indian communities extant in the national society, thereby unmasking its colonial nature and its supportive ideology. (Dostal 1971:278–80)

Some additional points may be made in considering this matter. First, as I mentioned earlier, most anthropologists assume a "realist" position— that extinction of indigenes is inevitable, either biologically or through assimilation (Bodley 1990:179–207). Second, the values of cultural evolutionism and salvage ethnography have led most anthropologists to ignore or neglect cultural change (Fabian 1983; Gruber 1970; Pandian 1985; Sponsel 1985:95–98, 1989). Third, most anthropologists have avoided direct involvement in the change process under the fallacious pretense of preserving scientific objectivity through neutrality (Marquet 1964). Fourth, studies of cultural change and applied anthropology have never been valued by the profession as prestigious. When anthropologists have participated in the process of cultural change, it has usually been as consultants for a government or other external agents of change, perhaps with the hidden agenda of making the changes less painful and more humane for the indigenes.

A fifth point is that most anthropological field research is conceived, designed, and, after implementation, analyzed, reported, and published solely within the framework of academia. During the entire research process there is little, if any, consideration of the interests, priorities, problems, and issues of the local indigenous community in which the anthropologist is privileged to live and work. Rarely does the anthropologist report the results of the research to the local community. Instead, most publications are directed toward the intellectual entertainment of colleagues and students and more generally toward some sort of contribution to Western knowledge and science (Sponsel 1991, 1992b).

Sixth, except perhaps for reporting human rights abuses to appropriate government authorities, human rights organizations, and/or news media, most anthropologists are relatively powerless economically and politically, albeit not in comparison to the indigenous community. Anthropologists working in foreign countries are especially vulnerable because their visas and research permits can be readily revoked if they cause perceived problems or expose embarrassing violations of human rights (Sponsel 1990, 1991, 1992b). The anthropologist's previous research investment and continued career development naturally translate into a strong interest in maintaining access to an area for research, and this interest tends to preempt much if any involvement in the problems that confront the host community. Admittedly, dealing in the field with serious problems such as human rights can be dangerous personally for anthropologists as well as for members of the host community.

Finally, another factor that can easily become a rationale for procrastination is that the anthropologist must first understand the details and complexity of a situation before considering appropriate action. However, this factor does not prevent the design of basic research, and accordingly there is no reason why it should prevent the design of applied or advocacy research, especially if it is conducted in close collaboration with members of the host community as knowledgeable colleagues. In any field research, the anthropologist must proceed with special caution and sensitivity.

Advocacy and Human Rights

Seldom have anthropologists acted directly on behalf of the survival, rights, and other practical concerns of indigenous communities, although since the 1960s such action has progressively emerged as advocacy anthropology. It is practiced by a relatively small number of anthropologists and a few organizations such as Cultural Survival, Survival International, the International Work Group for Indigenous Affairs, Rainforest Action Network, and Rainforest Alliance (Hecht and Cockburn 1989:193–209; Miller 1993; Paine 1985; Rainforest Action Network 1990; Warry 1990; Wright 1988).

In this respect, several developments of the early 1990s are important: the Society for Applied Anthropology published a report on the relationship between human rights and the environment (Johnston 1993); the American Anthropological Association (AAA) established its Commission for Human Rights and made human rights the main theme for its 1994 annual convention (Alfredsson 1989; Sanders 1989); and the European Association of Social Anthropologists established its Network on Human Rights and Indigenous Peoples. Thus there appears to be a growing concern for human rights within the profession of anthropology.

The increased interest in human rights within the AAA would appear in part to be a natural development from its "Statement on Ethics: Principles of Professional Responsibility" (American Anthropological Association 1976:1), especially these points:

> In research, an anthropologist's paramount responsibility is to those he studies. When there is a conflict of interest, these individuals must come first. The anthropologist must do everything within his power to protect their physical, social, and psychological welfare and to honor their dignity and privacy.

In the modern world there is general agreement that all human beings and societies have certain basic rights that all nations should respect (Donnelly 1989). This international recognition of human rights has been a promising development in global politics and international law since World War II. However, there is less agreement on the specifics of human rights and on whether they should be narrowly or broadly defined. Human rights that are now part of international agreements approved by many countries include the following (also see Downing and Kushner 1988; Miller 1993):

1. The right to life and to personal integrity free from physical or psychological abuse

2. The right to a nationality
3. The right to freedom from genocide, torture, and slavery
4. The right to seek and enjoy in other countries asylum from persecution
5. The right to freedom from arbitrary arrest and imprisonment
6. The right to a fair trial in both civil and criminal matters
7. The right to freedom of movement, including the right to leave and return to one's own country
8. The right to privacy
9. The right to own property
10. The right to freedom of speech, religion, and assembly
11. The right of peoples to self-determination
12. The right to preserve culture, religion, and language
13. The right to adequate food, shelter, health care, and education (Indian Law Resource Center 1984:1–2)

Human rights offer anthropologists one very practical focus and set of priorities for a research agenda, whether their personal emphasis is on basic or applied work. For example, a little reflection will reveal that ecological anthropology and all 13 of these basic human rights are mutually relevant, at least indirectly. The direct mutual relevance of ecological anthropology and human rights numbers 1, 3, 7, and 9–13 should be obvious, and they have been touched on in various ways in many of the previous chapters. *The rights to life, movement, land, resources, food, shelter, health care, education, culture, language, religion, and self-determination are basic for the survival, adaptation, and welfare of indigenes in Amazonia.* Ecological anthropologists can help document, defend, and promote these needs in traditional and acculturated societies (e.g., Clay 1988:69–73; Messer 1993).

Paradigm Shift

Research in ecological anthropology in Amazonia needs to go far beyond the traditional approach; it must add and emphasize a whole new dimension—*indigenous adaptations to the new challenges of Western society's encroachment on their society and environment* (Table 13.1). Some of the frontiers for future research in ecological anthropology may be itemized as follows:

1. Basic considerations of territory, land, resources, nutrition, health, demography, education, language, and religion
2. Adaptations to spatial and temporal variation in natural ecosystems

Table 13.1 Paradigm Shift for Ecological Anthropology in Amazonia

Category	Past	Future
Ethics and politics	Covert	More overt and examined
Research emphasis	Knowledge as end in itself as good, i.e., basic research	Knowledge as means to an end; applied and advocacy research including systematic critique and lobby of government, missionaries, and other external change agents
Framework	Cultural evolutionism and salvage ethnography	Advocacy as well as ecology of adaptation: survival, well-being, identity, and self-determination
Environment	Static, pristine, homogeneous	Dynamic, heterogeneous, deforestation, indigenous environmental impact, historical ecology
Culture	Indigenous society as isolated, static, and pristine	Dynamic: interaction of indigenous and Western societies
Challenges	Uneven distribution and scarcity of natural resources; natural hazards	Western society and world system as hazards, in addition to natural resources and hazards
Focus	Subsistence economy as influences culture in interplay with environment and population	Political economy and human rights; market as well as subsistence economy, economic alternatives; resource use, management, and conservation; relations with nutrition, health, and demography
Audience	Academia and Western society, including state government	Indigenous society for empowerment and enhanced adaptation

3. Adaptations to Western society and the changes it causes in the indigenous society and environment
4. A more systematic, sustained, and vocal defense of the indigenous society, as well as a critique of Western society
5. Sociocultural restoration and revitalization of indigenous societies and their adaptations

6. The political as well as the economic, ecological, and sociocultural dynamics of the preceding items, including human rights issues
7. Relevant information provided directly to the leadership of indigenous communities and organizations for their own use, empowerment, and self-determination

This paradigm shift does not necessarily require the abandonment of the previous concerns of ecological anthropology, but only the addition of new ones, together with a redefinition of priorities—including our priorities in terms of audience. For example, basic research in archaeology, ethnohistory, and ecological anthropology can provide valuable documentation for the land-rights claims of indigenous societies, as well as information for the anthropological profession and its general audience. It remains important to document the usually ecologically sound values, knowledge, and technology of indigenous peoples (Clay 1988; McNeely et al. 1990a, 1990b; Posey et al. 1990; Sponsel 1986, 1992a). It is important to document cases in which indigenes are influenced by and/or involved in deforestation, and also to help them develop alternative, non-consumptive, sustainable economic activities such as the regulated ecotourism being conducted in the Manu Park in Peru (Anderson 1990b; Plotkin and Famolare 1992; Redford and Padoch 1992).

In addition to research on such standard topics as the history of patterns of settlement and land and resource use and management, ecological anthropologists can turn to some additional topics that are oriented more toward applied and advocacy anthropology: agroforestry, extraction reserves, ethnopharmacology, aquaculture, game ranching, ecotourism, international peace parks, and restoration ecology. The careful development of some of these endeavors, along with just compensation for intellectual property, could generate the cash income indigenes require to meet critical needs such as medicines, material goods, education, and legal assistance from Western society (Cultural Survival 1991; for more traditional lists of research agendas, see Clay 1988; Moran 1979, 1982; Sponsel 1986).

Information arising from anthropological research needs to be made available in meaningful ways directly to appropriate leaders of indigenous communities and organizations. An important element in this paradigm shift is the acknowledgment of indigenes as *colleagues* rather than simply as informants, and therefore the addition of indigenes to the team that designs, implements, reports, and uses the research (e.g., Warry 1990; Wax 1991). This is not a new idea, but it is potentially revolutionary in its consequences. The first International Congress of Ethnobiology (Posey et (al. 1990:I:8), for example, published a document called *Declaration of Belém*, which, among other things relevant to ecological anthropology, recommends that:

(1) henceforth, a substantial proportion of development aid be devoted to efforts aimed at ethnobiological inventory, conservation, and management programs;

(2) mechanisms be established by which indigenous specialists are recognized as proper authorities and are consulted in all programs affecting them, their resources, and their environments . . .

(4) procedures be developed to compensate native peoples for the utilization of their knowledge and their biological resources . . .

(7) ethnobiologists make available the results of their research to the native peoples with whom they have worked, specially including dissemination in the native language;

(8) exchange of information be promoted among indigenous and peasant peoples regarding conservation, management, and sustained utilization of resources.

A major challenge for ecological anthropologists in the future is to translate these ideas into practice. This will be accomplished by more creative and responsive research conducted in ways appropriate to the individual anthropologist and the particular situation. It will not be easy or without controversy. This paradigm shift recognizes the intrinsic as well as the extrinsic value of indigenes and environments. If this change is not made voluntarily, then it will be forced upon anthropologists by the circumstances of the increasing impact of Western society on indigenes and ecosystems and by the concerns and demands of indigenes themselves. Indeed, this sort of pressure is already being felt in many areas of the Amazon. In Venezuela, half the indigenous groups no longer welcome anthropological researchers. This shift can help promote the survival of indigenes and environments in the endangered world of Amazonia, although, of course, much more has to happen in other arenas as well. The shift will also promote ecological anthropology, among other things, through the mutual feedback between theory and practice. Obviously, ecological anthropology will not survive if its subject matter becomes extinct, except perhaps as a variant of archaeology and ethnohistory.

Perhaps the main criticism of the new paradigm is that it introduces morality and politics into science, which can remain objective only by preserving neutrality. But the myth that science is necessarily amoral and apolitical should have been dispelled long ago by the role of science in Nazi ideology and in medical experiments at death camps, and later, in another way, by the role of science, including anthropology, in the UNESCO *State-*

ment on Race and the UN *Declaration of Human Rights,* among other things.

The conflation of objectivity and neutrality is neither valid nor useful. Neutrality is elusive and not always desirable. A medical doctor applies science in an objective manner but is not neutral in dealing with disease and death. The persistent argument that science can only be objective by being neutral, and therefore amoral and apolitical, is either remarkably naive or purposefully deceptive. The "neutrality" many anthropologists express in the face of the continuing holocaust in the Amazon contributes, at least indirectly, to genocide, ethnocide, and ecocide. Such inaction is tantamount to complicity, even if the latter is inadvertent. If anthropology does not become more of the solution, then it will remain more of the problem in the holocaust in Amazonia. Political involvement of some kind is increasingly unavoidable for the ecological anthropologist, simply because indigenous societies and environmental concerns are increasingly political.

The proposed paradigm shift would also allow ecological anthropology to make a significant contribution as part of the broader and varied movement of radical ecology. This movement has been described by the respected environmental historian from the University of California at Berkeley, Carolyn Merchant (1992:1):

> Radical ecology emerges from a sense of crisis in the industrialized world. It acts on a new perception that the domination of nature entails the domination of human beings along lines of race, class, and gender. Radical ecology confronts the illusion that people are free to exploit nature and to move in society at the expense of others, with a new consciousness of our responsibilities to the rest of nature and to other humans. It seeks a new ethic of the nurture of nature and the nurture of people. It empowers people to make changes in the world consistent with a new social vision and a new ethic.

Conclusions

To conclude this chapter, I would reiterate that a paradigm shift is required in ecological anthropology to focus much more attention on the survival, well-being, identity, and self-determination of indigenous peoples as they adapt to the challenges of Western society in the contexts of political economy, human rights, and sustainable use of the unique tropical forest ecosystems of Amazonia. A new component—indigenous communities and organizations—is added to the team designing, implementing, and reporting this research, toward the end of contributing to indigenous people's information and thereby to their empowerment and self-determination. The significance and urgency of greater collaboration between indigenes and ecological anthropologists is underlined by the gravity of the deforestation crisis with all of its human, as well as biological, ramifications.

This chapter was intentionally written to be provocative, but constructively so. I hope this review and its recommendations will provoke healthy individual introspection, along with collective retrospection, debate, and change in at least some of the research and teaching being done by specialists on the anthropological aspects of the human ecology of Amazonia. And in doing so, perhaps it will make some contribution to advance indigenous causes. If there is any hope for the future of the Amazon, it lies with the descendants of the original people of the region. For millennia, these people have developed the land, generally in ways that used land and resources on a sustained basis without major, irreversible environmental degradation and destruction (Sponsel 1992a). In Amazonia, in various ways, indigenes are to a large extent the key to environmental ethics, ecological knowledge, sustainable land and resource use and management, and the conservation of biodiversity, ecosystems, and wildlife. Anthropologists who develop more meaningful collaboration with indigenes may make some contribution toward the survival of the people and ecosystems of the increasingly endangered world of the Amazon.

References Cited

Albert, Bruce
1992   Indian Lands, Environmental Policy, and Military Geopolitics in the Development of the Brazilian Amazon: The Case of the Yanomami. *Development and Change* 23:35–70.
1993   The Massacre of the Yanomami of Hashimu. *Folha de São Paulo* (Brazil), October 10.
Alfredsson, Gudmundur
1989   The United Nations and the Rights of Indigenous Peoples. *Current Anthropology* 30(2):255–59.
Allegretti, M. H.
1990   Extractive Reserves: An Alternative for Reconciling Development and Environmental Conservation in Amazonia. In *Alternatives to Deforestation: Steps Toward Sustainable Use of the Amazon Rain Forest*, edited by Anthony B. Anderson, pp. 252–64. New York: Columbia University Press.

American Anthropological Association
1976   *Statement on Ethics: Principles of Professional Responsibility.* Washington, D.C.: American Anthropological Association.

Amnesty International
1992   *Brazil, "We Are the Land,": Indigenous Peoples' Struggle for Human Rights.* New York: Amnesty International.

Anderson, Anthony B.
1990   Deforestation in Amazonia: Dynamics, Causes, and Alternatives. In *Alternatives to Deforestation: Steps Toward Sustainable Use of the Amazon Rain Forest,* edited by Anthony B. Anderson, pp. 3–23. New York: Columbia University Press.

Appell, George N.
1975   The Pernicious Effects of Development. *Fields Within Fields* 14:1–45.
1988   Costing Social Change. In *The Real and Imagined Role of Culture in Development,* edited by Michael R. Dove, pp. 271–84. Honolulu: University of Hawaii Press.

Arvelo-Jiménez, Nelly, and Andrew L. Cousins
1992   False Promises: Venezuela Appears to Have Protected the Yanomami, But Appearances Can be Deceiving. *Cultural Survival* 16(1): 10–13.

Barrau, Jacques
1982   Plants and Men on the Threshold of the Twenty-First Century. *Social Science Information* 21(1):127–41.

Barrett, Suzanne W.
1980   Conservation in Amazonia. *Biological Conservation* 18:209–35.

Berwick, Dennison
1992   *Savages: The Life and Killing of the Yanomami.* London: Hodder and Stoughton Ltd.

Bodley, John H.
1985   *Anthropology and Contemporary Human Problems.* Menlo Park, Calif.: Cummings.
1990   *Victims of Progress.* Mountain View, Calif.: Mayfield Publishing Co.

Bodley, John H., ed.
1988   *Tribal Peoples and Development Issues: A Global Overview.* Mountain View, Calif.: Mayfield Publishing Co.

Browder, John O.
1992   The Limits of Extractivism. *BioScience* 42(3):174–82.

Bunker, Stephen G.
1984   Modes of Extraction, Unequal Exchange, and the Progressive Underdevelopment of an Extreme Periphery: The Brazilian Amazon 1600–1980. *American Journal of Sociology* 89(5):1017–64.

Bunyard, Peter
1987   The Significance of the Amazon Basin for Global Climatic Equilibrium. *The Ecologist* 17(4/5):139–41.
1989   Guardians of the Forest: Indigenist Policies in the Colombian Amazon. *The Ecologist* 19(6):255–58.

Bunyard, Peter, ed.
1993   *New Responsibilities: The Indigenous Peoples of the Colombian Amazon.* Cornwall, U.K.: Wadebridge Ecological Centre.

Burger, Julian
1987   *Report from the Frontier: The State of the World's Indigenous Peoples.* Atlantic City, N.J.: Zed Books, Ltd.

Buschbacher, Robert J.
1986   Tropical Deforestation and Pasture Development. *BioScience* 36(1): 22–28.

Carneiro, Robert L.
1988   Indians of the Amazonian Forest. In *People of the Tropical Rain Forest,* edited by Julie Sloan Denslow and Christine Padoch, pp. 73–86. Berkeley: University of California Press.

Chagnon, Napoleon A.
1992   *Yanomamo.* New York: Harcourt Brace Jovanovich College Publishers.

Clay, Jason W.
1988   *Indigenous Peoples and Tropical Forests: Models of Land Use and Management from Latin America.* Cambridge, Mass.: Cultural Survival, Inc.
1989   Defending the Forests. *Cultural Survival Quarterly* 13(1):1.
1991   Cultural Survival and Conservation: Lessons from the Past Twenty Years. In *Biodiversity: Culture, Conservation, and Ecodevelopment,* edited by Margery L. Oldfield and Janis B. Alcorn, pp. 248–73. Boulder, Colo.: Westview Press.

COICA (Coordinating Body of the Indigenous Peoples' Organizations)
1990   We Are Concerned. *Orion Nature Quarterly* 9(3):36–37.

Cook, Allison G., Anthony C. Janetos, and W. Ted Hinds
1990   Global Effects of Tropical Deforestation: Towards an Integrated Perspective. *Environmental Conservation* 17(3):201–12.

Crosby, Alfred W.
1972   *The Columbian Exchange: The Biological and Cultural Consequences of 1492.* Westport, Conn.: Greenwood Press.
1986   *Ecological Imperialism: The Biological Expansion of Europe, 900–1900.* New York: Cambridge University Press.

Cultural Survival
1991   Intellectual Property Rights: The Politics of Ownership. *Cultural Survival Quarterly* 15(3):1–52.

Dickenson, J. P.
1989   Development in Brazilian Amazonia: Background to New Frontiers. *Revista Geográfica* 109:141–55.

Donnelly, Jack
1989   *Universal Human Rights in Theory and Practice.* Ithaca, N.Y.: Cornell University Press.

Dostal, W., ed.
1971   *The Situation of the Indian in South America.* Geneva, Switzerland: World Council of Churches.

Downing, Theodore E., and Gilbert Kushner, eds.
1988   *Human Rights and Anthropology.* Cambridge, Mass.: Cultural Survival, Inc.

Eden, Michael J.
1990   *Ecology and Land Management in Amazonia.* New York: Belhaven Press.

Ehrlich, Paul R., and Anne H. Ehrlich
1992   The Value of Biodiversity. *Ambio* 21(3):219–26.

Fabian, Johannes
1983   *Time and the Other: How Anthropology Makes Its Object.* New York: Columbia University Press.

Farnworth, Edward G., Thomas H. Tidrick, Webb M. Smathers, Jr., and Carl F. Jordan
1983   A Synthesis of Ecological and Economic Theory Toward More Complex Valuation of Tropical Moist Forests. *International Journal of Environmental Studies* 21:11–28.

Fearnside, Philip M.
1986   Settlement in Rondonia and the Token Role of Science and Technology in Brazil's Amazonian Development Planning. *Interciencia* 11(5): 229–36.
1989a   Brazil's Balbina Dam: Environment Versus the Legacy of the Pharaohs in Amazonia. *Environmental Management* 13(4):401–23.
1989b   The Charcoal of Carajas: A Threat to the Forests of Brazil's Eastern Amazon Region. *Ambio* 18(2):141–43.
1989c   Forest Management in Amazonia: The Need for New Criteria in Evaluating Development Options. *Forest Ecology and Management* 27:61–79.
1989d   Extractive Reserves in Brazilian Amazonia. *BioScience* 39(6):387–93.
1990a   The Rate and Extent of Deforestation in Brazilian Amazonia. *Environmental Conservation* 17(3):213–26.
1990b   Estimation of Human Carrying Capacity in Rainforest Areas. *Tree* 5(6):192–96.

Ferguson, R. Brian
1992   A Savage Encounter: Western Contact and the Yanomami War Complex. In *War in the Tribal Zone: Expanding States and Indigenous Warfare,*

edited by R. Brian Ferguson and Neil L. Whitehead, pp. 199–227. Santa Fe, N.M.: School of American Research Press.

Foresta, Ronald A.
1991   *Amazon Conservation in the Age of Development: The Limits of Providence.* Gainesville, Fla.: University of Florida Press.

Godfrey, Brian J.
1990   Boom Towns of the Amazon. *The Geographical Review* 80(2):103–17.

Godoy, Ricardo, and Ruben Lubowski
1992   Guidelines for the Economic Valuation of Nontimber Tropical-Forest Products. *Current Anthropology* 33(4):423–33.

Gómez-Pompa, A., T. C. Whitmore, and M. Hadley, eds.
1991   *Rain Forest Regeneration and Management.* Park Ridge, N.J.: Parthenon Publishing Group.

González, Nicanor
1992   We Are Not Conservationists. *Cultural Survival Quarterly* 16(3): 43–45.

Gribel, Rogerio
1990   The Balbina Disaster: The Need to Ask Why? *The Ecologist* 20(4): 133–35.

Grove, Richard H.
1992   Origins of Western Environmentalism. *Scientific American* 267(1): 42–47.

Gruber, J. W.
1970   Ethnographic Salvage and the Shaping of Anthropology. *American Anthropologist* 72:1289–99.

Guimaraes, Roberto P.
1991   *The Ecopolitics of Development in the Third World: Politics and Environment in Brazil.* Boulder, Colo.: Lynne Rienner Publishers.

Hawkes, J. G.
1989   The Domestication of Roots and Tubers in the American Tropics. In *Foraging and Farming: The Evolution of Plant Exploitation*, edited by D. R. Harris and G. C. Hillman, pp. 481–503. Boston: Unwin Hyman.

Head, Suzanne, and Robert Heinzman
1990   *Lessons of the Forest.* San Francisco, Calif.: Sierra Club.

Hecht, Susanna B.
1989   The Sacred Cow in the Green Hell. *The Ecologist* 19(6):229–34.

Hecht, Susanna B., and Alexander Cockburn
1989   *The Fate of the Forest: Developers, Destroyers and Defenders of the Amazon.* New York: Verso.

Hemming, John
1987   *Amazon Frontier: The Defeat of the Brazilian Indians.* London: Macmillan.

Hern, Warren M.
1992   Family Planning, Amazon Style. *Natural History* 101(12):30–37.

Hiraoka, Mario
1985   Mestizo Subsistence in Riparian Amazonia. *National Geographic Research* 1(2):236–46.
1989   Agricultural Systems on the Floodplains of the Peruvian Amazon. In *Fragile Lands of Latin America: Strategies for Sustainable Development*, edited by John O. Browder, pp. 75–101. Boulder, Colo.: Westview Press.

Hvalkof, Soren
1989   The Nature of Development: Native and Settler Views in Gran Pajonal, Peruvian Amazon. *Folk* 31:125–50.

ICHI (Independent Commission on International Humanitarian Issues)
1986   *The Vanishing Forest: The Human Consequences of Deforestation*. London: Zed Books.

Indian Law Resource Center
1984   *Indian Rights, Human Rights: Handbook for Indians on International Human Rights Complaint Procedures*. Washington, D.C.: Indian Law Resource Center.

Jablonski, David
1991   Extinctions: A Paleontological Perspective. *Science* 253(5021):754–57.

Johnston, Barbara R., ed.
1993   *Who Pays the Price? Examining the Sociocultural Context of Environmental Crisis: A Society for Applied Anthropology Report on Human Rights and the Environment*. Oklahoma City.: Society for Applied Anthropology.

Katzman, Martin T.
1975   The Brazilian Frontier in Comparative Perspective. *Comparative Studies in Society and History* 17(3):266–85.

Katzman, Martin T., and William G. Cale, Jr.
1990   Tropical Forest Preservation Using Economic Incentives. *BioScience* 40(11):827–32.

Kemf, Elizabeth, ed.
1993   *The Law of the Mother: Protecting Indigenous Peoples in Protected Areas*. San Francisco: Sierra Club Books.

Lugo, Ariel E.
1991   Cities in the Sustainable Development of Tropical Landscapes. *Nature Resources* 27(2):27–35.

Lugo, Ariel E., John R. Clark, and R. Dennis Child, eds.
1987   *Ecological Development in the Humid Tropics: Guidelines for Planners*. Morrilton, Alaska: Winrock International.

Lutzenberger, Jose
1987   Brazil's Amazonian Alliance. *The Ecologist* 17(4/5):190–91.

McNeely, Jeffrey A., Kenton R. Miller, Walter V. Reid, Russell A. Mittermeier, and Timothy B. Werner
1990a *Conserving the World's Biological Diversity.* Washington, D.C.: World Resources Institute.
1990b Strategies for Conserving Biodiversity. *Environment* 32(3):16–20, 36–40.

McNeely, Jeffrey A., and David Pitt, eds.
1984 *Culture and Conservation: The Human Dimension in Environmental Planning.* New York: Croom and Helm.

McNeil, John R.
1986 Agriculture, Forests, and Ecological History: Brazil, 1500–1984. *Environmental History Review* 10(2):123–34.

Malm, O., C. P. Pfeiffer, C. M. M. Souza, and R. Reuter
1990 Mercury Pollution Due to Gold Mining in the Madeira River Basin, Brazil. *Ambio* 19(1):11–15.

Margolis, M.
1977 Historical Perspectives on Frontier Agriculture as an Adaptive Strategy. *American Ethnologist* 4:42–64.

Marquet, J.
1964 Objectivity in Anthropology. *Current Anthropology* 5:47–55.

Martinelli, L. A., J. R. Ferreira, B. R. Fosberg, and R. L. Victoria
1988 Mercury Contamination in the Amazon: A Gold Rush Consequence. *Ambio* 17(4):252–54.

Merchant, Carolyn
1992 *Radical Ecology: The Search for a Livable World.* New York: Routledge.

Messer, Ellen
1993 Anthropology and Human Rights. *Annual Review of Anthropology* 22:221–49.

Miller, Marc S., ed.
1993 *State of the Peoples: A Global Human Rights Report on Societies in Danger.* Boston: Beacon Press.

Molion, Luiz Carlos B.
1989 The Amazon Forests and Climate Stability. *The Ecologist* 19(6):211–13.

Moran, Emilio F.
1979 *Human Adaptability: An Introduction to Ecological Anthropology.* Boulder, Colo.: Westview Press.
1982 Ecological, Anthropological, and Agronomic Research in the Amazon Basin. *Latin American Research Review* 17(1):3–42.
1983 *The Dilemma of Amazonian Development.* Boulder, Colo.: Westview Press.
1988 Following the Amazonian Highways. In *People of the Tropical Rain Forest,* edited by Julie Sloan Denslow and Christine Padoch, pp. 155–62. Berkeley: University of California Press.

Mowat, Linda
1989   *Cassava and Chicha: Bread and Beer of the Amazonian Indians.* Ayles-
        bury, U.K.: Shire Publications.

Myers, Norman
1992   *The Primary Source: Tropical Forests and Our Future.* New York: W. W.
        Norton.

Myers, Norman, ed.
1993   *Gaia: An Atlas of Planet Management.* Garden City, N.Y.: Anchor Press.

Padoch, Christine
1988   People of the Floodplain and Forest. In *People of the Tropical Rain Forest,*
        edited by Julie Sloan Denslow and Christine Padoch, pp. 127–40.
        Berkeley: University of California Press.

Paine, Robert, ed.
1985   *Advocacy and Anthropology.* St. Johns: University of Newfoundland Press.

Pallemaerts, Marc
1986   Development, Conservation, and Indigenous Rights in Brazil. *Human
        Peace Quarterly* 8(3):374–400.

Pandian, Jacob
1985   *Anthropology and the Western Tradition: Toward an Authentic Anthropol-
        ogy.* Prospect Heights, Ill.: Waveland Press.

Peters, Charles M., Alwyn H. Gentry, and Robert O. Mendelsohn
1989   Valuation of an Amazonian Rainforest. *Nature* 339:655–56.

Pimentel, David, Ulrich Strachow, David A. Takacs, Hans W. Brubaker,
Amy R. Dumas, John J. Meaney, John A. S. O'Neil, Douglas E. Onsi, and
David B. Corzilius
1992   Conserving Biological Diversity in Agricultural/Forestry Systems. *BioSci-
        ence* 42(5):354–62.

Plotkin, Mark J.
1991   Traditional Knowledge of Medicinal Plants: The Search for New Jungle
        Medicines. In *The Conservation of Medicinal Plants,* edited by Olayiwola
        Akerele, Vernon Heywood, and Hugh Synge, pp. 53–63. New York:
        Cambridge University Press.

Plotkin, Mark, and Lisa Famolare, eds.
1992   *Sustainable Harvest and Marketing of Rain Forest Produce.* Washington,
        D.C.: Island Press.

Poelhekke, Fabio G. M. N.
1986   Fences in the Jungle: Cattle Raising and the Economic and Social Inte-
        gration of the Amazon Region in Brazil. *Revista Geográfica* 104:33–43.

Posey, Darrell A., et al., eds.
1990   *Ethnobiology: Implications and Applications,* vols. 1–2. Proceedings of
        the First International Congress of Ethnobiology. Belém, Brazil: Museu
        Paraense Emílio Goeldi.

Rainforest Action Network
1990   *Amazon Resource and Action Guide.* San Francisco: Rainforest Action
        Network.

Ramos, Alcida, and Kenneth Taylor
1979   *The Yanomami in Brazil 1979.* Copenhagen: International Work Group
        for Indigenous Affairs, document 37.

Raup, David M.
1988   Diversity Crises in the Geological Past. In *Biodiversity,* edited by E. O.
        Wilson and Francis M. Peter, pp. 51–57. Washington, D.C.: National
        Academy Press.

Redford, Kent H.
1990   The Ecologically Noble Savage. *Orion Nature Quarterly* 15(1):46–48.
1991   The Ecologically Noble Savage. *Cultural Survival Quarterly* 9(1): 41–44.
1992   The Empty Forest. *BioScience* 42(6):412–22.

Redford, Kent H., and Christine Padoch, eds.
1992   *Conservation of Neotropical Forests: Working from Traditional Resource
        Units.* New York: Columbia University Press.

Repetto, Robert
1987   Creating Incentives for Sustainable Development. *Ambio* 16(2–3):
        94–99.
1990   Deforestation in the Tropics. *Scientific American* 262(4):36–42.
1992   Accounting for Environmental Assets. *Scientific American* 264(6):94–
        100.

Ribeiro, Darcy
1972   *The Americas and Civilization.* New York: E. P. Dutton.

Robinson, John G., and Kent H. Redford, eds.
1991   *Neotropical Wildlife Use and Conservation.* Chicago: University of
        Chicago Press.

Ryan, John C.
1992   Conserving Biological Diversity. In *State of the World 1992,* edited by
        Lester R. Brown, pp. 9–26. New York: W. W. Norton.

Salati, Eneas
1987   The Forest and the Hydrological Cycle. In *The Geophysiology of Amazo-
        nia: Vegetation and Climate Interactions,* edited by Robert E. Dickinson,
        pp. 273–96. New York: John Wiley Sons.

Sanders, Douglas
1989   The UN Working Group on Indigenous Populations. *Human Rights
        Quarterly* 11:406–33.

Schmink, Marianne, and Charles H. Wood
1992   *Contested Frontiers in Amazonia.* New York: Columbia University Press.

Schwartz, Tanya
1989   The Brazilian Forest People's Movement. *The Ecologist* 19(6):245–47.

Schwartzman, Stephen
1989   Extractive Reserves: The Rubber Tappers' Strategy for Sustainable Use of the Amazon Rainforest. In *Fragile Lands of Latin America: Strategies for Sustainable Development*, edited by John O. Browder, pp. 150–65. Boulder, Colo.: Westview Press.

Sioli, Harald
1987   The Effects of Deforestation in Amazonia. *The Ecologist* 17(4/5): 134–38.

Smith, Nigel J. H.
1978   Agricultural Productivity Along Brazil's Transamazon Highway. *Agro-Ecosystem* 4:415–32.

Smith, Nigel J. H., and Richard Evans Schultes
1990   Deforestation and Shrinking Crop Gene-Pools in Amazonia. *Environmental Conservation* 17(3):227–34.

Smith, Nigel J. H., J. T. Williams, Donald L. Plucknett, and Jennifer P. Talbot
1992   *Tropical Forests and Their Crops*. Ithaca, N.Y.: Cornell University Press.

Sponsel, Leslie E.
1979   A Note on the Urgency of Research Among the Yanomama of the Brazilian Amazon. *Review of Ethnology* 7(1–9):72.
1981   Situación de los Yanomama y la civilización. *Boletín Indigenista Venezolano* 20(17):105–16.
1985   Ecology, Anthropology, and Values in Amazonia. In *Cultural Values and Human Ecology in Southeast Asia*, edited by Karl Hutterer, Terry Rambo, and George Lovelace, pp. 77–122. Ann Arbor: University of Michigan Southeast Asia Studies Center.
1986   Amazon Ecology and Adaptation. *Annual Review of Anthropology* 15:67–97.
1989   Foraging and Farming: A Necessary Complementarity in Amazonia? In *Farmers as Hunters*, edited by Susan Kent, pp. 37–45. New York: Cambridge University Press.
1990   Does Anthropology Have Any Future? *Anthropology Newsletter* 31(3): 32, 29. Washington, D.C.: American Anthropological Association.
1991   Sobrevivirá la antropología al siglo XX? Reflexiones sobre la mutua relevancia entre indígenas y antropólogos. *Arinsana* 7(13):65–79.
1992a   The Environmental History of Amazonia: Natural and Human Disturbances, and the Ecological Transition. In *Changing Tropical Forests: Historical Perspectives on Today's Challenges in Central and South America*, edited by Harold K. Steen and Richard P. Tucker, pp. 233–51. Durham, N.C.: Forest History Society.
1992b   Information Asymmetry and the Democratization of Anthropology. *Human Organization* 51(3):299–301.
1993   The Yanomami. In *Who Pays the Price? Examining the Sociocultural Context of Environmental Crisis: A Society for Applied Anthropology Report on*

Human Rights and the Environment, edited by Barbara R. Johnston, pp. 163–72. Oklahoma City: Society for Applied Anthropology.

Steward, Julian H.
1955   *Theory of Culture Change: The Methodology of Multilinear Evolution.* Urbana: University of Illinois Press.

Stone, Roger D.
1993   *Dreams of Amazonia.* New York: Penguin Books.

Survival International
1991   *Yanomami: Survival Campaign.* London: Survival International.

Treece, Dave
1989   The Militarization and Industrialization of Amazonia. *The Ecologist* 19(6):225–28.

Turner, Terry
1991   Major Shift in Brazilian Yanomami Policy. *Anthropology Newsletter* 32(6):1, 46. Washington, D.C.: American Anthropological Association.

Warry, Wayne
1990   Doing Unto Others: Applied Anthropology, Collaborative Research and Native Self-Determination. *Culture* 10(1):61–73.

Wax, Murray
1991   The Ethics of Research in American Indian Communities. *American Indian Quarterly* 15(4):431–56.

Weatherford, Jack
1988   *Indian Givers: How the Indians of the Americas Transformed the World.* New York: Fawcett Columbine.

Wilson, Edward O.
1989   Threats to Biodiversity. *Scientific American* 261(3):108–16.
1992   *The Diversity of Life.* Cambridge, Mass.: Harvard University Press.

Wolf, Eric R.
1982   *Europe and the People Without History.* Chicago: University of Chicago Press.

Wright, Robin
1988   Anthropological Presuppositions of Indigenous Advocacy. *Annual Review of Anthropology* 17:365–90.

Contributors

Nelly Arvelo-Jiménez is a professor in the Department of Anthropology
at the Venezuelan Institute for Scientific Investigations in Caracas.
She holds M.S. and Ph.D. degrees in anthropology from Cornell University and has specialized in the political and religious institutions of
indigenous societies in the Venezuelan Amazon. She has been active
in applied and advocacy anthropology, working closely with Ye'kuana,
Kariña, and Pemon peoples of southern Venezuela. She has also
worked with urban Piaroa, Guahibo, and Wakuenai of Puerto Aya-
cucho in the federal territory of the Amazon in Venezuela.

Michael Baksh is principal anthropologist with Tierra Environmental Services in San Diego, California. He formerly was an assistant researcher
in the School of Public Health and in the Latin American Center at
the University of California, Los Angeles. He holds a Ph.D. in anthropology from UCLA. Baksh spent almost two years on four field trips
between 1977 and 1988 with the Machiguenga in the Peruvian Amazon. More recently he has worked on cultural ecological studies in
the Amazon using satellite imagery.

William Balée, an associate professor in the Department of Anthropology
at Tulane University, earned his Ph.D. at Columbia University. He
has conducted extensive fieldwork on cultural ecology and ethnobotany in the Brazilian Amazon. His publications include *Footprints
of the Forest: Ka'apor Ethnobotany* (1994).

Robert L. Carneiro is curator of South American ethnology at the American Museum of Natural History in New York City. He received his Ph.D. from the University of Michigan. He has done extensive fieldwork in Brazil, eastern Peru, and southern Venezuela. He pioneered in the quantitative approach to cultural-ecological field research in Amazonia and is also noted for his circumscription theory of the origin of the state. His main interests are cultural ecology, cultural evolution, and political organization.

Janet M. Chernela is an associate professor in the Department of Sociology and Anthropology at Florida International University, where she is a participating faculty member of the graduate program in international studies. Chernela received her Ph.D. in anthropology from Columbia University. She has carried out fieldwork and consulting in Honduras, Colombia, Ecuador, and Brazil, publishing extensively on the interface between environmental preservation and indigenous peoples in Latin America. Her publications include *The Wanano Indians of the Brazilian Amazon: A Sense of Space* (1993).

Avecita Chicchón studied at Pontifica Universidad Católica del Peru in Lima, where she earned a bachelor's degree in social sciences with a major in anthropology. She was awarded an M.A. in anthropology from the University of Cincinnati, and a Ph.D. in anthropology from the University of Florida. Her ethnological fieldwork includes studies among the Ashaninka of Satipo, the Nomatsiguenga of Pangoa, and the Aguaruna of Alto Mayo in Peru. In 1988–89, she carried out her dissertation research among the Chimane of the Beni, Bolivia. She currently works for Conservation International as the in-country coordinator for the Peru program.

Carlos E. A. Coimbra, Jr., is a researcher in the Department of Epidemiology at the National School of Public Health, Oswaldo Cruz Foundation, in Rio de Janeiro, Brazil. He holds a B.S. from the University of Brasilia, and an M.A. and Ph.D. from Indiana University. His research focuses on the health and disease of indigenous populations, human nutrition, and the biological effects of sociocultural change. He is editor of *The Health of Indigenous Populations* (1991), a special issue of *Cadernos de Saúde Pública*.

Darna L. Dufour is an associate professor at the University of Colorado in Boulder. She holds an M.A. and Ph.D. from the State University of New York at Binghamton, with specializations in biological anthropology, nutrition, and human adaptation. She has worked extensively in the Amazon of Colombia with the Tukanoans, focusing on nutritional anthropology.

Kenneth Good is an assistant professor in the Department of Sociology and Anthropology at Jersey City State College. He holds an M.A. from Pennsylvania State University and a Ph.D. from the University of Florida. In 1991 he published the book *Into the Heart*, an autobiographical ethnography of his 14 years with the Yanomami in Venezuela. His research focused on the cultural ecology of foraging in relation to the animal protein hypothesis and warfare.

Rebecca Holmes holds a B.S. from the University of Michigan and an M.S. and D.Sc. from the Venezuelan Institute for Scientific Investigations in Caracas. She has worked for many years in Venezuela with the Curripaco and Karinya as well as the Yanomami, focusing on the influence of cultural change on nutrition and health.

Simeon Jiménez is a Ye'kuana who has worked extensively throughout the Venezuelan Amazon on behalf of indigenous survival, welfare, and rights with governmental and nongovernmental organizations. He has participated in numerous regional, national, and international conferences on indigenous affairs.

Betty J. Meggers is a research associate at the Smithsonian Institution. She holds a Ph.D. from Columbia University. She has specialized in the cultural ecology of Amazonia and has conducted archaeological investigations in Brazil, Ecuador, Guyana, and Venezuela. Since 1976 she has been coordinator of a long-term program of archaeological research in the Neotropical lowlands, involving fieldwork by local archaeologists. She is author of one of the classics on anthropology in lowland South America, *Amazonia: Man and Culture in a Counterfeit Paradise* (1971).

Emilio F. Moran is a professor at Indiana University. His Ph.D. is from the University of Florida. He is interested in cultural ecology, migration and rural development, social and environmental impact assessment, agrarian systems, applied anthropology, and the Brazilian Amazon. He is the author of *Human Adaptability: An Introduction to Ecological Anthropology* (1979) and *Developing the Amazon* (1981), and editor of *The Dilemma of Amazonian Development* (1983) and *The Ecosystem Concept in Anthropology* (1984).

Leslie E. Sponsel is an associate professor at the University of Hawaii, where he directs the ecological anthropology program and teaches courses on cultural ecology and human adaptation to tropical forest ecosystems. He received a B.A. from Indiana University and an M.A. and Ph.D. from Cornell University. He has conducted field research with Sanemá (a Yanomami subgroup), Ye'kuana, and Curripaco in the Venezuelan Amazon, and more recently in southern Thailand. Sponsel is coeditor of *Deforestation: The Human Dimension* (1995). He is chair of the Commission for Human Rights of the American Anthropological Association.

Allyn MacLean Stearman is a professor at the University of Central Florida in Orlando. Her Ph.D. is from the University of Florida. She has worked extensively with the Yuquí and Sirionó, the subjects of her books, *Yuquí: Forest Nomads in a Changing World* (1989) and *No Longer Nomads: The Sirionó Revisited* (1987). Her interests include cultural ecology, sustainable resource use, foraging and peasant societies, and women and development.

Index

Pleistocene, 16, 18
Policy, 13, 72, 112, 225–42, 245–59, 268
political ecology, 74, 83, 87; economy, 74, 87, 184, 279, 282; evolution, 51; involvement, 282; leadership, 64; mobilization, 273; organization, 50, 51, 53, 185
politics, 281; in anthropology, 279
polycropping, 265
population, 50, 53–54, 76, 79, 82–83, 121–22, 279; density, 17, 15, 33, 35, 60, 75, 85, 99, 187, 189, 190, 193, 195, 226, 265; growth, 47, 142, 190, 216, 219, 259; mobility, 72, 174; pressure, 12, 52, 226, 265; rebound, 174, 183–84, 271; size, 171, 174, 190
post-Columbian, 118, 131
postpartum sex taboo, 136
pottery, 19, 20, 30, 35, 53, 82, 115–16
pre-Columbian, precolonial, precontact, prehistoric, 15, 19, 27, 117, 121, 132
prehistoric environmental modification, 72; human skeletons, 55; mounds, 104
prehistory, 170
primary, pristine, forest, 105, 240
primates, 213, 215, 229, 232–33, 252
primitive, 274
procurement strategies, 191
productivity, 17, 33, 35–36, 48, 56, 71, 73, 75, 79, 80–81, 87, 114, 220, 267
progress, 263, 266, 269
protected area, 185, 225, 228–29, 241
protein, 4, 33, 49, 53–55, 59, 63–64, 112, 113–15, 119, 137, 139, 150, 158–61, 174, 193; debate, 113; deficient, 137; scarcity, 138
prussic acid, 151

puberty seclusion ritual, 169
pulp wood, 267

quality of life, 88, 183–84, 187–203, 225, 269

racial groups, 124, 132, 135, 140, 273, 282
racism, 268, 273
radical ecology, 5, 282; environmentalism, 5
raiding, 183, 189. *See also* warfare
Rainforest Action Network, 277
Rainforest Alliance, 277
raised fields, 62, 76, 104
ranchers, 100, 185. *See also* cattle
re-agriculturalization, 104
realist, 272, 275
reciprocity, 87, 238
Redford, Kent, 274
refugees, 62
Regional Indian Council of Cauca (CRIC), 253–54
religion, 4, 122, 167, 208, 278
relocation, 225, 265
reproduction rate, 142
reptiles, 231, 233
research priorities, 280; results, 280
reserve, 185, 226, 268
resguardos, 255, 259
resilience, 71, 263
resource, 245, 278; availability, 226, 240; competition, 12, 183–84, 190, 207, 217, 219, 220, 240–42, 250, 252, 254–55; concentration, 58; deficit, 220; depletion, 63, 215, 242; flushes, 211; management, 13, 73, 76–77, 83–84, 86, 106, 187, 246–47, 252, 267, 279–81, 283; patches, 211; poor, 84; scarcity, 213; stress, 217; use, 207
responsibility, 282
restoration, 247, 257–58, 267, 279, 280